The Imaginative Body

Psychodynamic Therapy in
Health Care

Dedication

For our children: Tara Rose; and Kate, Luke, Ben and Jake

The Imaginative Body

Psychodynamic Therapy in Health Care

Edited by
Aleda Erskine
Clinical Health Psychogist

and

Dorothy Judd
Principal Child Psychotherapist

Foreword by Henry Krystal

JASON ARONSON INC.
Northvale, New Jersey
London

Library of Congress Cataloging-in-Publication Data
pending
ISBN 1-56821-257-7

Jason Aronson Inc. offers books and cassettes. For information and catalog write to Jason Aronson Inc., 230 Livingston Street, Northvale, New Jersey 07647.

Photoset by Computape (Pickering) Ltd, North Yorkshire
Printed and bound in the UK by Athenaeum Press Ltd,
Newcastle upon Tyne

Foreword

The centenary of Freud's resolve to develop a scientific psychology has passed without any special notice or celebration. For much of this period, at least as far as the 'establishment' of the American Psychoanalytical Association was concerned, it looked as if there would be a steady refinement of theories and techniques of the treatment of the neuroses. All other conditions were to be viewed as a modification of the neuroses and the only legitimate material for research was to be derived from work in the classical psychoanalytical consulting room.

This is not surprising. It is now universally accepted (witness the 20 years' suppression of the current revolution in mathematics and physics) that every science is conservative, and naturally resists changes in its paradigm, until better ones 'break through' the structures of the particular discipline. Science is like a river; when a channel is blocked, it seeks alternative low ground, and then rushes on. Hence, despite the salience of the neuroses and drive theory, throughout the years there was a constant (largely unremarked) flow of discoveries in the field of affect development within psychoanalysis.

Within this development, I would note the contribution of Dashiel (1928) and the culminating work of Bridges (1930) on the theoretical model of the process of affect differentiation. (If anyone took much notice of this discovery, I have been unable to find any trace of it.) In the 1950s, Schur (1955) described affect regression in a dermatological patient. Later, Schmale's (1964) elaboration of the genesis of 'opposing pairs' of affects began to attract a wider interest. Importantly, the life-long work of Bowlby (e.g. 1969) permitted us to question Freud's economic view of attachment, based on nineteenth-century physiology. This was now replaced by a model which emphasised the 'hard wired' need of the infant (or any mammal) to make an attachment to a specific caretaker or couple. This included the importance of the infant's need for the empathic and congruent care by the mother or caretaker.

The results of this work led to the opening up of a whole new view of biology and medicine, and a new role for psychoanalysis within the medical field. It became clear that if we are going to work with medical patients, we cannot do so simply with techniques developed from the treatment of neuroses. This is fully argued by Taylor (1987), and by Taylor's chapter in this book.

As Taylor demonstrates, the nuclear conflict in many 'psychosomatic' patients is not an oedipal one, but one derived from earlier difficulties in object and self-representation. In my clinical experience, the resulting transference can, in extreme cases, be an idolatrous one, in which all the affective and life-enhancing parts of the self are attached to the (therapist as) object; the right to use those parts of the self is then exercised only under the (imaginary) 'franchise' derived from the object (Krystal, 1974).

Another signal of these early difficulties can be found in the alexithymic functioning commonly observed in these patients (see p. 5 of this Intro-duction). Alexithymic functioning encompasses both a regression to earlier stages of affective development and a cognitive disturbance, which the group of Parisian psychoanalysts call 'pensée operatoire' (Marty and de M'Uzan 1963).

This coincidence of the affective and cognitive is now more readily explained thanks to work such as that of Gaddini (1987) on transitional precursors and that of Horton and his associates (e.g. Horton, 1981) on 'solacing'. In the course of normal development the infant's 'myth' of omnipotence is renounced only very slowly. Some individuals relinquish it incompletely, or retain the ability to regress to it in times of perceived peril. This stage is the scaffold for the ability to play, develop wish-fulfilling phantasies, and probably for the entire capacity for abstract thinking. If the transitional process is interrupted by infantile or early overwhelming trauma, this leads to an arrest in development. The manifestations of this process are inhibitions in self-caring, self-solacing, self-soothing, and even biological self-regulation; later alexithymic characteristics may also be evident (Krystal, 1988).

The original assumption was that all preverbal memories are translatable into words; therefore we, as analysts, can lean back in our chairs and the patient will translate for us all their preverbal conflicts in due course. However, the work of the last few years indicates that there is an affective attunement between mother and child, which is at its height from 6 to 9 months. When language becomes available it is built 'on top of the ruins of the old structure', to borrow an image from archaeology (Stern, 1985). This fact – the difficulty of accessing early conflict through language – presents real clinical challenges.

As a result of these new and challenging developments, we find ourselves seriously in need of new techniques. It is more than ever essential that we work with all disciplines, hope to learn from each other, and in the process avoid the fragmentation of 'the patient'.

I therefore congratulate the editors and contributors to this volume, who make a brave attempt to deal with their patients as best they can. There is a helpful emphasis, not only on the imaginative aspects of the body, but on the body as subject to dysequilibrium and dysregulation. These imbalances can only be addressed to the extent that we are able to see the patient as a unique, whole and indivisible person.

References

BOWLBY, J. (1969). *Attachment and Loss*, Vol. 1; *Separation*, Vol. 2; *Loss*, Vol. 3. London: The Hogarth Press.

BRIDGES, K. M. B. (1930). A genetic theory of emotion. *Journal of Genetic Psychology* **37**, 517-527.

DASHIEL, J. F. (1928). Are there any native emotions? *Psychology Review* **35**, 319-327.

GADDINI, R. (1987). Early care and the roots of externalisation. *International Review of Psychoanalysis* **14**, 321-333.

HORTON, P. C. (1981). *Solace: the Missing Dimension in Psychiatry*. Chicago: University of Chicago Press.

KRYSTAL, H. (1974). The genetic development of affects, and affect regression. *Annual of Psychoanalysis* **2**, 98-126.

KRYSTAL, H. (1988). *Integration and Self-Healing: Affect, Trauma, Alexithymia*. Hillsdale, NJ: The Analytic Press.

MARTY, P. and DE M'UZAN, M. (1963). La 'pensée operatoire'. *Revue Française Psychoanalytique* **27** (suppl.), 1345-1356.

SCHMALE, A. H. (1964). A genetic view of affect: with special reference to the genesis of helplessness and hopelessness. *The Psychoanalytic Study of the Child*, vol. 19, pp. 287-310. New York: International Universities Press.

SCHUR, M. (1955). Comments on the metapsychology of somatisation. *The Psychoanalytic Study of the Child*, vol. 10, pp. 119-164. New York: International Universities Press.

STERN, D. M. (1985). *The Interpersonal World of the Infant*. New York: Basic Books.

TAYLOR, G. J. (1987). *Psychosomatic Medicine and Contemporary Psychoanalysis*. Madison, CT: International Universities Press.

Henry Krystal, MD

Professor Emeritus of Psychiatry, Michigan State University

Lecturer, Michigan Psychoanalytic Institute

Acknowledgements

We are grateful to Mrs Marion Milner for kind permission to borrow the phrase 'The Imaginative Body' for our title, from *On Not Being Able to Paint* (1950, p. 106).

The cover illustration (Edvard Munch: Madonna 1895–1902) is reproduced with the permission of the copyright holders BONO, Oslo, Norway.

We would like to acknowledge the following people who have been helpful to either or both of us in various ways, either practically or inspirationally: John Cape, Hilary Crewes, Felicity Dirmiek, Fiona Erskine, Violet Gleeson, Shirley Hoxter, Denis Judd, Anne Kilby, Anne Lanceley, Kathy O'Hanlon, Judy Osborne, Shirley Pearce, Sandra Ramsden, Julia Segal, David Sonnenberg, Robert Souhami, and the staff of the Tavistock Joint Library.

Our publishers and editors could not have been more efficient and helpful; we would like to thank, in particular, Jane Sugarman and Sally Crawford.

We thank the *International Journal of Psycho-Analysis* for allowing us to reprint Chapter 6, from Vol. 74 (1993).

Editors' note

In this book, when the pronoun 'he' is used, we do, of course, mean 'he' or 'she', unless a specific male is being referred to. Throughout the authors have changed patients' names and identifiable details to protect confidentiality.

Preface

This book is about the application of psychoanalytic thinking to the health care of medical patients and those with body image disturbance and eating disorders. The chapters have been planned to reflect innovative practice and to illustrate the diversity of patients and settings with which psychodynamically oriented clinicians currently engage. Our focus is on therapy with individuals (rather than groups or families) and on consultation with health care workers.

The idea for this book was conceived when we met on a course convened by Dorothy Judd at the Tavistock Clinic. This was a multidisciplinary working discussion group to think about the impact of illness and disability not only on patients but on their families and carers, and on ourselves as helping professionals. We became aware of the need for a book which brought together psychodynamic theory and practice, helped us to make better sense of our work and pointed the way forward to new ways of intervention. Our hope is that this book will be such a resource for other clinicians working therapeutically in health care, and will also stimulate a wider interest in this field.

Aleda Erskine
Dorothy Judd
London, 1993

For the making of any drawing, if it was at all satisfying, seemed to be accomplished by a spreading of the imaginative body in wide awareness and this somehow included one's physical body as well as what was being drawn.

Marion Milner (1950)

Contents

Chapter 6   145

The psychotherapeutic application of a dysregulation model of illness
Graeme J. Taylor

Chapter 7   165

Working with the false body
Susie Orbach

Chapter 8   180

The value of emotional awareness in general practice
Sotiris Zalidis

Chapter 9   200

'The body goes mad': hospital liaison psychiatry in sickle-cell disease
Sebastian Kraemer

Contributors

Aleda Erskine is a consultant clinical psychologist at the Whittington and University College Hospitals, London and head of specialty, psychological services to medicine and surgery within Camden and Islington Community Health Services NHS Trust. She trained in clinical psychology at the Institute of Psychiatry, London and thence developed a growing interest in health psychology and later in the application of psychodynamic thinking to health care. Her research interest is in chronic pain and she has published articles and chapters on this subject.

Peter Fonagy is a member of the British Psycho-Analytical Society, Freud Memorial Professor at University College London (UCL) and coordinator of research at the Anna Freud Centre. He is co-organiser of clinical psychology training at UCL and has been a member of the Executive Council of the International Psychoanalytical Association since 1989. His research interests include attachment and borderline personality disorder as well as the psychological treatment of chronic physical illness.

Dorothy Judd is head of child psychotherapy in oncology at the Middlesex and University College Hospitals, London, with responsibility for psychological support and therapy for patients, families and staff on the paediatric and adolescent oncology wards. Her first degree was in fine art, from whence she taught art, and trained as an art therapist. Later, she trained as a child psychotherapist at the Tavistock Clinic, London, where she has also recently undertaken adult psychotherapy training. She is a visiting teacher at the Tavistock Clinic and teaches infant observation there and in Dublin. She also teaches on the Psychodynamic Approaches to Cancer course (Tavistock), is a counsellor at University College School, London, and is on the Training Committee of the Centre for Psychoanalytic Psychotherapy. She has a small private practice. She has given papers and seminars in many places and is the author of *Give Sorrow Words - Working with a Dying Child* (1989) as well as many articles on child psychotherapy.

Jon Jureidini trained in child psychiatry and psychotherapy in Adelaide, Sydney and London. He is director of adolescent psychiatric services at the Women's and Children's Hospital in Adelaide, where for five years he has been the consultant responsible for paediatric psychiatry liaison. He is a clinical lecturer in psychiatry at the University of Adelaide, and has research interests in play and child abuse. He has published papers on psychotherapy with the physically disabled, Munchausen-by-proxy syndrome and project-ive identification. His clinical work is predominantly concerned with dis-turbed adolescents, young offenders and physically ill children.

Sebastian Kraemer trained in paediatrics before taking up psychiatry, which he studied at the Maudsley Hospital, later specialising in child and adolescent psychiatry at the Tavistock Clinic. Since 1980 he has been consultant in child and family psychiatry at the Whittington Hospital and at the Tavistock Clinic. His principal interests are the training of child psychia-trists, liaison work in hospitals and the promotion in social policy of a realistic understanding of the needs of children and parents. He has published papers on family therapy and liaison psychiatry and, more recently, on the historical origins and current problems of fatherhood.

Mary Sue Moore received her PhD in Clinical Psychology from the Cali-fornia School of Professional Psychology at Berkeley, in 1981. Her child clinical training was supervised by Bruno Bettelheim. Her thesis research, on the drawings of learning-disabled children, showed a strong correlation between patterns of indicators on a child's drawing and the specific dis-ability of the child. Since 1983, this research has been extended to include study of the drawings of children with chronic illness and physically or sexually abused children. She held an adjunct faculty position and was lecturer at the University of Texas at Austin from 1981 to 1984. In 1985, she founded an Interdisciplinary Child and Family Training Program at the University of Texas supported by the Hogg Foundation for Mental Health. Awarded a Fulbright Collaborative Research Grant in 1986 (under the supervision of Dr John Bowlby), she joined scholars at the Tavistock Clinic and various training hospitals in London investigating early disturbance in attachment and the occurrence of psychosomatic illness in children and adults. In 1990, she became clinical lecturer in the Department of Psychol-ogy, University of Colorado, and consultant for psychology and psycho-therapy at the Boulder County Mental Health Center, in Boulder, Colorado.

George Moran was a child psychoanalyst and member of the American Association of Child Psychoanalysis. He was the Director of the Anna Freud Centre between 1985 and his premature death in 1992. He was also an Honorary Senior Lecturer in the Department of Psychology at UCL where he contributed to the clinical psychology training course. His research interests included play, the technique of child psychoanalysis and the nature of its therapeutic effects. He had a long-standing interest in the treatment of children with physical disorders and worked in the Paediatrics Department of the Middlesex Hospital in London.

Deirdre Moylan trained as a clinical psychologist with the South East Thames Regional Health Authority after studying psychology at University College, Dublin. During her work in the psychiatric department of a general hospital, she became interested in primary care and work with general practitioners. A greater interest in psychoanalytic ideas led to a four-year training as a psychoanalytic psychotherapist at the Tavistock Clinic. Here her growing interest in the psychodynamics of institutions was also fostered. She now works as a consultant psychotherapist in the Adolescent Department of the Tavistock Clinic. She is interested in consultation to institutions, and in the wider application of psychoanalytic ideas, particularly in a medical setting; she also has a small private practice.

Susie Orbach co-founded the Women's Therapy Centre, London, an outpatient clinic, in 1976 and, in 1981, the Women's Therapy Centre Institute, a postgraduate training centre for psychotherapists in New York. She has a practice in London seeing individuals and couples, and supervises the work of other therapists. She is the author of *Fat is a Feminist Issue* (1976), *Fat is a Feminist Issue II* (1982), *Hunger Strike: The Anorectic's Struggle as a Metaphor for our Age* (1986) and *Towards Emotional Literacy* (1994). With Luise Eichenbaum she has written *Understanding Women: A Feminist Psychoanalytic Account* (1982), *What Do Women Want: Exploring the Myth of Dependency* (1983) and *Bittersweet: Love, Competition and Envy in Women's Relationships* (1988). She writes a column for *The Guardian*, on emotional issues.

Joan Raphael-Leff is a member of the British Psycho-Analytical Society and the International Psychoanalytical Association. She is also a social psychologist and serves on the Steering Committee of the Royal Society of Medicine's forum for maternity and the newborn. Over the past 20 years of specialisation, she has written several books, including *Psychological Processes of Childbearing* (1991) and *Pregnancy – The Inside Story* (1993), and has published over 40 papers on intrapsychic and interpersonal processes of reproduction. She teaches on a variety of professional training programmes and lectures worldwide.

Graeme J. Taylor is Professor of Psychiatry at the University of Toronto and a consultant psychiatrist at the Mount Sinai Hospital in Toronto, Canada. In addition to his contributions to psychosomatic theory and the psychoanalytic approach to illness and disease, he has conducted extensive research on alexithymia and associated disorders of affect regulation. He is the author of *Psychosomatic Medicine and Contemporary Psychoanalysis* (1987), and of numerous scientific articles.

Sotiris Zalidis is a general practitioner in Hackney, London. Born in Athens, Greece, he came to London after graduation from the Medical School of Athens and acquired experience in general psychiatry, psychoanalysis and general medicine. He has a long interest in psychosomatic medicine and found general practice to be a unique setting in which he could integrate his medical and psychological experience. For the last seven years he has been a partner at the Well Street Surgery, London, a training group practice of six partners and a professor of general practice. He is a member of the Balint Society, the Society for Psychosomatic Research and the Hellenic Society for the Study of Psychosomatic Problems.

Introduction

Aleda Erskine and Dorothy Judd

> Her pure and eloquent blood
> Spoke in her cheeks, and so distinctly wrought,
> That one might almost say, her body thought.
>
> *The Second Anniversary*,
> John Donne (1573-1630)

> The live body, with its limits, and with an inside and outside, is felt by the individual to form the core for the imaginative self.
>
> D.W. Winnicott (1965, p. 244)

The quotations above are striking because they stretch the possibilities of language, with its inherent dualism, to conjure up a sense of a live, dynamic interpenetration between 'mind' and 'body'. This holistic approach is easily claimed, but harder to practice in a culture informed by notions of 'flesh' versus 'spirit', 'physical' versus 'psychological', 'organic' versus 'functional' or 'psychosomatic', etc.

The prevailing Western 'medical model' has been summarised by Engel (1977, p. 130), an analyst and physician:

> The dominant model of disease today is biomedical, with molecular biology its basic scientific discipline. It assumes disease to be fully accounted for by deviation from the norm of measurable (somatic) variables. It leaves no room within its framework for the social, psychological and behavioural dimension of illness.

The complementary danger of psychogenic models – psychological reductionism – has been more neglected. An example is Groddeck's (1926) statement about tuberculosis: 'He alone will die who wishes to die, to whom life is intolerable'. In her powerful critique, *Illness as Metaphor*, Sontag (1983) writes:

> Psychologizing seems to provide control over the experiences and events (like grave illnesses) over which people have in fact little or no control. Psychological understanding undermines the 'reality' of a disease. That reality has to be explained. (It really means; or is a symbol of . . . .) (p. 59)

1

Although biological reductionism leads to the neglect of a patient's emotional needs, any form of psychotherapy inspired by psychological reductionism can lead to the phenomenon of blaming the victim. The patient in therapy whose physical condition does not improve ends up by bearing not only the illness, but also a sense of failure, and possibly guilt.

Engel (1977) described a non-reductionist 'biopsychosocial' model of health and illness. He drew on systems theory to describe bodily functioning in terms of a hierarchy of natural systems, ranging from subatomic particles to the level of the tissue, the organ and the nervous system. The central level of the hierarchy, the person, is also a component of systems such as the couple, family, community and nation. Each system is at once an organised dynamic whole and integral to higher systems. Hence body, mind and social setting are treated as inseparable, and any hard and fast distinctions between 'health' and 'illness' are rejected. Engel's work also gave new emphasis to the role of factors such as the doctor–patient relationship, social support and the inner world of object relations in a patient's presentation.

The imaginative body

However convinced we may be about the theoretical interdependence of body and mind, it is quite a different matter, for most of us, to experience that unity. Winnicott (1972) emphasised that the subjective integration of body and mind is a (reversible) achievement of the mature personality which, for some, is never achieved, or is delayed or later fragmented.

For women, arguably, that integration may always be more difficult to maintain because of the counterpointing of negative cultural stereotypes concerning menstruation, sexuality and reproduction, with unreal and tyrannous norms of the body beautiful. The link between a woman's body as an object of scrutiny and her sense of self has been eloquently expressed by Berger (1972):

> The social presence of woman . . . has been at the cost of woman's self being split into two . . . *men act* and *women appear*. Men look at women. Women watch themselves being looked at. (pp. 46–47)

Ussher (1989) traces a recurrent pattern of tendencies to splitting within the self throughout a woman's life cycle. She describes how this can lead to '. . . the splitting in the adolescent, who cannot assimilate the changes in her developing body and thus separates them from herself; the splitting in the pregnant woman who is faced with the dichotomy of sexuality and motherhood, within the archetype of woman as mother; and the splitting in the menopausal woman who cannot reconcile the archetype of uselessness and redundancy with her own experiences . . .' (p. 140). These dysjunctions among a woman's self, body and sexuality have been extensively explored by feminist psychotherapists such as Orbach (see Chapter 7).

Under the stress of pain, illness or disability, it is particularly hard to hold on to an integrated body/mind consciousness. Here, Klein's (1946) work on anxiety is helpful. She developed the concept of the oscillating shift between the 'paranoid–schizoid position', in which splitting and persecution rule, and the 'depressive position', in which integration, guilt and depressive anxieties predominate. With stress, primitive paranoid–schizoid anxieties are more likely to arise and more depressive feelings of sadness, loss and grief, which frequently accompany illness, are then not experienced or are ejected or destroyed.

Rosenfeld (1964) describes how, under the influence of persecutory anxieties, the abnormal splitting of good and bad objects (the inner representations of people or parts of people) can lead to the splitting off of bad objects into the body or into external objects and then their withdrawal back into the body or particular body organs. One everyday example is the tendency to use sadistic metaphors or images to describe the experience of pain. Adjectives such as 'punishing', 'cruel', 'fearful', etc. are commonly applied (Melzack, 1975). Images such as that of a knife being twisted or a screw being bored into the body are also commonly elicited from patients in pain. This is only one instance of the mechanisms by which the body can at times – for all of us – become a 'theatre' (McDougall, 1989) in which fantasies, symbolic processes and non-symbolic, preneurotic processes are enacted.

Our ability to tolerate and work through the distress accompanying and interacting with ill health depends in part on our pre-existing internal resources and in part on the support and receptivity of the people around us. We will now give one brief example of a case where such resources were lacking and specialist psychotherapeutic help was used.

Carl B.

Carl was a 13-year-old boy who became depressed and aggressive following the emergency amputation of his right leg because of cancer. He began to attack his younger brother physically, became sullen and morose, and was unable to articulate his distress. His oncologist referred him to the psychotherapist.

After several months of psychotherapy the meaning of Carl's distress grew clearer. He was besieged by an overwhelming sense of worthlessness and loss, and this had impaired his ability to harness his considerable inner strengths and environmental support. It also became clear that Carl felt the loss of his leg as a punishment, a pre-ordained doom for life-long aggression and oedipal longings. At this point, Carl's previous history came to the fore. When he was six months old his mother had been hospitalised for tuberculosis. She eventually returned home pregnant and gave birth to Carl's brother six months later. It emerged that Carl's brother – of whom he had always been jealous – represented his denied helplessness, and evoked his rage at the premature loss of his mother as well as the actual loss of his leg.

Carl's sudden disability was indeed terrible; however, his psychotherapy revealed the ways in which he had attached to it even more terrible and complex fantasies of retaliation, castration, his wickedness, and the sense that valued objects are always lost. These punitive fantasies, as well as his parents' difficulties in acknowledging his distress, impeded the inevitably hard task of re-integrating his disability into his body image.

One common thread running through the various case studies in this book is the therapists' attention to the patient's 'imaginative body' – that multifaceted, dynamic interplay between actual and perceived bodily form, cultural and social bodily norms, physiological processes, the syntax of gesture and posture and dress, internalised objects and part objects, conscious and unconscious thoughts, attributions, feelings and fantasies. (More precisely, we should speak of imaginative *bodies*, as Joan Raphael-Leff and Susie Orbach suggest in this book.)

Psychodynamic theorists have given us maps – however partial and inexact they may be – to help us explore unconscious and preconscious processes. Such theories can be used as a way of comprehending the complexity of the imaginative bodies of patients with illness, pain and body image disturbance. Psychodynamic therapy can also play an important role in the response to the distress of such patients. As we outline below, the current practice of psychodynamic therapy in health care owes much to important changes in the psychoanalytic understanding of health and illness over the last 20 years.

Recent developments in psychoanalytic approaches to health and illness

The early psychosomatic disease models (e.g. Alexander, 1950; Deutsch, 1959) influenced most psychoanalytic therapy of medical patients up to the early 1970s. These models were applied primarily to the so-called 'classical psychosomatic diseases': essential hypertension, bronchial asthma, rheumatoid arthritis, neurodermatitis, thyrotoxicosis, ulcerative colitis and peptic ulcer. Based on Freud's instinct theory of neurosis, such theories employed a dualistic linear concept of causality – the 'mysterious leap' from mind to body – and produced generally unimpressive clinical results.

A notable exception was the pioneering work with children of Anna Freud (1952) and her colleagues (e.g. Robertson, 1956; Bergmann, 1965).

They paid attention to the effects of illness, hospitalisation, anaesthesia and surgery on the child. The interplay of stages of development, environmental adversity, such as medical procedures, and the ill child's fantasy life was all brought to bear on the assessment and psychoanalytic treatment of ill or disabled children.

From the 1970s, the rising disciplines of behavioural medicine and (later) health psychology, both based on cognitive–behavioural theory, began to demonstrate effective short-term interventions in diverse fields such as chronic pain, hypertension, cardiac rehabilitation and preparation for surgery. These results contrasted with the clinical limitations of the classical model.

Nevertheless, it was also true that during this period important theoretical revisions were being made in this field by analysts such as Marty, de M'Uzan and David (1963), Nemiah and Sifneos (1970), McDougall (e.g. 1974, 1989), and Krystal (e.g. 1979). With varying emphases, they moved away from drive theory to explore the impact of failures in emotional processing on the development of illness. The concept of alexithymic functioning gained prominence. Alexithymia, a controversial concept, is described in more detail on pp. 50–53 and 90, but has been used to denote characteristics such as the inability to describe and discriminate between emotions, together with a tendency to somatise distress, an impoverished fantasy life and poor dream recall. Such characteristics were thought by many psychoanalysts to present a bar to psychodynamic therapy. Thus, for example, Sifneos (1974) writes:

> ... psychodynamic psychotherapy, which requires a patient to interact emotionally with his therapist is, in my opinion, contraindicated for such individuals, because what appears as denial of emotions, is an absence of feelings. Such a treatment tends to lead to frustration. In my patient, it may have aggravated his peptic ulcer or further elevated his blood pressure. It is also possible that it might give rise to another heart attack in the future. (p. 154)

McDougall (1982) described alexithymia, not as a psychological or neuroanatomical defect, but as a pre-neurotic, desperate defence against psychotic fears in the context of a failure to internalise a benign maternal object. She warned against psychotherapy where the dangers of destabilising such defences were excessive. However, her sympathetic and detailed case studies (e.g. McDougall, 1989) of psychoanalysis with certain 'anti-analysands' (as she used to call patients with alexithymic characteristics) have inspired other clinicians to follow on.

Krystal (1978) saw alexithymia as a response to trauma. In infancy or childhood it develops through arrested affective development, whereas in adulthood it represents a fluctuating and reversible regression to earlier stages of affective functioning; in both cases an impairment in the self-care and self-soothing functions is predicted.

For Krystal (1988), psychoanalytic work is rarely if ever indicated for the cases of arrested affective development, but he has developed a modified form of therapy for other patients. This includes: (1) helping the patient observe the nature of the alexithymic disturbance; (2) helping the patient to develop tolerance of emotions; (3) helping the patient to identify, verbalise and, if necessary, desomatise his or her emotions and begin to use them as signals which can aid self-care and self-regulation.

In addition to his contribution to the empirical measurement and study of alexithymia, Taylor (1987, 1992a,b) has also developed a biopyschosocial dysregulation model of illness. Drawing on general systems theory, Taylor has developed this model of illness which integrates psychoanalytic object relations and self theory with findings from developmental biology and the biomedical sciences. One of his essential notions is that relationships can function as external regulators, of biological as well as psychological processes. When early mother–infant relations lead to defective object relations, both the inner world, social relations and physiological functioning can become disturbed or vulnerable to disturbance. (See also Chapter 6 of this book by Graeme Taylor.)

As with the work of Krystal and McDougall, Taylor's theory leads to a renewed role for psychoanalytic involvement with somatic distress. Like Krystal (1988) he advocates a modified form of psychoanalytic psychotherapy where alexithymic characteristics prevail (Taylor, 1987):

> The aim of contemporary psychoanalytic treatment [with such patients], based on a theory of object relations and self, is not to increase patients' awareness of infantile wishes and drives so that these may be relinquished, but to promote further maturation of psychic structures, which will increase the capacity for self regulation. Repeated confrontations of defenses and interpretations of instinctual conflicts are often experienced by patients as empathic failures on the part of their analyst.   (pp. 257–258)

Lastly, as well as intervening directly with individual patients, psychodynamic therapists have also developed modes of consultation to groups of health care professionals. Major influences on this work have been general systems theory, group analytic theory, psychoanalytic familial interventions (e.g. Campbell and Draper, 1985), and the writings of Menzies-Lyth (e.g. 1970) demonstrating the ways in which institutions evolve structural defences against anxiety. Chapters 10 and 9 by Dierdre Moylan and Jon Juriedini, and Sebastian Kraemer illustrate this important development.

Recent psychodynamic interventions in health care

In the field of mother–infant interaction, psychoanalysts and psychotherapists have drawn upon developmental psychology, observational studies (Brazelton, Koslowski and Main, 1974; Stern, 1985; Trevarthen,

1985) and the 'infant' part of the adult as revealed in clinical practice, to intervene in a range of paediatric settings. These include neonatal units (e.g. Bender and Swan-Parente, 1983) and baby clinics where, for example, sleep problems in infancy have been addressed (Daws, 1989).

This involvement has extended to the understanding of the unborn child. Such research is exemplified by the psychoanalyst Piontelli (1992). Her observational, longitudinal studies use ultrasound to follow the developing fetus, through birth to infancy. Piontelli highlights the interaction *in utero* between fetus and placenta/mother or placenta/twin. She also documents the remarkable continuity of characteristics in infants pre- and postnatally and this stimulates profound questions about when and how mental life starts, with its rudimentary notions of 'me' and 'not me'.

In the field of reproductive medicine, Raphael-Leff's work draws on her clinical experience as an analyst, together with social psychological and anthropological research, to examine the influences of cultural, medical, individual conscious and unconscious processes on all aspects of reproduction: pregnancy, child birth, infertility, etc. (Raphael-Leff, 1991). She advocates the use of psychodynamic psychotherapy (individual or group) in pregnancy. This is especially recommended for 'at risk' women such as those with acutely conflicted feelings towards the pregnancy, psychologically vulnerable women and women with complicated pregnancies, because of either medical factors or concurrent psychophysical conditions including substance abuse or eating disorders. She points out that the accessibility of unconscious material during pregnancy makes a woman more insightful and amenable to change (Raphael-Leff, 1980). (See also Chapter 1 in this book by Joan Raphael-Leff.)

In the child disability field, Fraiberg's (1977) longitudinal studies of blind babies and children show that, throughout development, blindness can be an impediment to 'representational intelligence' (i.e. the ability to organise the object world). Above all, blindness can delay the establishment of a sense of 'I' and 'you', even in a group of educationally advantaged blind children with no neurological impairment. However, by the age of five the blind children had more or less caught up with sighted children in this respect; they were able to make qualitatively good human attachments, provided they had been nurtured in an environment that 'lures the child into discoveries of himself and the external world' (p. 282). By attention to fleeting communications and special body language, Fraiberg offers insights and strategies for parents and professionals to help blind children compensate for their disability and facilitate development.

Hoxter (1986) explores the impact in the counter-transference of working with physically disabled children who have experienced a range of traumas, including the risk of death, surgical intervention, dependency and the deprivation of various functions such as mobility. Hoxter suggests that by bearing some of the impact of the patients' traumas and their unconscious phantasies around their disability, as well as the ability to bear uncertainty, the psychotherapist can begin to contain and process that which is often avoided. Perhaps the painfulness of this area, imbued as it is with phantasies around a biological 'mistake', partly explains the paucity of clinicians working in this field and writing about it.

Yorke (1980) explores 'coping mechanisms' used by physically disabled children dealing with a painful reality. He concludes that for those patients who ascribe all their difficulties to the disability, the analysis proper can only take place after this emphasis has been successfully analysed and undermined.

Two papers have given detailed accounts of psychoanalytic psychotherapy with congenitally disabled children. Lussier (1980) describes the analysis of a boy born with two small deformed arms. The analysis uncovered a passionate desire within the boy to have his body accepted and validated, a desire which triggered fantasies both manic and ultimately, with the help of the analysis, 'ego-building'. Judd's (1990) paper on psychotherapy with an adolescent with spina bifida is an example of the ways in which a patient's physical damage can lead to psychical deficiencies and secondary cognitive and emotional burdens. This patient's incapacity to hold onto thoughts and to symbolise parallelled the paralysis of her lower body and lack of sphincter control. Through attention to the counter-transference, the psychotherapist found that the patient's verbal flow denied the reality of having to have enemas, catheters and a draining stunt in her head. In time, therapy helped her to discriminate between actual physical damage and the additional psychical and secondary cognitive burdens she was carrying.

Sinason (1992) has made a major contribution to the psychoanalytic understanding of learning disability. She has also described the way in which 'secondary' and 'opportunist' cognitive and emotional handicaps can be brought into play by patients without primary mental handicap, as ways of deadening longings and memories of past trauma, including that of illness or physical disability. Importantly, she has alerted workers in the field to pay attention to what they are *not* seeing, to attempt to know their own handicapping, 'going stupid' and not being able to think at times, when faced with extremes in their patients which are hard to bear.

We have already briefly mentioned the work of feminist psychotherapists (p. 170). Psychodynamic psychotherapists have combined feminist analysis of patriarchal social and family structures with the work of object-relations analysts (such as Fairbairn, 1952; Guntrip, 1974). In the context of distorting social and familial relations, the mother–daughter relationship is described as often disturbed; this impairs the gratification of the infant girl's early dependency needs and undermines the separation–individuation phase of development (Eichenbaum and Orbach, 1983). In turn this complicates the girl's relationship to needs, appetites and desires of all kinds, and increases vulnerability to psychological and body-image disturbance. These theories have in fact been most notably applied to the psychotherapy of women with disorders such as anorexia, bulimia and compulsive eating (e.g. Orbach, 1986; Dana and Lawrence, 1988). (See also Chapter 7 of this book by Susie Orbach.)

In the field of chronic life-threatening illness the analysts George Moran and Peter Fonagy have applied psychoanalytic psychotherapy to the treatment of diabetic children and young adults whose lives were constantly disrupted by life-threatening episodes of hypoglycaemia and ketoacidosis (e.g. Moran and Fonagy, 1987; Fonagy and Moran, 1991). Their studies are notable in two ways. They illuminate those unconscious and destructive processes involved in the patients' presentation and the ways in which these processes were able to be worked through in the therapy. (See also Chapter 3 by Peter Fonagy and George Moran in this book.) Importantly, they have used empirical outcome measures – for example, glycosylated haemoglobin, a cumulative measure of blood sugar control – to demonstrate the clinical efficacy of their methods. This research is particularly significant given the dearth of empirical evaluative studies in this whole field.

The problems of psychoanalytic research in health care are, of course, not to be underestimated. In brief, they include the fact that a major aim of psychoanalytic psychotherapy is to produce structural changes in the personality which are often unconscious and so inimical to self-report. Patients' self-reports may be 'contaminated' by an analyst's suggestions received under the influence of a positive transference. Drawing on his own research, Fonagy (1991) suggests that the way forward for psychoanalytic research lies in the choice of the following components: (1) a readily definable client group who tend to respond poorly to less intensive treatments; (2) a clinically relevant outcome variable which is robust to contamination from the treatment process; and (3) complementary process studies which offer suggestive evidence of the effective components of the treatment. Edelson (1984, 1989) and Wallerstein (1986) give full discussions of the many complex issues involved in the development of psychoanalytic research methods.

The issue of empirical means of evaluation in this field is important for reasons other than the need to monitor efficacy. It will open up communication with the wider scientific community – for example, within health psychology, liaison psychiatry and cognitive science – allowing for greater cross-fertilisation of theoretical and clinical ideas. Although more recognition is now given to the benefits of counselling within health care – perhaps in part because of the impetus of AIDS – nevertheless, resource allocation in terms of personnel and training remains poor. Psychodynamic therapies can be more complex, long term and costly than their alternatives. There is all the more need, therefore, to demonstrate their clinical efficacy to health care purchasers. For example, in the studies by Fonagy and Moran, mentioned above, all their patients had been through various expensive medical and psychological treatments before entering psychoanalytic psychotherapy. Although the latter was costly and labour-intensive, in the end the efficacy of the treatment may well have rendered it also cost-effective.

Conclusion

We are concerned that those who struggle with pain, illness, eating disorders or body-image disturbance should be able to access counselling or psychotherapy alongside good medical care. We emphasise, however, that the help offered should always be based on skilled assessment which can identify the patients' needs, capabilities, wishes and vulnerabilities.

Some patients may need only brief supportive counselling to enhance their coping strategies. Others may benefit from more structured, cognitive–behavioural interventions. Where there is sufficient readiness to look in greater depth at the presenting problem and its resonances in the patient's inner world and past life, the need may be for psychoanalytic counselling or psychotherapy. A few may be prepared to embark on a longer journey of psychoanalysis, whereby understanding the illness becomes a means of changing the structure of the personality itself.

References

ALEXANDER, F. (1950). *Psychosomatic Medicine*. New York: Norton.

BERGER, J. (1972). *Ways of Seeing*. London: Pelican.

BERGMANN, T. (1965). *Children in the Hospital*. New York: International Universities Press.

BRAZELTON, T., KOSLOWSKI, B. and MAIN, M. (1974). Origins of reciprocity: early mother–infant interaction. In: M. Lewis and L. Rosenblum (Eds), *The Effect of the Infant on its Caregivers*, pp. 49–76. London: Wiley-Interscience.

CAMPBELL, D. and DRAPER, R. (Eds) (1985). *Applications of Systemic Family Therapy: The Milan Approach*. London: Grune & Stratton.

DANA, M. and LAWRENCE, M. (1988). *Women's Secret Disorder: A New Understanding of Bulimia*. London: Grafton Books.

DAWS, D. (1989). *Through the Night – Helping Parents and Sleepless Infants*. London: Free Association Books.

DEUTSCH, F. (1959). *On the Mysterious Leap from the Mind to the Body*. New York: International Universities Press.

EDELSON, M. (1984). *Hypothesis and Evidence in Psychoanalysis*. Chicago: University of Chicago Press.

EDELSON, M. (1989). The nature of psychoanalytic theory: implications for psychoanalytic research. *Psycho-Analytic Inquiry* 9, 169–192.

EICHENBAUM, L. and ORBACH, S. (1983). *Understanding Women: A Feminist and Psychoanalytic Approach*. New York: Basic Books.

ENGEL, G. (1977). The need for a new medical model. *Science* 196, 129–136.

FAIRBAIRN, W.R. (1952). *Psychoanalytic Studies of the Personality*. London: Tavistock.

FONAGY, P. (1991). What is scientific about psychotherapy? *Newsletter, British Psychological Society Psychotherapy Section* **11**, 18-29.

FONAGY, P. and MORAN, G. (1991). Individual case study. In: L. Luborsky and N. Miller (Eds), *Handbook of Psychoanalytic Research*. New York: Basic Books.

FRAIBERG, S. (1977). *Insights from the Blind*. London: Souvenir Press.

FREUD, A. (1952). The role of bodily illness in the mental life of children. *Psychoanalytic Study of the Child*, Vol. 7, pp. 69-81. New York: International Universities Press.

GRODDECK, G. (1926). *The Book of the Id*. New York: Vintage Books.

GUNTRIP, H. (1974). Psychoanalytic object relations theory: the Fairbairn–Guntrip approach. Reprinted from: S. Areiti (Ed.), *American Handbook of Psychiatry*, 2nd edn, Vol. 1: *The Foundations of Psychiatry*. New York: Basic Books.

HOXTER, S. (1986). The significance of trauma in the difficulties encountered by physically disabled children. *Journal of Child Psychotherapy* **12** (1), 87-102.

JUDD, D. (1990). Psyche-Soma Issues for an adolescent with spina-bifida and mental handicap. *Journal of Child Psychotherapy* **16** (2), 83-98.

KLEIN, M. (1946). The psychogenesis of manic depressive states. In: *Envy and Gratitude*. London: Hogarth (1975).

KRYSTAL, H. (1978). Self-representation and the capacity for self care. *Annals of Psychoanalysis* **6**, 209-246.

KRYSTAL, H. (1979). Alexithymia and psychotherapy. *American Journal of Psychotherapy* **33** (1), 17-31.

KRYSTAL, H. (1988). *Integration and Self-Healing*. New York: Analytic Press.

LUSSIER, A. (1980). The physical handicap and the body ego. *International Journal of Psycho-Analysis* **61**, 179-185.

McDOUGALL, J. (1974). The psychesoma and the psychoanalytic process. *International Review of Psychoanalysis* **1**, 437-459.

McDOUGALL, J. (1982). Alexithymia: a psychoanalytic viewpoint. *Psychotherapy and Psychosomatics* **38**, 81-90.

McDOUGALL, J. (1989). *Theatres of the Body – A Psychoanalytic Approach to Psychosomatic Illness*. London: Free Association Books.

MARTY, P., DE M'UZAN, M. and DAVID, C. (1963). *L'Investigation Psychosomatic*. Paris: Presses Universites.

MELZACK, R. (1975). The McGill Pain Questionnaire: major properties and scoring methods. *Pain* **1**, 275-299.

MENZIES-LYTH, I. (1970). *The Functioning of Social Systems as a Defence against Anxiety*. London: Tavistock Institute of Human Relations.

MILNER, M. (1950). *On Not Being able to Paint*. London: Heineman Educational Books.

MORAN, G. and FONAGY, P. (1987). Psychoanalysis and diabetic control: a single case-study. *British Journal of Medical Psychology* **60**, 357-362.

NEMIAH, J. and SIFNEOS, P. (1970). Affect and fantasy in patients with psychosomatic disorders. In: O.W. Hill (Ed.), *Modern Trends in Psychosomatic Medicine*, Vol. 2. London: Butterworths.

ORBACH, S. (1986). *Hunger Strike: The Anorectic's Struggle as a Metaphor for our Time*. London: Faber.

PIONTELLI, S. (1993). *From Fetus to Child – An Observational and Psychoanalytic Study*. London: Tavistock/Routledge.

RAPHAEL-LEFF, J. (1980). Psychotherapy with pregnant women. In: B. Blum (Ed.), *Psychological Aspects of Pregnancy, Birthing and Bonding*. New York: Human Sciences Press.

RAPHAEL-LEFF, J. (1980). *Psychological Processes of Childbearing*. London: Chapman and Hall.

ROBERTSON, J. (1956). A mother's observations on the tonsillectomy of her four year old daughter, with comments by Anna Freud. *Psychoanalytic Study of the Child*, Vol. 2, pp. 410-433. New York: International Universities Press.

ROSENFELD, H. (1964). The psychopathology of hypochondriasis. In: *Psychotic States*. London: Maresfield Reprints, 1965.

SIFNEOS, P. (1974). A reconsideration of psychodynamic mechanisms in psychosomatic symptom formation in view of recent clinical observations. *Psychotherapy and Psychosomatics* **24**, 151.

SINASON, V. (1992). *Mental Handicap and the Human Condition - New Approaches from the Tavistock*. London: Free Association Books.

SONTAG, S. (1983). *Illness as Metaphor*. London: Penguin.

STERN, D. (1985). *The Interpersonal World of the Infant*. New York: Basic Books.

TAYLOR, G. (1987). *Psychosomatic Medicine and Contemporary Psychoanalysis*. Madison, CT: International Universities Press.

TAYLOR, G. (1992a). Psychoanalysis and psychosomatics: a new synthesis. *Journal of the American Academy of Psychoanalysis* **20**, 251-275.

TAYLOR, G. (1992b). Psychosomatics and self regulation. In: J. Barron, M. Eagle and D. Wolitzky (Eds), *Interface of Psycho-analysis and Psychology*. Washington DC: American Psychological Association.

TREVARTHEN, C. (1985). Facial expressions of emotion in mother–infant interaction. *Human Neurobiology* **4**.

USSHER, J. (1989). *The Psychology of the Female Body*. London: Routledge.

WALLERSTEIN, R. (1986). Psychoanalysis as a science: a response to new challenges. *Psychoanalytic Quarterly* **56**, 414-451.

WINNICOTT, D. (1965). *The Maturational Processes and the Facilitating Environment*. London: Hogarth.

WINNICOTT, D. (1972). Basis for self in body. *International Journal of Child Psychotherapy* **1** (1), 7-16.

YORKE, C. (1980). Some comments on the psychoanalytic treatments of patients with physical disabilities. *International Journal of Psycho-Analysis* **61**, 187-193.

Chapter 1
Imaginative bodies of childbearing:
visions and revisions

Joan Raphael-Leff

The imaginative body does not just spring from within – it is a psychosocial product of its time and place. While growing up, a child's body-images are shaped by the forces that form and inform the interpersonal matrix of his or her 'intra-psycho-somatic' world. Social concepts of our reproductive bodies have altered dramatically in recent times as a result of widespread availability of contraception and safe abortion, as well as rising incidence of infertility coupled with extraordinary new reproductive technologies for combating this. These in turn have enabled us to discriminate between impulse, compulsion and choice, and to appreciate finer distinctions between sexuality (both male and female), feminine or masculine gender identity, and biochemical/physiological reproductive processes. Thus we may delineate a desire to be pregnant from a wish for a baby or a need to parent. Conversely, discrepancies between the high-flying imaginative body and the harsh limitations of corporeal reality are heightened by contemporary psychosocial factors – illusions of contraceptive control, the unconquerability of AIDS, the existential disillusionments of infertility and the fact of prenatal screening.

Engagement in childbearing brings the internalised 'generative' body-image into sharp focus. Obstacles to its fulfilment not only underscore fantasy figurations but revitalise archaic doubts about creativity and theories of how babies are made and where they come from. These reactivated representations of inner space, ovum, sperm, gestation, placenta and birth permeate the pregnancy, and a baby thus conceived may be moulded as much by preconceptual ideas in the minds of his or her progenitors as by exchanges with those parents pre- and postnatally.

Before addressing the imaginative bodies of reproductivity, there are three interrelated presuppositions about body-image in general that I want to pose:

1. Many different imaginative bodies may coexist.

13

2. Body-images fluctuate continually in relation to internal and external events.
3. As experienced and observed, our bodies are never solipsistically our own.

To explain the first point, I will attempt first to collate some distinctions made in the literature between diverse constructs which constitute the body-image totality (these are adapted from authorities such as Shonz, 1974; Cash and Pruzinsky, 1990; and others):

1. *Body schema*: the body as sensory register and processor; source of biological needs, reflexes, etc.; closely related to neurological processes.
2. *Body concepts or percepts*: a private world of cognitive bodily images of body appearance, size, competence, boundaries, gender, experiences and memories.
3. *Body ideal*: the concept against which these are measured.
4. *Body self*: the body as self-stimulus and instrument of purposive action.
5. *Body-image affect*: derived from the body as expressive instrument and social stimulus to others.
6. *Body-image attitude*: ideas and rules which organise our view of the physical self.

To these dimensions, I would propose adding another – that of expanding or contracting *personal dominion*: the psychic extension or intrusive projection of the self into internal objects or bodies and minds in the surrounding space beyond body boundaries.

Most researchers seem to concur that the fundamental sense of self as embodied and differentiated – the body self – is related to emotional and cognitive aspects of self-perception. Also implied is an assumption that the multifaceted body-image operates as a totality of interrelating levels of body experience filtered through social reality.

However, clinical experience in dealing with reproductive issues has led me to realise that not only do we operate simultaneously, but on many experiential levels (as implied above), we also conjure up diverse body percepts retained from different developmental phases. In addition, we engage differentially with various subsets of the imaginative body-selves that make up personal identity – ourselves as gendered, generative, genital, sexual, creative, procreative, etc.

This idea of a plurality of imaginative bodies which I propose to elaborate here accords with the idea held by some contemporary British psycho-analysts of the independent tradition who argue for multi-layered, multi-tracked consciousness and the existence of a plurality of internal selves and voices (see, for instance, Kennedy, 1993). In other words, I am suggesting we might envisage a variety of imaginative body-selves drawing on imagery both subjectively esoteric and objectively exoteric, metaphorically tumbling over each other in the inner 'space' they come to inhabit. Some remain within corporeal restrictions; others meander fantastically across intrapsychic spaces, sexes and ages or fluidly spill out, gliding through membranous borders into the skins of others. It seems to be the case that some internal imagos reside harmoniously side by side whereas others (for instance, maternity and sexuality in late pregnancy and particularly during lactation) coexist uneasily. Among yet other body-selves, conflicts rage, as social bodily selves encased in worldly trappings of gender solidarity and subcultural definition vie with the unself-conscious loose image-boundaries of the sloppy-slippered bedtime-child. Nevertheless, despite describing this internal medley, I would endorse the general formulation that through a process of symbolisation and self-awareness of bodily experience, body-image and self-image normally cohere to form a sense of self-identity, providing a relatively stable internal frame of reference, continuous over time, space and state (Krueger, 1990).

However, my thesis here is that crucial bodily experiences or technological advances, such as contraception, assisted conception and prenatal screening, may fracture this internal coherence. During nodal points of transition – for example, adolescence, awaited impregnation, pregnancy, menopause – body-image distinctions between the core-components of sexuality, reproductivity, generativity and gender are heightened and become disjointed.

The second point, that developmentally and daily an oscillating interplay of external and internal, conscious and unconscious, time past and present events modify and update ongoing bodily images, was first remarked upon by the originator of the 'body-image' concept, Paul Schilder:

> The image of the body thus shows characteristic features of our whole life. There is a continual change from crystallized rather closed entities to states of dissolution and to a stream of less stabilized experiences, and from there a return to better form and changed entity. It is therefore the continuous building up of a shape which is immediately dissolved and built up again.
>
> (Schilder, 1935, pp. 209–210)

In health, we hardly notice as our body texts shift their metaphors in accordance with the changing content of daily life. At other times, psychological changes in self-perception may take the form of over- or under-cathexis of the body or parts of it, as in states of hypochondria or anaesthesia (see Szasz, 1957). Internal conflicts may manifest in dramatic ways, as in hysterical conversions and psychosomatic states, when the body expresses its meanings in symptom or action without resorting to intermediating thought. In some borderline conditions, inner components are so fragmented that each behaves as a separate personality not acknowledging the existence of others (what Ferenczi, 1933, called 'atomization'). Each component may be attributed to a body organ or function (for instance, dichotomous right/left female/male body-cleavage as described by Anthi, 1986). In cases of 'multiple personality' (a psychiatric rarity despite the current 'epidemic' of this DSM-III-R diagnosis which is seemingly used cynically in the USA for purposes of reimbursement by health insurers), bodily posturing may differ flamboyantly, as the person remains in the grip of insular selves. In more projective conditions, when internal components are so antagonistically split that their battles are too violent to contain, aggressor and/or victim self may be ejected, expelled into others and converted into sado-masochistic interpersonal enactments. Conversely, rigidity of body limits, paucity of representations or distorted stylised images, like the unrelenting mannequin-ideal of anorexia or the monomania of fetishistic triggers, equally indicate disorders of the imaginative body.

Disturbance may be transient – temporarily exacerbated by emotional turbulence or bodily trauma. It may be permanently in evidence or accentuated by regressive de-differentiation under stress. Interest in non-verbal manifestations during psychoanalytic treatment have led to the documentation of a variety of archaic kinaesthetic, thermal, acoustic, vestibular and tactile features of the body-image reasserting themselves on the couch under conditions of analytic regression (Peto, 1959). Such experiences have variously been described as the dangerous leakage or drainage of non-distinguished mental and physical contents (Kafka, 1971); collapse of the sense of self-cohesion with reawakening of an autistic–contiguous ordering of sensory experience (Ogden, 1989), or regression to a dimension of autistic 'shapes' (Tustin, 1984); revival of primitive anxieties of boundlessness and spillages (Rosenfeld, 1984), and bodily enactments of addictions, somatisation, perversions and risk-taking (Hopper, 1991). The latter links these enactments to psychic representations of fusion/confusion with abandoning objects and lost parts of the self; such objects become encapsulated as a defence against annihilation anxieties caused by failed attachments in early relationships.

Thus I come to my third point. Experienced and observed, our bodies are never solipsistically 'our own'. Our body-images are social products. For we 'learn' our bodies through the hands, faces and minds of significant carers and their bodily ministrations. Depending on the developmental theory they hold, each psychoanalytic researcher emphasises different aspects of the process in describing how acquisition of a sense of embodied self takes place. To Freud, the ego is 'first and foremost a body-ego' (1923, p. 27) initially derived from bodily sensations, and enhanced, as he was later to suggest, by the mother's physical care (1933, p. 120). Margaret Mahler, too, stresses that internal proprioceptive experiences come to be supplemented by interchange within the mother–infant 'symbiotic' duality; the separating–individuating baby gradually internalises the mother's organising patterns of caring behaviour, thus shaping the nature of the body-self (Mahler and McDevitt, 1982). From a self-psychology viewpoint, Lichtenberg (1975) suggests that a cohesive sense of self is born of gradual, experiential blending of bodily self-images, self-images in relation to objects and images of the grandiose self associated with idealised self-objects. Finally, drawing on neonatal research, Daniel Stern (1985) focuses on the development of diverse dimensions of self including agency, physical cohesion and continuity; this occurs through the aggregation and distillation of cross-modal experiences in addition to feedback from the attuned/misattuned (m)other, all of which provide grounds for the development of a unified, pervasive sense of 'self being' as well as recognition of a core other.

Whatever the language used, inevitably, all theoreticians tacitly assume physical as well as emotional give-and-take between caregiver and infant during the process of elaborating body boundaries and representations. However, few acknowledge the sheer sensual bodiliness of the exchange and the primal nature of fluids and substances involved – amnion, blood, milk, sweat, saliva, tears, urine, excreta – a primitive interactive foundation which lasts for life. Indeed, right into adulthood, a web of associative connections link the flesh of our permeable bodies in our most intimate moments to the bodies of others. Even in the privacy of masturbatory acts and within the secret realms of bulimic activity or self-mutilating solitude, their imagined responses guide erotic fantasy or relentlessly dictate cruel standards. Furthermore, through an interplay of processes of projective identification and merger, not only their responses but the body-images of others are themselves also absorbed into the imaginative body-self.

Clearly then, the imaginative body is a social acquisition, bound and shaped by subtle cultural standards and aesthetic categories which are as effective to psyche as Chinese foot-binding is to flesh. They are as somatically influential as diverse childrearing customs in creating foundations of bodily experience through such things as infant swaddling, buggy-riding or the continuous vestibular stimulation of the mother's carrying body and readily accessible breast (see Raphael-Leff, 1991d, for transcultural perinatal variations of intake, labour, feeding, etc.).

Schilder (1935) recognised both the social and culture-bound aspects of body-image. Despite bowing to the concept of 'autoerotic narcissism' prevalent at the time, in a conclusion remarkable for its day, he stated that:

> . . . body images are never isolated. They are always encircled by the body-images of others . . . . There is a continuous interchange between parts of our own body-image and the body-images of others.   (pp. 240–241)

Again, drawing the circle wider, he stated:

> . . . a body-image is in some way always the sum of the body-images of the community.   (p. 302)

Configurations of the reproductive body

In this chapter I wish to focus both on psychosocial pressures and unconscious representations underpinning the imaginative body, with a special emphasis on its generative aspects. My ideas are based on intensive psychoanalytic or psychotherapeutic work with some 200 individuals and couples preoccupied with childbearing, seen over the last 20 years. This work is supplemented by questionnaire studies and analysis of videoed mother–baby observations. Illuminating the text is a subtext of quotes from all these sources.

Pregnancy

Let us begin at the beginning. We have each started our lives as a connected-duality within the inner space of a female body. In our wildest dreams and most intimate sexual and emotional moments, we transcend bodily boundaries of separateness and sexed dividedness, striving to recapture undefined fusion. Ferenczi (1938) traced the male's intrauterine recapitulation to a momentary return to the womb through his penis in coitus. Deutsch (1945) suggested that, for a woman, the penetrating penis is both breast and baby – 'an object of maternal libido' to the woman's sucking/suckling vagina (in Deutsch's view, provided she has renounced the claim of the clitoris to be a 'penis surrogate'); later the penis will be supplanted by the child in her womb. Thus, not only briefly in intercourse, but during the prolonged state of pregnancy, a woman may recapitulate her bodily origins.

Pregnant, a woman is in the strange position of actually having the continuous presence of an Other within her body – two people reside under her skin. In some cases pregnancy promises fulfilment of a woman's ancient desire for merger; to another it offers reparation of her own severance by means of the umbilical connection to the baby inside her. Taking an imaginative leap into identification with the fetus residing in her womb as she was carried by her own mother, an expectant mother may revel in a prelapsarian ideal, fancifully undoing the expulsion of her own birth. Her imaginative body expands with gestation as, holding logic in abeyance, she replays the elusive vision of herself like her own mother – creatively swelling with herself *in utero*; identifying with her baby, she luxuriates in oceanic weightlessness, sprouting finger-buds and features, while somersaulting within the repossessed maternal uterus.

However, for the expectant mother, this state is not necessarily blissful. Twosomeness can prove troubling for some women, threatening hard-won independence. Pregnancy always entails loss of freedom and autonomy, and may also constitute a physical drain, an unwanted life event or burdensome necessity, a loss of self: the growing fetus may feel like an invasive, parasitic being feeding within her, or an internal saboteur beyond her control. According to her mood and circumstances, imagery of the 'tethered tandem' fluctuates. I have suggested that these variations may be conceptualised as permutations of positions along two axes – good/bad and self/fetus – ranging from idealised visions of herself as a bountiful source of nutrients for a grateful good baby, to persecutory images of a bad exploitative fetus sapping her energy; to herself as a damaging or stingy provider for a vulnerable baby or a state of mutually deleterious exchange of poisonous substances or bad feelings (Raphael-Leff, 1989).

The pregnant woman's conscious identity as a separate, single, intact, female being is in question. Objectively, her body, as she has known it since adolescence, is in the throes of rapid and dramatic physical changes with which her body-image cannot keep pace. Not only singularity but gender, too, is affected. Paradoxically, while engaged in this quintessentially female reproductive function, there is a good chance that she contains a male fetus within her, as well as having incorporated the foreign residue of her male impregnator. She may feel a sense of excitement as the whirlpool of kaleidoscopically rotating imagery poses intoxicating potentialities. However, the re-establishment in reality of the lost intrauterine world inside her own inner space, the ambiguous hybrid nature of her sexed body, her vivid dreams and heightened emotionality, and the need for constant identity reappraisal, all at times feel alarming, drawing her into use of primitive defences to preserve her sense of self (Raphael-Leff, 1993b).

For onlookers, too, a fruitbearing body heavy with archaic meaning propels us into another register of imaginative thought. Like iron filings in a magnetic field, we may feel drawn to the writhing mound of life being generated. In its compelling presence, concepts of ordinary bodies are reformulated. By unconscious comparison to the pregnant one, body-imagery becomes reframed on a gradient of essential distinctions replete with primal symbolism. This comparison leads to revision of both the onlooker's body-self and the view of the pregnant other in the following ways:

1. The body as generatively male or female.
2. A female – sexually attractive, maternal and forbidden, goddess-like and/or menacing.
3. A feminine body – sealed in virginity, receptively open or impregnatedly closed.
4. The woman – as full or empty container – unfecundated or electrified by fertilisation.
5. The pregnant body interior as creative or dangerous vessel rather than digestive tract.
6. The body taken-for-granted as owner-occupied appendage or a potential 'duplex'.
7. The onlooker's self-perceived neutral body contrasted with the pregnant body swelling with internal life-force.
8. A seemingly omnipotent female self-sufficiently engaged in the enigmatic secrets of life – rich mysteries of formation, preservation and transformation.
9. Depending on the onlooker's locus of identification, the pregnant mother may be deemed to be housing a cherished child, holding an inmate prisoner or putting up with a wily intruder.

10. The pregnant body seen as never-ceasing placental powerhouse circu-
    lating life-giving oxygen and growth-promoting nutrients while acting
    as a processing plant and clearing-house for fetal waste products.
11. The maternal body as enclosed site of paradisiacal placental fullness
    destined to be cord-severed with impending parturition – spelling
    expulsion, loss and division.

Intrauterine existence

For us all, from the outset, internal sensations are filtered through external
stimulation. After what seems aeons of curiosity, new techniques of fibre-
optic fetoscopy have made it possible to see what a baby is actually doing in
the womb and how she or he responds to different situations. What has
now been experimentally demonstrated, beyond doubt, is that the fetus
reacts to subtle changes in both the internal and external environment, and
is discriminating in response to physical experiences (of dark–light, movements, sounds, tastes, touch), social stimulation (conversation, singing,
dancing, music, external stroking and twin interaction) and maternal
emotional changes (transmitted in biochemical changes and through variations in metabolic and/or heart rate). Even within the occluding uterine
boundaries, the human baby is being influenced by the specific culture of
the external environment, as fetal hearing homes in on the mother's voice
to the accompaniment of her pulsating heartbeat and gurgling digestive
system. Thus, the baby inside is growing to know a world beyond the
womb, both directly, through the impact of maternal biorhythms and
hormonal influences, and indirectly through the fluctuating patterns of
movement, sleep, intake and social activities. No longer can we see life as
beginning with birth. Researchers such as De Casper and Fifer (1980) have
demonstrated the newborn's preference for his or her mother's voice, and
recognition of pieces of music or even of stories heard prenatally. Nor is the
baby a passive recipient, but initiates changes in the fetal environment,
competing with the mother over scarce resources, altering the composition
of amniotic fluid through swallowing and urinating, determining the spiralling shape of the cord's windings through movement, and possibly triggering labour too (see Raphael-Leff, 1993b, for a more detailed review).
Furthermore, using baby-observation techniques during ultrasound scans
and the first years postnatally, Italian psychoanalyst Alesandra Piontelli
(1992) has established a diversity of individualised prenatal behavioural
patterns seen to persist in later years. Clearly, then, the fetus is already a
complex and competent little being who responds to both incentives and
impingements and acts in a way which makes sense.

The foundations of the imaginative body are in the process of being laid
down in the womb. Whether consciously acknowledged or denied, pregnancy is already a time during which, like impulses from nerve endings

sparking across neurons in electrical discharge, social transmissions occur across uterine boundaries. Thus, as mothers have suspected throughout time, in subtle ways, mild as well as intense, properties of each fetus affect the mother in specific ways and the pregnant woman's own particular emotional and material world have a cumulative influence on her baby's well-being *in utero*. In many societies, the expectant mother's and sometimes the father's personal influences are socially controlled during pregnancy through tabooed foods, herbal applications, necessary or forbidden activities (such as plaiting, knot-tying, fishing), permitted and restricted contacts, and protective ritual ceremonies. Some of these reflect an underlying dread of the unknown, heightened during parturition. Freud, writing about prohibitions surrounding menstruation, pregnancy, childbirth and 'lying in', noted the following:

> Wherever primitive man has set up a taboo he fears some danger and it cannot be disputed that a generalized dread of women is expressed in all these rules of avoidance. Perhaps this dread is based on the fact that woman is different from man, for ever incomprehensible and mysterious, strange and therefore apparently hostile. The man is afraid of being weakened by the woman, infected by her femininity and of then showing himself incapable.   (1918, p. 198)

Birth

During labour, each woman, in the grip of a process beyond her control, is thrust back into uncharted depths of experience shared by the chain of mothers throughout time and mammals across the species. Given a choice, some parturients, willing to relinquish conscious control, risk following their bodies into the primordial event; others resist, or take fright at various points along the way, as they hang betwixt and between primitive and modern, past and future worlds. Others cling to cultural aids to bind or bypass the powerful forces unleashed by labour.

In societies where the male body is unconsciously upheld as a standard, the female one is treated as defective and lacking. Observing births transculturally, it seems that when 'delivery' is wrested from women, men take it upon themselves to manipulate, direct and improve the inferior female version. Control over the alarmingly unpredictable female body and its 'uncanny' interior is often justified by equating childbearing with dysfunction. In the West, we may trace a three-pronged take-over-bid – from female to male midwifery; home care to centralised hospital provision; and a general pathologisation of childbirth. (See, for instance, Moscucci, 1990, on historical developments in obstetrics.)

In patriarchal societies where male envy of female procreativity must be denied and negated, the act of giving birth may be construed as equivalent to defaecation; the birth canal is equated with the alimentary canal – a tube with an opening at either end (Mead, 1949), the same in both sexes.

Imagery of the female body affects the management of labour. Visualised as a vessel containing an internal cavity it may raise fantasies of the baby or the placenta rising up into the chest during labour to choke the parturient. To prevent this, in different societies, various measures are deployed, such as upright delivery, binders to prevent placental ascent or massage to ensure its descent. If internal organs are believed to be interconnected, delivery of the placenta by pulling the cord is avoided for fear it may remove other essential parts, or (as in some parts of Kenya) a stone may be tied on to prevent its return inside. Thus, configurations of the body interior, which vary according to unconscious body-image and psychosocial beliefs, come to influence both ritual practices and intrapsychic experience. A pregnant patient of mine who conceptualised her body as hollow dreaded internal vaginal examinations fearing the doctor's hand would reappear through her throat; another was anxious that once the 'plug' came out in early labour, all her internal organs would fall out.

Based on my analysis of many World Health Organization studies of childbearing patterns in various societies, I have proposed that the rich diversity in management of birth which exists around the world reflects cultural values and local beliefs about women and their bodies and these shape maternity care practices. More importantly, once internalised, these values are the stuff of which each female's reproductive body-image is moulded, subtly influencing a labouring woman's self-esteem and experience, as folk models of bodily functioning intertwine with personal imagery. For example, where parturition is believed to render a woman 'open' and vulnerable, the danger to a labouring woman from leakage or threatened invasion (by spirits or germs) is counteracted by speed and closure. If she is deemed to be in possession of dark powers, or is regarded as dirty or defiling, seclusion and magical or 'hygienic' protective measures are employed, often followed by purging and purifications. And, if labour is seen to be affected by a disharmony of humours, commensurate measures are taken to induce restoration of balance (Raphael-Leff, 1992b).

In Western cultures, where an efficiency model operates, technicians often attempt to streamline the birth (seemingly identifying with the baby, unconsciously seen as endangered within the incompetent parturient). Until the recent outcry from women, augmentation of labour, routine episiotomies (cuts across the perineum), a high rate of instrumental deliveries and a rising rate of caesarean sections were common features of modern obstetrics. Thus, in our own culture too, we may infer a variety of unconscious paradigms underlying birth practices, with procedures such as routine enemas, pubic shaving, fetal monitoring and acceleration of labour based on male perceptions and control of the dreaded female body.

If there is a female physical anxiety equivalent to male castration, genital surgery (such as clitoridectomy and circumcisory mutilation still practised in many societies and episiotomy widely practised in our own) looms large in the unconscious. In the months leading up to the birth, many pregnant women helplessly dread the humiliation, outrage and pain of being cut against their will. In addition to trepidation about the baby's birth battering her internal organs and stretching her orifices (a fear that may be so great as to cause some women to want a caesarean section), there are worries about iatrogenic damage – whether once sewn up, her vaginal opening and perineum will ever be the same. Compared to anxieties about having to face the painful hours of labour and birth, this concern is a long-term one. And indeed, in reality, her genital area never will return to its previous state. As with assisted conception, forceps deliveries and caesarean sections, a mother's generative self-esteem and reproductive body-image often feel violated by an inflicted procedure which proclaims her inability to produce a baby without artificial intervention. In addition to a deep sense of failure, regrets and guilt about not having provided her baby with a 'natural' beginning, incapacitation due to the presence of painful stitches affects initial caregiving. The very real genital damage often also has inhibitory effects on sexuality (for both partners) and may distort a woman's genital-dimensions of feminine selfhood.

Infancy and elaboration of the imaginative body

Following the birth, a mother's contact with her girl or boy baby's body draws its feel from her own mental-configuration of this alien–familiar being, grown inside and expelled from her body. Neonatal research has demonstrated that babies are primed to be exquisitely sensitive, influential and proficient in using the interactive environments into which they are born for the unfolding of their capacities. With reference to the emergent embodied self, I argue here that in addition to actual caregiving, the psychosexual gendered body is elaborated within the matrix of the imaginary bodies of significant others, through unconsciously perceived 'body syntax' as well as the quality, intensity, frequency, proximity and valence of their actual contact.

We may assume that the infant's concept of embodiment is gradually acquired in the form of self-representations. These are moulded through growing awareness of his or her own bodily experiences of touch and internal sensations, in the context of the caregiver's tactile bodily attunement, and matching or divergent ascriptions.

A mother's palpating hand, charged with affect, reflects her relation to male and female bodies, as well as the positive or negative forces unconsciously invested in her baby and feelings towards her own feminine bodiliness and fecundity, her unconscious representations of maternity, sexuality and gender. Micro-analysis of video films of mothers and fathers with their infants reveals fine-tuned differences between them in handling and intonation, which also vary according to the assigned sex of the child.

On the whole, interaction of non-primary caregiver fathers tends to be more vigorous and arousing, and more sex-typed than that of mothers, who tend to be soothing rather than stimulating (see, for example, Yogman, 1982, or Pederson, Anderson and Kain, 1980). However, clinical experience shows that who or what the sexed baby signifies varies not only from parent to parent but within the same mother or father at different developmental stages of infancy and at different times during the day and night. To a mother, the baby may at first signify completion of her own fertile identity; alternatively, representing some facet of her internal world, she or he is greeted as a beloved or hated reincarnation of a significant figure in her emotional life. She or he may be invested with an idealised female baby-self or ascribed repudiated aspects of the mother's self-image depending on her unique psychohistory (Raphael-Leff, 1986b, 1991a, 1993b). To other mothers, the child may become sexualised as a phallic extension (Deutsch, 1945), or invested with phallic desire (Lacan, 1958). My point is that, at any one time, whatever the parental fantasy, it transmits itself through the mother's fingertips, infusing her voice, gestures and demeanour as surely as, in Freud's words, secrets are unconsciously betrayed as they 'ooze out' at every pore (Freud, 1905, p. 78). Likewise, her partner's gingerly, harsh, tender or eroticised handling of the baby conveys his own personal and intergenerational unconscious gender attributions.

On an observational level, watching a parent feeding, bathing or changing an infant's nappy, we see how subtly basic bodily suppositions are conveyed and how early and unheedingly the fundamental notion of body ownership may be violated between five to ten times a day. Feelings about intake and expulsion, purity and pollution, me/not-me, genitalia, sexuality, cleanliness, propriety and spontaneous creation are concretely manifested in the caregiver's way of dealing with the infant's bodily excretions. The clotted faeces of a breast-fed baby may seem reciprocal gifts to one bountiful mother who has nourished her baby with her own bodily juices; anxious about the quality of her milk/motherliness, another may peer a fraction too closely or hesitate too long at the yellow cottage-cheese-like substance, seeking to determine whether her 'badness' has been absorbed or her 'goodness' rejected ('Why is he straining like that?'). To an obsessional mother, the soiled body in hand becomes a surface to be cleaned. As she concentrates on the bottom area, grasping the convenient 'handles' of the legs – nothing else seems to exist but this dirty object. Aversion to odours may indicate a caregiver's distaste or fear of being polluted by something wildly primitive or foreign that comes out of the little body. Compulsive expurgation of familiar-smelling faeces may reflect a mother's persecutory feeling that, having come out of her own body, the baby is associated with, has been affected by and/or reveals to the world, her own internal muck. To another carer, nappy-changing constitutes a moment of prime interaction, as, legs freed, the gurgling baby wriggles and kicks, and the playful adult swoops and tickles, initiates and responds to the excited infant's merriment or waning interest in the game. Yet another parent may find nappy-changing intensely enraging as the wriggling baby evades control or pees in the clean nappy. Another is embarrassed by the undisguised pleasure the baby takes in exploring the uncovered genital area. To others, danger lurks in exposed orifices, necessitating quick, harsh measures in dealing with the task in hand to overcome an irresistible temptation to do as she or he was done by. Tantalised by the enticing offer, another mother or father may be drawn to tease, allowing wiping to slip into caressing, whereupon arousal – generated like an electrical current – is transmitted, often unwittingly, from the carer's hand to the sensitive body in its care.

The psychosexual gendered body-image

I shall not dwell here on details of developmental phases in gendered body-image acquisition. Much psychoanalytic work has been carried out on the topic, including a prolonged debate over a period of decades about determining aspects of respective genitalia: vaginal awareness in both sexes, and whether the penis is to be regarded as a primary female lack or prized masculine possession of phallic narcissism which renders the boy vulnerable to castrative anxieties not experienced by the little girl. Indeed a whole generation of psychoanalysts was preoccupied with the extent to which a female deals with her 'castrated state' and seemingly incompatible clitoral and vaginal urges. Later analysts have debated the double deprivation of females in terms of both oppression and the difficulty of incorporating hidden genitalia into her body-image and mental representation.

In my own contribution here I would like to focus on the imaginatively conceptualised gendered body in terms of process rather than schema. A distinction has been made between various aspects of acquired gender identity. *Core gender identity* – the sense of maleness or femaleness – begins with hormonal influences on the fetus and lived-in bodily anatomy as well as parental handling following sexual assignment. *Gender role identity* – the intrapsychic representations of femininity or masculinity – is based on social ascriptions and identifications with same-sexed peers and carers as well as those of the other sex. A third aspect, *sexual partner orientation*, pertains to the love object chosen as the outcome of the positive and negative oedipal phase of bisexual conflict. From my work on issues of reproductivity, I feel it is useful to delineate an additional developmental aspect of gender identity – that of *generative identity* (Raphael-Leff, 1993a).

In my view this generative aspect of self-representation arises out of the child's growing disillusionment with what has been termed the initial 'undifferentiated matrix' of belief in unlimited potentialities (Fast, 1978). I propose that as the distinction between the sexes becomes paramount for the toddler, body-image constructs come to be elaborated in generative terms. In other words, in conjunction with other facets of gender identity, body-image is construed not only by male or female anatomy and specific genitalia (i.e. sexed body-image) and growing awareness of masculine or feminine psychosocial roles and normative appearance (gendered body-image) or even in terms of hetero-, homo- or bisexual coupling (erotic body-image), but specifically in relation to the imaginative body as a source of future generativity – *a reproductive body-image*.

Of relevance here is Judith Kestenberg's work tracing developmental sequences in the struggle of both sexes to acknowledge the existence of what she has termed the 'inner genitals' (Kestenberg, 1968). In a paper decades ahead of its time, she suggested that universal repudiation of femininity could be attributed to the anxiety these inner genitals arouse, with female vulnerability and fear of internal injury exceeding that of males who externalise their inner sensations through 'phallic dominance'. Concrete proof of the existence of inner genitals with the onset of menses and emissions in puberty brings about a reorganisation of the internal image, involving female recognition of her 'receptacle' (versus inner baby or penis) and the reversal of male avoidance of the 'dangerous, dark and bloody' female inside. In Kestenberg's view, 'Adult genital organization cannot be achieved without the acceptance of the role of internal genital organs in coitus and reproduction' for both sexes (1968, p. 516). The prepubertal situation she describes accords with Melanie Klein's view of the primary female anxiety as fear of internal damage due to persecutory maternal retaliation for fantasied attacks on the mother's body (Klein, 1955, p. 133). This fear can become compelling in some cases of subfertility, as I shall illustrate.

I am suggesting that the concept of generative identity comprises unconscious representations, desires and conscious beliefs about one's body as capable of impregnating and/or being pregnant, growing, birthing and suckling a baby. Generativity is not postulated as a hermetically sealed, time-bound, teleological facet of identity but one that has wider intrapsychic and interpersonal repercussions. For instance, societal conflation of creativity and procreativity may mislead girls to a fallacious (!) conviction of having to await activation of their own internal creative capacities by a seminal male contribution, resulting in psychosocial dependence and undervaluation of female agency (Raphael-Leff, 1993a). (It is possible that people prone to these conflations have, for various reasons, maintained a generative identity that precludes identification with *both* parents in procreative union, necessary for creativity.) Similarly, unconscious psychosocial equation of mothers' and placental functioning (the idea of a 'container' mother) has contributed to a widespread collusive expectation of female nurturing, processing and waste-disposal (Raphael-Leff, 1991c).

Body-image traumas

Although I have emphasised that body-image is not contiguous with bodily boundaries, nevertheless, orifices serve as gateways between the imaginative internal body and the world – eyes, ears and mouth as sensory organs, mouth, nose, anus, urethra and vagina as avenues of elimination and expulsion as well as channels of ingestion and incorporation. These orifices may also serve as loci for incorporative fantasies, through which desired properties of significant others may be introjected or threats propelled outwards. Disturbances of the imaginative body can arise from uninvited or intolerable cumulative or sudden traumatic crossing of skin surface or sphincter barriers – violence, circumcision and surgical invasions, sexual abuse, force feeding or intrusive hygienic care. Similarly, disturbances arise from violations of the wider sphere of personal space – inappropriate visual impacts such as the obvious impingement of a 'flasher', disturbing television sights and those that introduce alien fantasy or are beyond the ego's capacity for digestion. In less dramatic ways, the body-image scheme can be disturbed by unpleasant or suggestive sounds or noise, intolerable because too loud, grating or sudden; likewise shocking gestures, unexpected temperature extremes, over-intimate handling, uninvited criticism, incongruous gossip or even something as simple but perturbing as distraction from musing.

Perhaps less evident are the traumatic effects of too little physical contact – acknowledged in their dramatic forms, like marasmus in institutionalised babies (Spitz, 1945) and Rumanian orphanages. However, other common forms of tactile deprivation are only slowly being recognised as such: for some time now there has been evidence of improved physiological wellbeing of premature babies in so-called 'kangaroo' skin-to-skin contact with the parental body rather than incubator, indications of closer bonding with unseparated newborns (Klaus and Kennell, 1983) and reduced vulnerability to cot death (sudden infant death syndome, SIDS), in infants who sleep in contact with their mothers (McKenna, 1986; McKenna et al., 1993).

As my clinical experience grows, I am coming to believe that 'indigestible' bodily experiences remain encapsulated in concrete form. I have argued that the original carer's body language and silent encounters become absorbed into the body-image or imprinted as an unconscious imagery or commentary on the self. However, some intense bodily experiences, particularly those pertaining to the reproductive body, can remain defensively embodied in primitive concretisations which I have termed 'geodes'. I have chosen this term to convey their archaic nature and sealed, ossified structure. Bypassing thought, physical imagery thus retained is later enacted compulsively in concrete ways: such as breast enlargement or reduction, trans-sexualism, multiple abortions, sterilisation, giving birth and relinquishing a child for adoption, baby snatching, infanticide, self-mutilation, etc. I am suggesting that very real experiences of sibling damage or death, stillbirth or maternal miscarriage, as well as adoption, incidents of childhood sexual abuse, physical invasions by neonatal surgery and household violence, may be too overwhelming to be metabolised. The sense of parental disloyalty, the incestuous breach of confidence or the impact of discovering the frailty or failure to protect, combined with the *undeniably real and irreversible* nature of the early trauma, leave young victims with geodic pockets of imaginative rigidity which obstruct sublimation. The omniscient imaginary body becomes tethered to harsh realities of death, manipulative control or submission. Imagination as a protected reservation of playful ideas, in which everything is possible, becomes shattered when forbidden fantasy is played out as a morbid or incestuous physical reality. Not only the body but the safety of thought itself is violated, leading to concrete enactment of counterphobic measures.

On a body-image level, defensive measures may result in a young child having to contract his or her physical essence to a hard nugget of fiercely held separateness or forced liveliness. Yet this image is one which nevertheless, jelly-fish-like, still remains enveloped by a hypersensitive sense of vulnerable transparency – tendrils aquiver to every imagined approach of deathliness, criticism or high-tension current.

Puberty and generative identity

With her first menstruation, the female imaginative body undergoes further development as the girl is enlisted into a cyclical lunar calendar of monthly hormonal waxing and waning. No longer a constant, body-image fluctuates with each phase of ripening, decline, bleeding and regeneration, unconsciously affecting daily negotiation with both internal and external worlds. Depending on its flexibility, the imaginary body is restructured and stretched during adolescence, able to take the stress of tensions inherent in the growing, rapidly changing, sexually ripening body with resultant alterations in body-image; alternatively, there is a struggle to maintain its defensive fixity despite obvious changes.

Menarche has been identified by many psychoanalysts as both a reactivator of old inadequacies, disgust and fear of soiling and loss of control, alongside a new pride and sense of feminine maturity, necessitating a revision of a girl's bodily image, both like and unlike her own mother's (a contradiction often conveyed in the combination of teenage cult-clothing and shared wardrobes). In itself, periodic bleeding may exacerbate a young girl's tendency to bodily shame and secrecy, heightening her sense of mysterious inner processes. However, developing breasts which cannot be concealed proclaim to the world that the teenager is maturing and taking on undeniable female characteristics, reminiscent of her early mother's.

Identification with the maternal, sexual, fertile and lactating body may be fraught with ambivalence, as adolescence, in common with other transitional phases, reactivates earlier conflicts of dependency and identity. An insecure girl may conform to peer dress-dictates, use food intake to mould her bodily shape to non-maternal standards or physically negate her childbearing potential by re-imposing the prepubertal criteria of her imaginary body on the maturing corporeal one. Arrival of her periods may arouse intense anxiety at separateness and loss of the unchallenging safety of childhood, possibly leading to a rebellious path of bodily risk-taking or regressive anorexic demands to be fed and looked after, sometimes resulting in amenorrhoea. Egle Laufer (1991) has suggested that, for some adolescents, the maturing sexual body represents loss of the prepubertal idealised body-image, which for them still contains the unrelinquished early infantile mother–infant couple. To combat this threat they may engage in perverse or self-destructive behaviour in an attempt to preserve an illusion of omnipotent control over change. Dinora Pines (1993), too, has examined some of the unconscious uses to which the female body may be put in adolescence or pregnancy to avoid conscious affects and fantasies which have felt overwhelming in childhood.

After puberty, some teenagers become impatient, experiencing the inner reproductive body, like a coiled spring, awaiting fruition. Pregnancy may be consciously pursued ('I don't care! I want a baby of my own to love me now'), or unconsciously expressed in contraceptive risk-taking or impulsive precocious sex. As I suggested above, a troubled girl may have unconsciously associated procreativity with creativity – holding her talents and intellectual capacities in abeyance and keeping her life in suspended animation as she hibernates, awaiting impregnation. This may take the form of emotional investment in day-dreaming, of compliant waiting or defiant denial of the importance of her femininity, until conception finally starts her life-clock ticking.

To threatened, damaged or empty children, the idea of future pregnancy may assume magical properties. Healing may appear to reside in reproductivity – with overdetermined symbolism: a swelling belly is seen to demonstrate publicly that there is something good inside after all; its substance negates the sense of self-fragility; it provides evidence of sexual desirability; it is proof that she was not internally impaired by abuse, and has potent/formative capacities. To teenagers with a history of family tragedy, pregnancy may constitute a concrete compensation for a destructive assault on the mother's body or babies (the imagined cause of the reality of sibling perinatal death) or the baby itself may be seen as a sacrificial life-giving replacement for a dead sibling or tangible reversal of fate in the case of a damaged child. Above all, it is a material enactment that hopes to challenge stasis: as a woman born to replace a brother who died a 'cot-death' says:

'I have nothing inside. It makes me feel I could kill myself. No, it's not nothing but something I can't communicate; there are no words – as if I grew up in silence, ignored while my mother mourned her dead baby. A baby of my own would fill me and free what got stuck when I was a baby.'

Whereas many budding adolescents find reassurance in the menstrual cycle as a monthly reminder of bodily operativeness, to an anxious girl, bleeding from within may become a recurrent cursed sign of internal morbidity, chaos or waste rather than promise of future fulfilment. ('Whenever my period's due I keep losing things and feel people are out to cheat me.') Likewise, to a teenager who has been molested, periodic bleeding triggers unwanted alarming representations of processes within her beyond her control, and bodily anxieties about internal damage caused by sexual violation. ('Something's wrong – the blood comes in fits and starts as if something heavy is sort of strangling it inside.')

Precocious sexual activity or promiscuity may represent a plea for help. It may constitute a girl's simultaneous bid for close contact and independence in an attempt to break away from an overinvolved or disengaged mother or father, as well as an attempt to establish bodily ownership and a separate, secret life of her own. Repeated abortions are often pursued by teenagers as compulsive confirmation of life- and death-dealing powers and to sustain a fragile illusion of omnipotence and control. Driven hetero- or homosexual activity may disguise a desperate desire not for sex but merger – intercourse as a fantasy of exclusive possession of the mother's body rather than identification with maternal sexuality.

I have found that adopted children often contain parallel sets of reproductive body-images – life-giving associated with real abandonment, and caregiving associated with infertility. In adolescence, for some, attempting to try out their fertility may take on a forbidden or secretive quality, or be accompanied by acts of wild abandon to counteract the fear of divine retribution. This may manifest in repeated acting out of these paradoxical structures in bodily ways such as conception and abortion, psychogenic infertility necessitating intervention, etc. (Raphael-Leff, 1992d).

Similarly, I have found that the denial of the parent's reproductive capacities or the reality of their sexual relationship can lead to developmental disturbance of the generative body-image which comes to be enacted in adulthood reproductive behaviour. These enactments may variously conceal an infantile magical belief in parthenogenesis, a desire for hermaphroditic self-sufficiency or life-creating superpowers, in identification with the archaic omnipotent joint parents/mother, or, conversely, a denigration of one's own reproductive capacities, fears of internal damage or assumptions of inner destructiveness. Thus, in adulthood, the fertile body may be compelled to enact the imaginative one, through 'immaculate' routes to conception, such as self-insemination by anonymous donor, psychogenic infertility, Munchausen-by-proxy, etc.

In general, disturbances due to preoedipal throwbacks differ from ongoing oedipal conflicts which interfere with adult generativity. Failure to conceive may be symbolically associated with preoedipal archaic symbiotic entanglement: 'I feel I'm not allowed to have a baby – as if my mother put a curse on me because she wants to keep me all for herself' says one woman. It may be linked to persecutory anxieties: 'My mother can't let me have a baby – she wants to be the only mother' says another; or to oedipal retaliation: 'Sometimes, it's as if I'm forbidden to have a baby – or that it's a punishment for something' says a third. In the last two cases, repeated abortions, too, might reflect an underlying unresolved oedipal conflict and prohibition on keeping an 'incestuous' pregnancy.

Miscarriage

Coming in the midst of a creative momentum, miscarriage has far-reaching implications for the generative body-image. It is not a rare occurrence – in the United Kingdom, about one in six confirmed pregnancies end in spontaneous abortion, and possibly half of all conceptions. Three-quarters of all miscarriages occur in the first trimester, and often come as a shock to a woman whose omnipotent reproductive body-image contains no possibility of loss. In Western societies, where hospitalisation and the taboo on mentioning death remove perinatal loss from the public eye, it is not uncommon for a woman who miscarries to feel inexplicably singled out. This inevitably sharpens the sense of alone-ness with her reproductive destiny. When an established emotional trajectory of hope and procreativity is interrupted by death or destruction, the trauma suffered by the imaginative body can feel as tangible as the physical one. The process of accommodation to non-pregnancy takes time; as the emotional disequilibrium of pregnancy slowly subsides, some women are caught by surprise by the intensity of their bereavement and its long-lasting effects, particularly when miscarriage has stirred up previous losses and anxieties about death and helplessness.

The loss of a fetus also entails loss of all the aspirations and expectations invested in the baby, loss of the unquestioned sense of being special and creative during pregnancy, and loss of innocent trust in her generative body's reliability, doubts which will accompany her into the next pregnancy. Many women feel a deep sadness at not having protected the baby from harm, and blame themselves for failing to sustain the pregnancy. Some couples experience a profound sense of bewilderment and grief at the loss of their joint baby, which, if expressed to each other, can deepen their relationship. However, in other cases, the loss seems to symbolise their inability to foster growth of something that is a mixture of them both. Silent or voiced recriminations may begin to poison the joint flow of their lives. Similarly, asymmetry of emotional distance from the epicentre of pain and

lack of reciprocity and mutual exchange may change the partners' relationship, sometimes irrevocably.

> 'When my first miscarriage happened I had not planned to become pregnant', says
> a barrister who had come to consult me about difficulties in her marriage. 'It was
> like a dream, so fleeting . . . . I was just beginning to come to terms with it when it
> was taken away. That was another shock but I suppose I shrugged it away. When I
> had my second miscarriage, I was blown away. Emotionally I was numb for six
> weeks afterwards, and instead of getting better it just got worse. I desperately
> needed to be recognised as bereaved – there was this enormous sense of loss and
> grief which was going nowhere. I became totally unable to deal with everyday
> things, avoided colleagues, pregnant women and small kids and in my mind was
> acutely preoccupied with reliving every moment of the short pregnancy. It had
> been like having someone at the centre of me who was snatched away. It took on
> enormous significance in my life but my husband couldn't understand it at all. I felt
> very lonely and sad that he didn't value the child we'd made together. No one
> could help – I felt so vulnerable and abandoned and although my sister came with
> me to hospital when I had the D & C, I felt barriers rising inside me and hugged my
> feelings to myself with the covers over my head rather than talk to her about his
> callousness. His lack of understanding instigated a downward spiral in our relation-
> ship which seems to have continued in a state of decline ever since.'

Modern technology has a profound effect on the imaginative body.
Ultrasound, with its capacity to reveal the interior of the body, can dispel
internal mysteries, disrupt fantasy elaborations and, in the case of miscarriage, may increase the loss experienced when expectant parents have
previously seen their baby actually moving within the womb. Prenatal
screening sometimes presents parents with a terrible choice either of
aborting a fetus diagnosed to be malformed or impaired, or resolving to live
with the difficulties. This ethical and emotional dilemma is often exacerbated by having become familiar with the baby on the screen. In some
scans, side by side with the live fetus, an empty sac revealed on the
ultrasound screen indicates that there had been twins, one of whom has
been aborted. Juxtapositions of life and death, creativity and destructiveness, like the painful decision of eugenic abortion or the dark paradox of
stillbirth, life ending before it has begun, are strange occurrences which
touch off an existential crisis in various child and adult members of ber-
eaved families, distorting unconscious representations.

In terms of the imaginative body, miscarriage constitutes a shattering of
the naive belief in uncomplicated gestation, confirming the doubts some
abused or deprived women may have retained about internal creativity.
Nevertheless, despite their impact, major life events such as miscarriage,
enforced abortion or even stillbirth may be casually dismissed by others
('never mind, you'll have another one') or at times treated by a detached
woman herself as if nothing much has occurred – a 'non-event' (Lewis and
Bourne, 1989). Normal grief reactions, and the outpouring of doubts,
anxiety or despair generated by loss, are often regarded by professionals and

friends alike as excessive. A couple's sexual relationship with its failed generative connotations may be disrupted for many months or another pregnancy pursued relentlessly to replace the first.

In a woman's inner experience, miscarriage is a brush with death, not just close by, but *inside* her own body, affecting her generative identity – her view of herself as potentially creative, transformative, retentive, nurturing – and blighting her vision of propagative capacities and her fruit-bearing inner space. Inevitably, loss of an awaited baby touches off a whole host of emotions, the working through of which requires time, space and possibly therapy. Failure to mourn gives rise to difficulties during subsequent pregnancies, and may result in various forms of acting out, such as having 'a replacement baby'.

Subfertility and the conquest of inner space

Infertility is on the increase and now affects one in six couples in the West, with male factors now found to be responsible for some 40% of cases. Clearly, non-conception cannot be indiscriminately attributed to psychological factors. With improved diagnostic techniques, failure to conceive previously ascribed to so-called psychogenic factors has been dramatically reduced. Only 10% of relationships where conception fails to occur are now unexplained. Nevertheless, psychological factors do figure and, as I have elaborated elsewhere, the impact of diagnosis itself has profound emotional repercussions even on stable individuals. Archaic fantasies are re-triggered; the destabilised generative identity and body-image affects sexuality, social relationships and work capacities. Problems may manifest in symptoms as diverse as depersonalisation, derealisation, hypochondria, anxiety and panic attacks, depression, guilt, obsessive ruminations with compulsive rituals, and a variety of phobic reactions, accompanied by changes in the conceptualisation of body, time and space (Raphael-Leff, 1986a, 1992a). In addition to reproductive failure, fertility treatment itself may be pathogenic. Repeated cycles of hope and despair cause prolonged distress and lowered self-esteem, whereas dependency on doctors emphasises lack of autonomy and infantalisation:

> 'We can no longer even take the simplest decision for ourselves – like when to make love and how to spend our money. We're always being geared to yet more treatment and we've become so unequal – I get pumped full of hormones and have to endure horrible procedures, and end up feeling completely alienated from my body, which can't even do what any animal can.'
>
> Woman having IUI (intrauterine insemination) with her husband's sperm

Pursuit of fertility often involves a couple in prolonged investigations, with a third term, the clinic, intruding into the privacy of their dyadic sexual relationship. Intimacy between the partners seems incestuously invaded by the parental fertility experts. The powerful presence of 'baby-making experts' and their hold over a couple's reproductive organs re-activate oedipal conflicts and primal-scene fantasies (Raphael-Leff, 1991a). Sex often feels mechanical and empty, bound to temperature charts in a cyclical timetable of enforced abstinence, intercourse on demand and postcoital tests. Sexual disturbances are common. That these are reactive rather than causal is clear from research findings of temporary impotence following diagnosis of infertility and even inhibited ovulation in the female partner following the diagnosis of male subfertility.

Intrapsychically, an infertile individual is thrust back into re-examining previously resolved issues now churned up afresh and constantly, repeti-tively reworked. 'In my twenties, I fathered two kids without a thought. Now I find myself continuously having to justify why I might want a baby and what it would mean to us,' says a man whose irreversible vasectomy makes donor insemination the only option for his new wife. Many who have difficulty conceiving suffer intense disappointment and loss of self-esteem as the imagined body of long-awaited generativity fails to actualise in impregnation.

A subfertile male finds investigatory procedures and masturbation-to-order humiliating. Both he and his partner may feel the previously un-questioned reproductive interior now seems twisted and sterile, limited and limiting. 'My work has suffered drastically. I can't write or think since I discovered my sperm count was low,' says a childless man. 'I feel I have a huge gaping hole inside where nothing can grow' is a common female lament. Inner space seems full of unacceptable emotions, as the subfertile person is flooded by uncharacteristic feelings: intense envy and hatred of expectant couples and pregnant women; vengeful resentment towards their own parents who cannot comprehend what it is not to have a child; bitterness towards the other partner who appears less affected or does not share in all the invasive treatment procedures. They feel rage, shame and panic at the recurrent desire to steal a baby and desperate, poignant, painful feelings of being cut off, set apart and excluded from the human race.

Internal imagery is projected onto facets of the partners themselves: 'She just sits there waiting for me to come home and liven her up – I feel trapped just thinking about her waiting,' says a man unconsciously equating his partner with her ovum awaiting fertilisation. 'It's so frustrating – he's so slow! He sludges around the flat and delays me,' says a woman after her partner's semen examination revealed a good count but poor motility ('sluggish sperm' as they are called). Infertility brings to the fore core-gender differences between the sexes. It also emphasises distinctions among a desire for parenthood, the wish to be pregnant and a yearning for genetic immortality or for a child. As such it highlights subsets of body-image – erotic, generative, fertile and reproductive or merely gendered and sexual.

Left to their own resources during the long years of awaiting conception, relationships can become embittered, festering with disappointments, silent recriminations and self-blame. In cases when one or both partners have not come to terms with the altered parameters of their generative identity, psychosomatic symptoms, extramarital affairs, suicidal breakdown or paranoid crises might erupt to avoid insight. Despite their gratitude for the hope granted by new reproductive technologies, some couples feel acutely humiliated and handicapped. Others feel pressurised, externally egged on to try ever more drastic measures to rectify their 'deficit' with not even menopause as a deadline. Imaginative bodies encompass the un-imaginable. Ovum donation now enables postmenopausal women to conceive, and there is even talk of ovary implantation from dead embryos. As treatment intrudes into the most intimate spheres of their bodily and emotional inner sanctums, intervention can alienate the couple not only from each other but even from their desired baby:

> 'IVF (in vitro fertilisation) is an admission of failure. It feels terrible – the embryo stuck back in my womb is like a fostered baby – they made it; it's their baby 'cos the magic hasn't happened inside where my husband and I can connect . . . what a loveless way to conceive.'
> Woman in analysis, just having come from embryo transplant

In addition to medical procedures, daily monitoring of her menstrual cycle and massive doses of hormones heighten a woman's bodily awareness to a nerve-jangling edginess. As inner functions are exposed, long-held body images are demolished. The sharp edge of new knowledge obliterates fuzzy-edged fantasy representations of the imaginative body. Technological innovations reveal the workings of the inner body in detail as ultrasound scans familiarise a woman with the mysteries of the hidden recesses of her innermost body, the amniotic seascape inside her uterus and the daily growth of her follicles. For the male partner, revelation of his oscillating sperm count and motility feel exposingly judgemental; potency and virility unconsciously intertwine, often leading to physical and creative impotence. In addition, reproductive treatments are usually physically invasive. When a woman who has been abused also suffers from subfertility, not only does it seem to confirm her persecutory fantasies of being internally defective, contaminated or punished, but the actual treatment procedures themselves may prove re-abusive; the result can be a triggering of geodic flash-backs and acute panic states in women who have little memory of the original violation as well as in those who have consciously struggled to come to terms with the past:

> 'Left with my legs in the air in stirrups with this vaginal probe inside me and the smell of sperm in the air – I just imploded inside – couldn't breathe or see out at all – I felt that something terrible was happening to me and nobody would ever find me.'
> Woman in therapy

Recent reproductive technologies not only shatter the idea of the fertile imaginative body but call forth new fantasies that border on science fiction. Donor sperm may enable an infertile couple to have a child, or split them assunder if the male partner feels excluded: 'We started off wanting to make a baby together, but it doesn't feel like a joint enterprise anymore and what will we tell the child?' As early as 1984 the Warnock Committee recommended 'openness' about a donor child's genetic origins and availability of counselling for all involved. However, this has been slow to be implemented. Nowadays impregnation may not only involve insemination with the sperm of a stranger but with the ovum of another woman, or both; thus, a woman may virtually give birth to an adopted baby, genetically related to neither partner. The woman in whose body a foreigner grows may find it hard to incorporate the unknown stranger's contribution into her familiar dream-child. Fantasies flourish and hang themselves on pegs of childhood 'family romances' and oedipal adventures. Nevertheless, invited and socially condoned, accepting the foreigner in her midst is usually less stressful for the donor recipient than for those impregnated by rape, or by hated or incestuous sexual partners. For these, the loved/hated blood-connected alien presence moving within her beyond her control serves as constant reminder of the events surrounding conception, fears of the child resembling her impregnator mingling with the bitter-sweet ambivalence towards the forming baby. Even in the case of surrogate birth-mothers, determination to remain emotionally detached may be undermined (see, for instance, the autobiography of the first surrogate, Elizabeth Kane, 1988).

Undergoing fertility treatment (or even during the course of pregnancy, for that matter), a couple are rarely given a chance to explore in depth the inevitably complex and unconscious psychological issues, many of them relating to inconceivable visions and revisions of the imaginative body. New reproductive technologies have raised ethical problems in their wake, the kinship status of fertilised embryos held in cold storage (Strathern, 1992), the morality of antenatal testing, abortions, euthanasia and research, and the dangers of genetic engineering and potential eugenics (Edwards, 1989), sex determination, artificial wombs, surrogacy, breeding and iatrogenic disorders, male control of female reproductivity (Corea, 1985) – the list is long.

Psychodynamic psychotherapy during childbearing

Psychotherapy during the course of childbearing can ease the anguish of those suffering from reactivated emotional trauma and the impact of unaccommodated pregnancy and birth, dilemmas of prenatal screening, or coming to terms with perinatal loss, infertility and the bizarre nature of its remedies. Individual therapy provides a safe space and time to focus and try to formulate nebulous feelings in words. People who have had no interest in therapy and repeatedly enact their conflicts rather than expressing them in words may seek help at crucial times in their childbearing and thereby come to recognise unconscious aspects of their 'geodic' behavioural pattern. Mother/infant therapy can work towards resolution of difficulties leading to failure to thrive, overinvolvement, abuse or neglect. Seen together, partners may have an opportunity to share doubts, air resentments and voice their expectations from the other, and, on another level, to reorganise bodily conceptions and re-examine their respective needs and aspirations. Above all, conjoint therapy allows a couple intent on childbearing space to regain the emotional partnership which can enable some to grieve their losses. They can also better face the uncertainty of future pregnancies or even come to terms with childlessness, or engage with the rollercoaster highs and lows of fertility treatment with greater equanimity. In addition, in cases of psychogenic infertility, therapy can be effective in reducing obstacles to conception, and even short-term cognitive counselling or suggestive techniques are proving effective in combating negative preoperative tensions. (Preliminary results from a randomised trial being conducted at the Hadassah Hospital in Jerusalem have shown a dramatic increase in conceptions among women undergoing relaxation counselling alongside in vitro treatment by comparison with non-counselled controls – Romani, 1993.) Likewise, brief psychotherapy has been found to be effective in delaying premature labour and relieving resistances to birth (Klaus, 1991).

Finally, as elaborated earlier, there are individuals whose psychohistory renders them more vulnerable to problems related to generative identity. They experience perinatal losses and being denied a baby more keenly than others, as this links to early engrossment with pregnancy as a means of escaping childhood hurts or rectifying deprivation.

Psychoanalytic psychotherapy or full-scale psychoanalysis can bring about a modification of the overwhelming overdetermined intensity of the wish for a child which in turn affects impregnation. In my own caseload, I have seen nine women with long-standing infertility who have conceived following an insightful breakthrough in psychotherapy. These women begin therapy with a monomania, a conviction that only pregnancy or mother–baby fusion is deemed capable of reversing an original loss or trauma. There seems to be no identity but the generative one. During the course of therapy, the imaginative body itself appears to undergo a sea-change as the barren internal 'hole' gradually is conceived of as a 'space', and this inner space comes to assume creative properties, no longer barren but a fertile 'garden' in which many types of emotional, intellectual and social produce may grow:

'Life seems full of possibilities – for so long I've been reluctant to see them for fear it would detract from my determination to conceive. I look around me and suddenly see I could have several things at once – I can afford a second-hand bicycle, and can spare an evening a week for a creative writing course and if I accept promotion in my job I could still continue with it even if I become pregnant in the next year.'   Woman in therapy

When and if conception occurs, it is no longer the stop-gap be-all and end-all of identity but a baby that is awaited. (It is at this point of internal modification that I have come to make written predictions of my patient's emotional readiness to conceive; in the cases cited above conception has occurred in that cycle or the following one, without the patient knowing of my prediction.)

Conclusions

My hypothesis is that the imaginative body of childbearing lies dormant until put to the test. Contraception and new technological devices highlight previously disguised distinctions among core components of body-image subsets – such as sexuality, reproductivity and gender, demanding revision of unconsciously held amalgams. In addition, reality, moulded to substantiate the internal schema of body imagery, at times rudely intervenes to change it. My exploration here has focused on a variety of abrupt conceptual transitions, such as infertility, prenatal diagnosis of abnormality, miscarriage and stillbirth, in which configurations of the psychosexual reproductive body abruptly come up against an undeniable reality which cracks the imaginative template. Furthermore, I suggest that an intense uncontrollable physical experience, such as egg-harvesting, embryo transfer, spontaneous abortion or prolonged labour and precipitous birth, forces a rapid, drastic revision of body-imagery, which can send a susceptible person spiralling into emotional upheaval as unplumbed depths of repressed or remembered traumatic experiences from the past are revived and revised. And, conversely, I suggest that emotionally unprocessed concrete traumas, such as incubation, early surgery, injury, physical/sexual abuse, possibly even birth complications, as well as perinatal death of a sibling and maternal obstetric complications, suffuse generative identity with particles of vulnerability and 'geodes' of primeval experience, and that these may be exposed under conditions of severe physical and emotional stress.

Finally, I stress that a caregiver's own infantile experiences are reactivated by the emotional/sensual experience of parenting. Exposure to a baby's cry, the evocative feel of an infant's naked fragility, and the pungency of concrete substances spilling out of every orifice, re-trigger a powerful resurgence of unformulated emotional residues from the carer's own early life. In health these unnamed residues may serve as the basis of empathic attunement. However, when identifications become uncontainably overwhelming and no one is there to hold the parent, bodily codes may burst their restraints or collapse under the strain, as the past becomes alive in the present and wanton cravings of the child imaginatively embodied within the adult begin to misappropriate the childcare situations. Occasionally, custodial hospitalisation or 24-hours-a-day monitoring may be necessary. In less dangerous cases, psychoanalytic understanding of unconscious forces offers the parent a safety valve – an alternative to literally or figuratively throwing the baby out of the window, or resorting to the myriad forms of squeezing, teasing, torturing and tormenting the psyche and the flesh.

When explosions are imminent, an accepting therapeutic relationship offers a safe space in which ancient 'geodes' may surface, be cracked open and explored to make the unbearable bearable through symbolisation and contact with air and light. Emotional 'geodes', like their geological counterparts, may be imagined as age-old sealed structures formed when volcanic lava solidifies around a gaseous bubble. Thus trapped, an imaginative moment, which normally would be fleetingly alive then gone, is preserved encapsulated in all its archaic bodily passion. Psychoanalytic therapy at a time when these strange wordless phenomena are exposed by childbearing, can prevent enactment and intergenerational transmission. Through live transferential understanding, the geodic lava is 'depetrified', releasing the captive moment and allowing it to evaporate.

References

ANTHI, P.R. (1986). Non-verbal behaviour and body organ fantasies. Their relation to body-image formation and symptomatology. *International Journal of Psycho-Analysis* **67**, 417–427.

CASH, T.S. and PRUZINSKY, T. (1990). *Body-images – Development, Deviance and Change*. London: Guilford Press.

COREA, G. (1985). *The Mother Machine*. London: The Women's Press.

DE CASPER, A.J. and FIFER, W.P. (1980). Of human bonding: newborns prefer their mother's voices. *Science* **208**, 1174–1176.

DEUTSCH, H. (1945). *Psychology of Women*. New York: Grune & Stratton.

EDWARDS, R. (1989). *Life Before Birth*. London: Hutchinson.

FAST, I. (1978). Developments in gender identity: the original matrix. *International Review of Psycho-Analysis* **5**, 265–274.

FERENCZI, S. (1933). Confusion of tongues between adults and the child. In: *Final Contributions to the Problems and Methods of Psychoanalysis*. London: Maresfield Reprints, 1955.

FERENCZI, S. (1938). *Thalassa – A Theory of Genitality*. London: Karnac, 1989.

FREUD, S. (1905). Fragment of an analysis of a case of hysteria. *The Complete Psychological Works of Sigmund Freud*, Standard Edition, Vol. 7, pp. 3–122. London: Hogarth Press.

FREUD, S. (1918). The taboo of virginity. *The Complete Psychological Works of Sigmund Freud*, Standard Edition, Vol. 11, pp. 193–208. London: Hogarth Press.

FREUD, S. (1923). The ego and the id. *The Complete Psychological Works of Sigmund Freud*, Standard Edition, Vol. 19, pp. 3–67. London: Hogarth Press.

FREUD, S. (1933). New introductory lectures on psycho-analysis, femininity. *The Complete Psychological Works of Sigmund Freud*, Standard Edition, Vol. 22, pp. 112–135. London: Hogarth Press.

HOPPER, E. (1991). Encapsulation as a defence against the fear of annihilation. *International Journal of Psycho-Analysis* **72**, 607-624.

KAFKA, E. (1971). On the development of the experience of Mental Self, the Bodily Self and Self Consciousness. *Psychoanalytic Study of the Child* **26**, 217-240.

KANE, E. (1988). *Birth Mother - the Story of America's First Legal Surrogate Mother*. London: Harcourt Brace Jovanovich.

KENNEDY, R. (1993). Aspects of consciousness - one voice or many? *The British Psycho-Analytical Society Bulletin* **29**, 16-25.

KESTENBERG, J. (1968). Outside and inside, male and female. *Journal of the American Psychoanalytic Association* **16**, 457-520.

KLAUS, M.H. and KENNELL, J.H. (1983). *Parent-Infant Bonding*. St Louis: C.V. Mosby.

KLAUS, P. (1991). Report to the Pediatric, Obstetric and Psychiatric (POP) Conference, London Hospital.

KLEIN, M. (1955). The psycho-analytic play technique: its history and significance, In: *Envy and Gratitude and Other Works*. London: Hogarth & Institute of Psycho-Analysis, 1984.

KRUEGER, D.W. (1990). Developmental and psychodynamic perspectives on body-image change. In: T.S. Cash and T. Pruzinsky (Eds), *Body-Images - Development, Deviance and Change*. London: Guilford Press.

LACAN, J. (1958). The significance of the phallus. In: *Ecrits - la selection*. London: Tavistock, 1977.

LAUFER, E. (1991). Body image, sexuality and the psychotic core. *International Journal of Psycho-Analysis* **72**, 63-72.

LEWIS, E. and BOURNE, S. (1989). Perinatal death. *Baillière's Clinical Obstetrics and Gynaecology* **3**, 935-953.

LICHTENBERG, J.D. (1975). The development of the sense of self. *Journal of the American Psychoanalytic Association* **23**, 453-484.

MAHLER, S.M. and McDEVITT, J.B. (1982). Thoughts on the emergence of the sense of self with particular emphasis on the body self. *Journal of the American Psychoanalytic Association* **30**, 827-848.

McKENNA, J.J. (1986). An anthropological perspective on the Sudden Infant Death Syndrome (SIDS): the role of parental breathing cues. Speech-breathing adaptations, *Journal of Medical Anthropology* **10**, 9-92.

McKENNA, J.J., THOMAN, E.B., ANDERS, T.F., SADEH, A., SCHECHTMAN, V.L. and GLOTZBACH, S. (1993). Infant-parent co-sleeping in an evolutionary perspective: implications for understanding infant sleep development and the Sudden Infant Death Syndrome. *Sleep* **16**, 263-282.

MEAD, M. (1949). *Male and Female - A Study of the Sexes in a Changing World*. London: Victor Gollancz.

MOSCUCCI, O. (1990). *The Science of Woman - Gynaecology and Gender in England (1800-1929)*. Cambridge: Cambridge University Press.

OGDEN, T. (1989). *The Primitive Edge of Experience*. Northvale, NJ: Jason Aaronson.

PEDERSON, F.A., ANDERSON, B. and KAIN, R. (1980). Parent-infant and husband-wife interactions observed at five months. In: F.A. Pederson (Ed.), *Father-Infant Relationship*. New York: Praeger.

PETO, A. (1959). Body image and archaic thinking. *International Journal of Psycho-Analysis* **40**, 223-231.

PIONTELLI, A. (1992). *From Fetus to Child - An Observational and Psychoanalytic Study*. London: Routledge.

PINES, D. (1993). *A Woman's Unconscious Use of her Body - A Psychoanalytical Perspective.* London: Virago.

RAPHAEL-LEFF, J. (1985). Facilitators and Regulators, Participators and Renouncers: mothers' and fathers' orientations towards pregnancy and motherhood. *Journal of Psychosomatic Obstetrics and Gynaecology* 4, 169-184.

RAPHAEL-LEFF, J. (1986a). Infertility: diagnosis or life sentence? *British Journal of Sexual Medicine* 13, 28-29.

RAPHAEL-LEFF, J. (1986b). Facilitators and Regulators: conscious and unconscious processes in pregnancy and early motherhood. *British Journal of Medical Psychology* 56, 379-390.

RAPHAEL-LEFF, J. (1989). Where the wild things are. *International Journal of Prenatal and Perinatal Studies* 1, 78-89.

RAPHAEL-LEFF, J. (1991a). *Psychological Processes of Childbearing.* London: Chapman & Hall; New York: Routledge, Chapman & Hall.

RAPHAEL-LEFF, J. (1991b). Psychotherapy and pregnancy. *Journal of Reproductive and Infant Psychology* 8, 119-135.

RAPHAEL-LEFF, J. (1991c). The mother as container: placental process and inner space. *Feminism and Psychology* 1, 393-408.

RAPHAEL-LEFF, J. (1991d). Childbearing practices across the continents - reflections of cultural metaphor and pregnant fantasies. Presented to the Annual Conference of the Society for Reproductive and Infant Psychology, Durham, September 1991 (unpublished).

RAPHAEL-LEFF, J. (1992a). The Baby-Makers - psychological sequelae of technological intervention for fertility. *British Journal of Psychotherapy* 7, 239-294.

RAPHAEL-LEFF, J. (1992b). Impact of Medicine on Reproductivity. Key note address, ISPOG Congress, Stockholm, 1992. In: K. Wijma and B. von Schoultz (Eds), *Reproductive Life: Advances in Research in Psychosomatic Obstetrics and Gynaecology.* Carnford: Parthenon.

RAPHAEL-LEFF, J. (1992c). When eternals change . . . invited commentary on reproductive issues and the National Health Service. *APP Psychoanalytic Psychotherapy Newsletter*, Summer.

RAPHAEL-LEFF, J. (1992d). Transition to parenthood - infertility. Creating a family. In: D. Reich and J. Burrell (Eds), *Infertility and Adoption.* London: Adoption Centre Publications.

RAPHAEL-LEFF, J. (1993a). Thoughts on gender and generativity. Presented to the '52 club', February 1993. To be published in *Female Experience* (Eds), J. Raphael-Leff and R. Perleberg.

RAPHAEL-LEFF, J. (1993b). *Pregnancy - The Inside Story.* London: Sheldon Press.

ROMANI, Z. (1993). Relaxation breeds fertility (Hadassah Study). Reported in *Mor, Health Supplement, Lalsha* Magazine, June, Israel.

ROSENFELD, D. (1984). Hypochondrias, somatic delusion and body scheme in psychoanalytic practice. *International Journal of Psycho-Analysis* 65, 377-388.

SAMUELS, A. (1985). The image of the parents in bed. In: A. Samuels (Ed.), *The Father.* London: Free Association Books.

SCHILDER, P. (1935). *The Image and Appearance of the Human Body.* London: Paul Trench Trubner.

SHONZ, F.C. (1974). Body image and its disorders. *International Journal of Psychiatry in Medicine* 5, 461-471.

SPITZ, R.A. (1945). Hospitalism: an inquiry into the genesis of psychiatric conditions in early childhood. *Psychoanalytic Study of the Child* 1, 53-72.

STERN, D. (1985). *The Interpersonal World of the Infant*. New York: Basic Books.

STRATHERN, M. (1992). *Reproducing the Future - Anthropology, Kinship and the New Reproductive Technologies*. Manchester: Manchester University Press.

SZASZ, T.S. (1957). A contribution to the psychology of bodily feelings. *Psychoanalytic Quarterly* **26**, 25–49.

TUSTIN, F. (1984). Autistic shapes. *International Review of Psycho-Analysis* **7**, 27–40.

YOGMAN, M.W. (1982). Observations on the father–infant relationship. In: S.H. Cath, A.R. Gurwitt and J.M. Ross (Eds), *Father and Child: Developmental and Clinical Perspectives*. Boston: Little, Brown & Co.

Chapter 2
The initial contact:
assessment for counselling in the medical context

Aleda Erskine

RECOGNISE '. . . to acknowledge by special notice, approval or sanction; to treat as valid, as having existence or as entitled to consideration; to take notice of (a thing or person) in some way'.   *Shorter Oxford English Dictionary*

Introduction

As a clinical health psychologist in a large inner city general hospital, part of my role is to take referrals from medical colleagues. These vary from the patient with chronic pain, to the patient in crisis following the diagnosis of life-threatening illness, to the 'worried well' patient with, for example, cardiac anxiety. The first step is to make an assessment and this chapter describes my approach to the task.

Although at times I use client-centred or cognitive–behavioural methods of intervention, my guiding theoretical framework is psychodynamic. My understanding of health and illness has been shaped by a biopsychosocial model (as described in the introduction to this book), which is based on the interdependence of the biological and psychosocial aspects of the person (Engel, 1977). I emphasise this holistic model, because dualistic models of illness are still influential in the literature on medical counselling and psychotherapy. For example, a current text on counselling in the medical context makes the following recommendation as to the counsellor's 'priority first step' (Abel Smith, Irving and Brown, 1989, p. 128):

> What kind of objectives or goals are being identified by those engaged in counselling in these settings? In some circumstances a principal initial aim may be to help the client become aware of the possibility that his or her symptom has a psychological cause, when he or she is expecting a response more akin to the 'illness model'.

The authors here are using a psychogenic model of illness no less dualistic than the medical 'illness model' which they reject. In both cases, the assumption is that a firm distinction can be made between 'psychological' and 'organic' causes. Their emphasis on confronting the patient's attributions to the symptoms is, I shall argue, not only theoretically untenable but also clinically mistaken. By contrast, I shall emphasise the vulnerability of many medical patients and the need for the counsellor to respond with empathy and flexibility so that, even in the earliest stages of therapy, the patient has the experience of being met with recognition.

The term 'counselling' is used in various ways and needs definition. Here, I use it to denote 'the specialist, highly skilled psychological endeavour of helping people with complex psychological and relationship problems' (Davis and Fallowfield, 1991, p. 25). I am assuming that the counsellor (from whatever profession) is qualified in this work and has an appropriate support system. There is of course overlap in the usage of the terms 'counselling' and 'psychotherapy' and any absolute distinctions are probably unreliable. I have chosen the term 'counselling' because it reflects the emphasis of this chapter on interventions which are not in the main open-ended or long term.

A final introductory note: my focus here is on the clinical issues within assessment. I do not deal with the issue of the use of empirical assessment measures in health care. For this, Karoly (1985) is a recommended text.

The assessment task

The form of any assessment must be related to its purpose and I shall suggest that the assessment of medical patients has its own typical objectives and characteristics. It is important to underline this because many counsellors come to work in the medical context after experience in mental health and may assume that they can approach assessment in the same way. In mental health, one common objective is to assess the patient's symptoms, mental state, behaviour problems and personal history in order to arrive at some kind of psychiatric diagnosis or psychological formulation. The primary thrust is diagnostic, although the assessment is also necessary to determine appropriate treatment.

Another common objective is to assess the extent to which a patient's presentation meets predetermined inclusion and exclusion criteria for a particular intervention. One example of this would be the assessment interview for psychodynamic psychotherapy or counselling.

By contrast, the primary objectives in assessing the medical patient should be: (1) to determine the patient's need for a psychological intervention, and (2) to determine what kind of therapy (if any) is appropriate. This more pragmatic approach follows on from the special characteristics of the patient group. First, by definition, the medical patient presents initially with a physical complaint and will only rarely initiate a referral to a counsellor. The counsellor may well have to create a 'mandate' for psychological intervention within the assessment period. The 'mandate' represents the shared understanding of the patient's presenting problems which the counsellor and the patient construct together and which then validates some form of psychological intervention. (Certain ways of doing this are suggested on page 53.) Any persistent enquiry into psychological or psychodynamic factors or personal history outside the 'mandate' may be experienced as irrelevant to the patient's health concerns and hence intrusive. Secondly, where a patient is seriously or terminally ill, the imperative is for the counsellor to work alongside medical colleagues to offer relief from distress as quickly as possible. The postponement of intervention for the sake of precise diagnosis in this situation is inhumane.

This pragmatic emphasis on 'need' in assessment has become common in the very different field of psychiatric rehabilitation. Brewin et al. (1987), writing in this context, usefully define the concept of 'need' as 'a condition of dysfunction due to some remediable or potentially remediable cause'. The 'need' (as defined) is met when it attracts a potentially effective intervention. More recently, Brewin, Bradley and Home (1991) have applied this model to the assessment of diabetic patients.

It follows that medical patients may have many 'problems' but no 'needs' if an appropriate intervention is not available. The 'need' is assessed on the basis of professional judgement, but it is crucial that the patient's wishes and priorities are taken into account. No intervention can be effective if it is not broadly acceptable. At the same time the identification of needs may shift over the course of the assessment in line with the developing relationship between counsellor and patient. It is not uncommon for a patient to underplay or deny a 'problem' at the beginning of the assessment which, by the end, has been explored and defined as a 'need' for which psychological help is appropriate. (This is illustrated by the case of Cecilia J., described on page 56.)

Difficulties in the first session

Robert F.

Robert F. was a tall, bronzed Canadian of 28 who had been referred by a cardiologist. He had finished a course of treatment for hypertension but had continued to complain of chest pain and anxiety – hence the referral.

I was told Robert F. had a family history of heart disease, was working in the UK as a part-time manual worker, and was in the middle of travelling around the world. He appeared at the session dressed in shorts and T-shirt and had a correspondingly easy-going manner, only thinly masking the underlying tension. Robert F. quickly let me know that he felt highly anxious because the cardiologist had chosen not to refer him for further tests before writing to me. He expressed polite bafflement over the referral. He went into great detail over the varieties of chest pain and palpitations he experienced and spoke of a sense of continuing malaise, regularly exacerbated by periods of fatigue and poor appetite. At these times he found it hard to do his job and he tended to be irritable and withdrawn from his wife, who had just come over to join him. He alluded repeatedly to the possibility of some as yet undiagnosed cardiac problem.

Like many medical patients, Robert F.'s referral to a counsellor came about as a result of a secondary or tertiary referral process and, as often happens, was made with little consultation with the patient. Robert F.'s reaction is an example of one important feature of assessment in the medical context: the fact that a substantial minority of patients will show strong ambivalence, suspicion or even hostility at their first appointment. Of course, this occurs in other fields, such as mental health, but it seems to be more salient in this context. Sometimes the reluctance is expressed indirectly: for example, through hinted scepticism or indifference; bewilderment about the purpose of the referral; or apparent interest in the counsellor's approach accompanied by 'yes but' statements. Such feelings may simply be expressed non-verbally, for example, in tension and wariness. It is critical that the particular reasons underlying the patient's ambivalence are explored and at least partially understood within the first session. Failing this, a meaningful assessment is unlikely. Some common reasons for a patient's reluctance are as follows:

- At the simplest level, many patients (unlike Robert F.) have been through a weary round of failed medical or surgical treatments before getting to the counsellor. The referral may imply the painful truth that they have reached the 'end of the line' in terms of conventional medical approaches. For either or both reasons, they may feel despairing over the likelihood of relief or cure.
- Like Robert F., patients may feel they have been 'fobbed off' with a psychological referral when further medical/surgical investigations or treatments are needed.
- They may feel that their problems are being dismissed as 'all in the mind' and the reality of their suffering is under question.
- They may feel accused of malingering.
- They may worry that they are suspected of madness.
- They may feel the referral is a sign that they are untreatable and that there is no prospect of cure or relief.
- Occasionally they may infer or be told by the referring doctor that the opportunity for further medical or surgical treatment will depend on the health counsellor's assessment and/or intervention.
- Many patients and many doctors adhere to a biomedical model of illness (see Introduction) which severs body and mind and excludes a valid role

for psychosocial factors in illness and its treatment. If the referring doctor has taken a subtly (or not so subtly) dismissive attitude to the referral, the patient's worries will intensify.

For other patients, adherence to a biomedical model is not just a matter of conditioning but is also defensive: a chronic symptom or illness tends to weave itself into the fabric of identity, social relations and lifestyle, all of which adapt accordingly. Almost inevitably, some form of 'primary gain' and/or 'secondary gain' will accrue. Pinsky (1975) offers a definition:

> Psychologically, the primary gain from a symptom is the freedom from anxiety and conflict achieved by the symptom's presence. The secondary gain consists of the practical advantages that can be achieved by using the symptoms to influence or manipulate others. Both operate largely at an unconscious level. . . . The second-ary gain of chronic pain and suffering behaviour has been the major focus of investigations and commentary largely because of its impact on the psychologi-cally important people in the patient's life . . . .

Examples of secondary gain could include a partner taking over responsi-bility for household tasks from the patient, the redesign of a job description at the workplace or the drawing of sickness benefit. The primary gain of symptoms or illness is usually more deeply repressed and may take many different forms. For example, primary gain occurs when the illness or pain gratifies unconscious unmet needs for nurturance, while simultaneously satisfying the internal demand that such dependency is unacceptable and merits punishment (Pinsky, 1975).

Both 'primary' and 'secondary' gain can make it harder for the patient to move on from a conventional medical view of a symptom or illness and begin to reconceptualise the distress in a holistic, biopsychosocial way.

Alan B.

Alan B., a 50-year-old man, presented at the multidisciplinary pain management clinic. He complained of chronic back pain following an assault at his local workplace, a Government Social Security office four years previously. He had felt outraged by the injustice of the attack and increasingly depressed. He had also responded poorly to the various treatments offered. He grew steadily more disabled to the point where he was medically retired and his wife took over all the household tasks. They moved to a different town in order to live in a bungalow and he gave up driving.

Up to the time of his assessment at the clinic, Alan had felt there was a direct, unquestionable causal link between his injury and his life as an invalid. He worried in case the referral meant his doctor no longer believed his pain and suffering were 'real'. It took a great deal of listening and discussion and appropriate education before Alan B. began even to contemplate the notion that the pain could be

both 'real' and also the expression of multiple factors: physiological, affective, cognitive and behavioural.

Sometimes unhappy patients present with what Winnicott (1966) called a
'scatter of responsible agents'. The patient comes for help to the counsellor
but also describes ongoing contacts with a number of other helping agents
such as general practitioner, acupuncturist, consultant, healer, osteopath,
etc. Alternatively, the patient may try to keep the helping agents responsible
for 'psyche' and 'soma' rigidly split apart. Winnicott explained this by
relating the patient's distress to developmental difficulties in uniting
'psyche' and 'soma' within the personality. Such a dissociation can lead to
problems in relating to whole objects and the use of splitting as a defence is
common. Winnicott advises caution in challenging such a presentation:

> Our difficult job is to take a unified view of the patient and the illness *without*
> *seeming to do so in a way that goes ahead of the patient's ability to achieve*
> *integration to a unit.*   (p. 515)

It is easier to manage this 'scattering' or splitting in a team setting. At the
multidisciplinary pain clinic, we are able to offer some compromise. We do
not accept patients for pain management if they are still pursuing medical or
complementary treatments, because our emphasis is on mobilising the
patient's own resources. However, the presence of doctors and physio-
therapists on the team reassures patients that the medical aspect of their
symptoms is being respected and monitored.

Another form of splitting may occur when a patient shows a dismissive,
irritated or contemptuous attitude to the counsellor and doctor while also
speaking about the superior help likely to be gained from another doctor/
second opinion/type of complementary medicine. Here, the patient may be
projecting rejected aspects of the self (e.g. anger, rage, inadequacy) into the
counsellor or the referring doctor; simultaneously, the 'good' aspects of the
self may be projected into an idealised but inaccessible alternative professional. Anger (often unconscious) in the presence of the counsellor or
the referring doctor may be exacerbated or inspired by envy of the
physically well professional (Adler, 1984). There can also be intense frustration if the experience of encountering a counsellor/doctor who has no
instant cure for suffering recapitulates early experiences of disappointment
or abandonment.

If the counsellor/doctor's own areas of vulnerability relate to these
projections, there is a risk that he or she may be provoked to retaliate or
withdraw emotionally. The aggressive response then punishes the patient
and may also confirm the view that the symptom, illness or physical
disability is unbearable to others as well as to themselves. It is possible for
the patient to experience several such encounters with medical personnel
before reaching the counsellor and his or her scepticism at the point of
referral will be all the stronger.

The therapist's recognition and response

Before considering ways of engaging the patient in the assessment process, I want to discuss the vulnerability of certain distressed patients who present in the medical context. Of course, given the diversity of medical patients, what follows applies only to a proportion – but nevertheless a significant proportion. Although this section is more theoretical than the rest of the chapter, my concern is with a key clinical issue: how we choose the values and priorities which shape our response to the patient.

In his essay on a rural general practitioner, Berger (1967) describes how the experience of illness tends to sever connections with the taken-for-granted world of daily living and relationships and encourages a fragmented form of self-consciousness. It tends to exacerbate a sense of uniqueness, especially when the illness is still undiagnosed. Berger goes on to make a link between this experience and that of unhappiness.

> It is a question of failing to find any confirmation of oneself in the outside world. The lack of confirmation leads to a sense of futility. And this sense of futility is the essence of loneliness . . . . Any example offers hope. But the conviction of being unique destroys all examples.
>
> An unhappy patient comes to a doctor to offer him an illness in the hope that this part of him at least (the illness) may be recognisable. His proper self he believes to be unknowable . . . . Clearly the task of the doctor . . . is to recognise the man (sic). If the man can begin to feel recognised – and such recognition may well include aspects of his character which he has not yet recognised himself – the hopeless nature of his unhappiness will have been changed . . . . (pp. 74–75)

Berger explicitly draws here on the work of Balint, but his own introduction of the notion of recognition seems particularly apt in the medical context.

Winnicott (1974) traces the earliest sense of recognition back to the mutual gaze between mother and infant:

> What does the baby see when he or she looks at the mother's face? I am suggesting that, ordinarily, what the baby sees is himself or herself. In other words, the mother is looking at the baby *and what she looks like is related to what she sees there.*   (p. 131)

Here Winnicott describes the 'good enough' mother's face as the child's first mirror, reflecting back and confirming the child in its being and aliveness. Winnicott goes on to suggest that the mother's failure to function in this way can lead to trauma. If the mother's face shows depression, distraction or fixity, the baby experiences a premature sense of the Other, of the Other's look and a consequent shocking impingement of self-consciousness.

Wright's (1991) book, *Vision and Separation*, presents a complex account of early development in which the face and the sense of sight are given new emphasis. Unlike the breast, the face as an object cannot be consumed. In a good enough mother/infant dyad, the dawning recognition of a mother's face implies separation and space. Wright describes this space as a precursor for the internal space necessary for healthy symbol formation and creative play. But when mother's face is not loving, Wright, like Winnicott, emphasises the trauma and the shame of being objectified, 'looked at', and contrasts this with the benign 'looking after' of the mirroring gaze. If the infant's distress and rage is again met by the Other in her 'Gorgon' aspect, the infant feels doubly repelled, repulsed and ashamed.

> My hypothesis is that it is this catastrophic consequence which leads the child to abandon its own ship as it were. He joins forces with this mother who looks, disowns the self which the mother could not contain and which caused the rupture, and thenceforward regards this threatening self as an Other that has the appearance the child imagined it had for the looking mother. This is a self that has been written off. It is one of the *desaparecidos*, one that has disappeared and has no name, has no loving mother keeping it alive in the memory or looking to refine it. It exists only in a kind of limbo . . . in a space where the mother is not and where things are not named or recognised.   (Wright, 1991, p. 46)

Wright echoes Winnicott in describing this as a 'false self' mode of functioning and he goes on to speak of the life of this self as one of: '. . . delivering up to the mother acceptable appearances, strung together to form a pseudo-cohesive envelope in her continuing positive regard'. Wright argues that there is a phobic relationship, engendered by shame, both with the dispossessed self and with the look of the Other (external or internalised) who regards that self. By contrast, the 'subjective self' is a self that has experienced the mother's mirroring and holding and is in touch with (not primarily seen by) the Other and the world. It is also a self that is identified both with the psyche and with the totality of bodily functioning.

Wright does not make any links between the 'dispossessed self' and the presentation of patients in the medical context. However, his description of the '*space where the mother is not and where things are not named or recognised*' seems to me to illustrate the concept of 'alexithymia', a word coined by Sifneos (1972) to describe certain characteristics of so-called 'psychosomatic' patients.

Alexithymia is a controversial concept, although it has stimulated much research. Its essential features include difficulties in describing and/or differentiating emotions, a tendency to somatise distress, externally oriented thinking and an impoverished fantasy life. The analyst, Joyce McDougall (1989), links alexithymia to the phenomenon of 'pseudonormality', whereby patients may present with superficially adjusted behaviour patterns, together with somatic symptoms and concealed disturbance. She stresses its origin in preoedipal developmental difficulties, in particular the failure to internalise a benign, care-taking maternal object. An inner sense of deadness or numbness is typical and can emerge in the therapist's counter-transference.

As early as 1979, the analyst Krystal anticipated research (e.g. Taylor, Parker and Bagby, 1990) which showed that alexithymia is not confined to 'psychosomatic' patients and is widespread among all patient and non-patient groups. He also emphasised that it is not an all-or-nothing quality and can fluctuate in severity and consistency within an individual. Importantly, he linked its manifestation to an origin in trauma (see p. 5).

Significant numbers of distressed medical patients have experienced trauma either in infancy or in adulthood or both. Other patients are (re)traumatised by the impact of an accident, a life-threatening illness, a disability, pain or a medical/surgical procedure. Trauma in early life is likely to result in that fracturing of the self which Wright described and the consequent subjective sense of an inner 'space . . . where things are not named or recognised'. This development of alexithymic characteristics, according to Krystal (1979), comes about because of an arrest in the young child's affective development. In adulthood, post-traumatic stress can lead to a regression of affect to earlier developmental stages of undifferentiated, mostly somatised and poorly verbalised emotions. Such a defence clearly reflects an overwhelming fear of feeling and there may be a corresponding anticipatory dread of meeting a counsellor who might not be sensitive to such fears. What I emphasise here is the vulnerability to appraisal and assessment within certain medical patients which renders this process particularly delicate and difficult.

With Berger (1967), I believe that the response of the health counsellor should be the offering of what he terms 'fraternal recognition': a quality of empathy linked to acceptance and self-knowledge. The counsellor's recognition has a paradoxical effect. On the one hand, the patient feels temporarily confirmed in the individuality she or he may find difficult to grasp; on the other, the lonely sense of uniqueness is temporarily dispelled because the counsellor's empathic response implies a commonality of experience. Without this quality the counsellor in the early stages of therapy can all too easily be experienced as the 'Gorgon Other'.

> This new sense of *holding* of the once banished self has to *precede* any renewed looking – premature interpretation would merely drive the self into hiding again. Only when the self has been drawn out by the safety of the therapy and the therapist's acceptance of what is 'bad' can there be a reviewing and a clearer understanding of this banished self.   (Wright, 1991, p. 290)

I link this recognition/holding process to the 'introspective–empathic' stance on the analyst's part advocated by Taylor (1987) in working with medical patients. The analyst's aim, according to Taylor, should be 'psychic maturation' – the repair of deficits in object relations through new internalisations – which can then increase the capacity for self-regulation. This stance can involve education about emotions, the analysis of the form and functions of communications and dreams as much as their contents, as well as the cautious use of interpretations.

I would like now to illustrate this discussion by describing a segment from the case of Theresa J.

Theresa J.

For the first two months of our contact, Theresa J., a 39-year-old woman, sat tensely, often looking down and avoiding eye contact. She suffered from menorrhagia (excessive menstrual bleeding) and the referral had come from her consultant gynaecologist who had become concerned by her condition which included depression and anxiety. In the first session, one of my key concerns was to understand and acknowledge Theresa J.'s fears about attending. She told me she had not slept the entire night before and had sat up smoking. She did not know why, although with a little prompting, a fear that she would be humiliated emerged. She had no idea why she was so depressed and said she felt 'blank' about it.

The next five sessions were an extended assessment. In addition to the presenting problems, Theresa J. suffered from social phobia (a disabling fear of social situations) and her compulsive eating occasionally involved vomiting. An Ulster-born Catholic, she had married a Protestant, and her family had disapproved of the marriage. She was an only child of a single-parent mother who had herself been battered by her boyfriend and had had little time for her child. At the age of six, Theresa J. was taken into care where, for the next five years, she was sometimes physically abused by a harsh female careworker. Aged eleven she had rejoined her mother.

Theresa J., a typist, described how her new (woman) office manager had been sadistic and abusive towards various members of staff. We were able to link this experience to the recent depression. Overeating was one way of 'blanking out' her misery, although it also made her feel worse about her body, which was overweight.

By this time, Theresa J.'s capacity to begin making links between her symptoms and her inner world convinced me that I had a mandate to offer her a contract for once-weekly psychodynamic counselling.

After two months, 'blankness' took over. In one session, I asked her to try to describe herself and the wordless blankness. She spoke of a sense of being in a 'mould' which was like a sarcophagus with a bandaged, mummy-like figure inside. Hidden inside the bandaged figure was a 'speck' – like a seed.

This important simile illuminated her initial presentation. When she came to counselling it felt as if she had left the outer mould and was dangerously exposed. As we explored her associations, the sarcophagus/mould seemed to represent her compliant, 'moulded' persona which felt both protective and painfully inauthentic. The bandages represented the layers of fat which seemed to be there to protect the inner 'mummy' figure. This figure seemed to refer punningly to her sense of a deadened self, identified with her depressed, deadened mummy/mother – but also wounded by her mother. Inside the 'mummy' figure lay the protected but inaccessible 'speck', which she called the seed of her true self. Another layer of meaning emerged when Theresa J. recaptured the experience from babyhood of lying alone in her cot/sarcophagus, covered with her blankets/bandages, with only the blank ceiling to stare at in the seemingly endless absence of her mother.

Theresa J.'s memory of the blank ceiling makes the link between the external physically and emotionally absent mother, the internal dead mummy object and her alexithymic blankness – a link predicted by McDougall (1989). Her case also shows how the early traumatic experiences of lack of recognition lead to a fracturing of the self-experience – the dispossession of the 'speck'/self and a developing phobic relationship both to others (her later social phobia) and to the self she felt was unacceptable. Krystal's work, as described, would also predict a greater likelihood of alexithymic functioning because of the trauma. Later experiences of traumatic abuse would only have confirmed the pre-existing alexithymic defences. Without prior experience of (relatively) safe understanding, together with a gradual exposure to the identification of feelings during the extended assessment, any engagement in therapy would have been impossible.

Engaging the patient in the assessment

Whenever possible, I prefer to see outpatients in a medical setting where I can be clearly identified as a member of the health care team. (Sometimes it is useful for the referrer to introduce me to the patient in person.) This offsets any tendency to see my province as the 'psychological' or 'psychosomatic' as opposed to the 'physical'.

Seeing inpatients on a hospital ward presents special problems. The lack of clear physical boundaries, privacy and the likelihood of interruptions can make it harder to establish and maintain therapeutic boundaries of role, confidentiality and time. The patient may feel particularly resentful in relation to a non-elected referral, given his or her relative powerlessness within the ward organisation. It is obviously necessary to do everything possible to arrange curtains, chairs, etc. to maximise privacy, or to interview in a side-room. It is also important to be alert for any problems the patient may voice or refer to indirectly in relation to the setting. It is helpful to arrange an ending time before getting into the session. This may need to be renegotiated on each occasion if the patient is very ill or in pain and only able to tolerate limited amounts of conversation.

With all patients, ambivalent, hostile or anxious feelings about the referral always need to be taken up right away, listened to and explored. It may be tempting to offer rapid reassurance but this may mean that the less obvious hesitations are passed over. Once the patient's reaction to the referral has been clarified, it is then possible to begin exploring the possibility of a 'mandate' for further assessment and intervention. (Sometimes this is best deferred until the presenting symptoms are assessed.) It may be useful to begin by explaining the counsellor's role within the health care team. How this is done depends on the nature of the patient's anxiety and the extent of any mis-information. Sometimes it is enough for me to explain that I work as a health psychologist exclusively with medical patients.

Sometimes I need to give a further rationale. For example, I might explain to a reluctant patient with newly diagnosed diabetes that the onset of such an illness leads to enormous changes in terms of initial loss of physical health, hospitalisation, diagnosis and the new demands of the diabetic regimen. Such changes are stressful and my job is to help people understand and cope in the best way with such stress. For the reluctant (or just curious) chronic pain patient, I might outline a relevant biopsychosocial model of pain, such as the 'gate theory' (Melzack and Wall, 1965) in order to validate my role within a multidisciplinary approach.

This process of building a shared model of understanding the symptoms with the patient is often difficult and can occasionally take several sessions. Always, it is essential to convey your belief in the reality of the patient's suffering. This belief may be tested and re-rested by the patient before a mandate for intervention becomes possible (Pinsky, 1975).

The next step may be to enquire into the presenting physical symptoms. These are usually uppermost in the patient's mind and the counsellor's interest signals a holistic (as against a narrowly 'psychological') approach. The interest should be informed and, for the non-medical counsellor, this often demands prior reading up on the illness. Sometimes the taking of an outline medical history can be the next step and this may lead on usefully to enquiries about the more personal details.

For some patients, the use of a 'psychodynamic life narrative' (Viederman and Perry, 1980) can be a way into the exploration of stress linked to illness. Here, the first two or three assessment sessions are spent in clarifying the patient's medical and psychological symptoms and associated thoughts, feelings, fantasies, conflicts and coping mechanisms; assessment is also made of past medical and personal history with special emphasis on pre-vious crises and associated conflicts and coping strengths. According to Viederman and Perry, the patient can then be given a written statement, which places the physical illness in the context of his or her life trajectory in such a way that his or her distress is viewed as a natural result of personal psychology rather than an inevitable consequence of the illness *per se*. The 'narrative' then forms the basis for further brief counselling or psychotherapy. I prefer to build up a verbal 'narrative' with the patient, as this is less fixed than the written variety. Clearly, this method is only possible when a patient has or quickly develops some interest in exploring the inner world.

Anthony K.

Anthony K. was a 25-year-old single researcher who became depressed soon after the diagnosis of insulin-dependent diabetes. He initially felt the diabetic regimen was a devastating 'life sentence' which would prevent him advancing in his career or attracting a future wife. He was, therefore, very unsure of the usefulness of counselling, although he was self-reflective by nature. In the remainder of the first session and in the second, I went on to assess Anthony K.'s personal history. By the third session we had together constructed a 'narrative' which went something like this:

> You were the only child of parents who had longed for a baby for 15 years. Perhaps partly as a result of that, your mother always tended to be over-anxious and over-protective. This only increased when you developed epilepsy as a tiny child. Although you outgrew this in your teens, it had the effect of making you feel 'different' from other children. You felt unsure about your appearance and attractiveness and it was hard to make many friends. Later when other young people began to date, you felt very shy and relationships with girls have always been a problem. When you then fell ill and were diagnosed with diabetes, it was only too easy to feel that this was an action replay: once again you were having to struggle with an illness that made you feel 'different'. Your mother was worried sick – but this time there is no possibility of out-growing it.

With the help of the 'narrative', we were able to discuss the possibility that it was Anthony K.'s own anxieties and memories which made the diabetes, however seriously it demanded to be taken, into something which took away all hope. There was no mandate to go beyond this and explore the early effects of his parenting and childhood illness. But it was possible to set up a short focused counselling intervention to work through the 'narrative'. This resulted in a significant improvement in Anthony K.'s mood and he began to make plans for the future.

Anthony K.'s case shows how important changes can be initiated within the assessment period itself. This can happen even with the most unpromising beginnings. In the case of Cecilia J., the problem was how to find a way of working with her derogatory and self-derogatory adherence to what she called her 'chronic psychosomatic personality'.

Cecilia J.

Cecilia J., a 28-year-old single secretary was referred by her general practitioner with various somatic and psychological symptoms. In the first session she spoke of her considerable cynicism over the referral. She told me about her chronic 'psychosomatic' symptoms of allergy, back pain and panic attacks which went back to childhood and which she felt were a sign of failure. She gave me an outline history with an almost bored detachment. My own response was to feel somewhat detached – almost bored – and pessimistic and I struggled to remain open.

In the second session, Cecilia J. began to speak with the same detachment, although the reluctant 'cynicism' had faded. She told me that her symptoms had eased since the doctor referred her because her demanding job had lightened; but in a month's time, as her workload increased, she could predict a return to illness and panic. I simply reflected this, while underlining that there was an implied inevitability about the illness to come. The crucial question, why she was here, was whether it was indeed true that nothing could be done.

There was a pause and then Cecilia J. told me that there were some things she had not gone into. We talked of two more symptoms both of which she described as 'ridiculous'.

Another pause and I was told that something had been omitted: the fact that at the age of sixteen, she had got pregnant and her parents, both successful and conventional, had put heavy pressure on her to have an abortion. At the time, she said, she had felt almost nothing, although she had quickly left home afterwards. I commented on this lack of feeling over such a distressing event and the contrast with the passionate anxiety and the pain which she experienced in her panic attacks and physical symptoms. I wondered if there was a pattern here. Cecilia J. seemed struck by this and the mood of the session changed. She became much more engaged. We discussed her parents' tendency to distance themselves from feelings – their's and hers – by indifference or even ridicule.

Cecilia J. accepted my point that it must have felt safer to distance herself from feelings, even at the expense of a greater vulnerability to the 'ridiculous' symptoms. At the end, she spoke with unmistakable feeling of her sense of a capacity for aliveness and life, largely unlived. By the end of the next session, we agreed on Cecilia J.'s need for long-term psychotherapy and a referral was made.

Clearly, part of my struggle here involved registering the way in which my counter-transference mirrored Cecilia J.'s hopelessness and numbness. This made it possible, with difficulty, to remain empathic – in Wright's terms, still able to 'look after' her rather than do what I was invited to do: 'look at' the 'psychosomatic' phenomena she tried to present.

Respect for the diversity of individual needs in the medical context leads on to an emphasis on flexibility and eclecticism in deciding on an intervention, even though that decision is always informed by psychodynamic understanding of the presentation. Ideally, the counsellor should have skills in several therapeutic approaches and/or know where to refer on as necessary. In the case of Robert F., whom I introduced on page 45, it became clear that there was no initial mandate for exploratory work, as I describe below.

Robert F. (continued from page 46)
My first concern was to listen to and acknowledge Robert F.'s anxieties about his heart and the possibility of undiagnosed disease. Further enquiry into his symptoms revealed that Robert F.'s hypertension had developed soon after his marriage a year previously. The marriage occurred without much prior planning. Robert F.'s UK visa was about to expire and by marrying his girlfriend, who was a UK citizen, he was able to stay on. His parents had divorced when he was in his 'teens and he recalled that his father had suffered from hypertension at that time. It also emerged that Robert F. tended to hyperventilate when stressed.

After discussion and an explanation from me about the physiology of hyperventilation, Robert F. somewhat grudgingly accepted the possibility of a link between his current symptoms and hyperventilation. He also accepted my point that he might spend many months in search of second opinions, further treatments, etc. for his symptoms but with no guarantee of cure at the end. It was also clear that my mandate extended only to offering help with the hyperventilation, as this was the one 'need' Robert F. could identify.

I taught Robert F. diaphragmatic breathing exercises and we worked on some stress management. Uneven progress was made, but the symptoms gradually abated and his working life eased. A trust developed and in the penultimate session he confided his fears of his marriage breaking down, like that of his parents. His wife's recent reappearance in the UK (after some months back in Canada) had only sharpened his fears. At that point he gradually accepted some sort of link between the stress that these fears had caused his somatic response and the tensions in his relationship with his wife – which had already begun to ease.

Summary

I have outlined an approach to assessment in which the patient's needs are identified through the dynamic interaction of the assessment process. The formulation of need implies the possibility of an effective intervention and I have emphasised flexibility in deciding the therapy of choice. I have also emphasised the difficulty a substantial number of medical patients have in engaging with a counsellor and the vulnerability to appraisal and assessment which a significant number share. I suggest that the counsellor's response should be one of recognition and acceptance.

Acknowledgements

Thanks to Dorothy Judd, Sebastian Kraemer, Stephen Pilling and Jane Serraillier Grossfeld for helpful comments on the chapter. Thanks also to Irene Edwards and Violet Gleeson for invaluable work on preparing the manuscipt.

References

ABEL SMITH, A., IRVING, J. and BROWN, P. (1989). Counselling in the medical context. In: W. Dryden, D. Charles-Edwards and R. Woolfe (Eds), *Handbook of Counselling in Britain*. London: Routledge.

ADLER, G. (1984). Special problems for the therapist. *International Journal of Psychiatry in Medicine* **14** (2), 91–98.

BERGER, J. (1967). *A Fortunate Man*. London: Penguin Books.

BREWIN, C.R., BRADLEY, C. and HOME, P.D. (1991). Measuring needs in patients with diabetes. In: C. Bradley, P. Home and M. Christie (Eds), *The Technology of Diabetes Care: Converging Medical and Psychosocial Perspectives*. Chur: Harwood Academic.

BREWIN, C.R., WING, J.K., MANGLEN, J.P., BRUGHA, T.S. and MacCARTHY, B. (1987). Principles and practice of measuring needs in the long-term mentally ill: the MRC needs, for care assessment. *Psychological Medicine* **17**, 971–981.

DAVIS, H. and FALLOWFIELD, L. (1991). *Counselling and Communication in Health Care*. Chichester: Wiley.

ENGEL, G. (1977). The need for a new medical model. *Science* **196**, 129–136.

KAROLY, P. (Ed.) (1985). *Measurement Strategies in Health Psychology*. New York: Wiley.

KRYSTAL, H. (1978). Self-representation and the capacity for self-care. In: *The Annual of Psychoanalysis*, Vol. 6. New York: International Universities Press.

KRYSTAL, H. (1979). Alexithymia and psychotherapy. *American Journal of Psychotherapy* **23** (1), 17–31.

McDOUGALL, J. (1989). *Theatres of the Body*. London: Free Association Books.

MELZACK, R. and WALL, P.D. (1965). Pain mechanisms: a new theory. *Science* **150**, 971–979.

NEMIAH, J. and SIFNEOS, P. (1970). Affect and fantasy in patients with psychosomatic disorders. In: O.W. Hill (Ed.), *Modern Trends in Psychosomatic Medicine*, Vol. 2. London: Butterworths.

PINSKY, J.J. (1975). Psychodynamics and psychotherapy in the treatment of patients with chronic intractable pain. In: B.L. Crue (Ed.), *Pain: Research and Treatment*. London: Academic Press.

SIFNEOS, P.E. (1972). *Short-term Psychotherapy and Emotional Crisis*. Cambridge, MA: Harvard University Press.

TAYLOR, G.J. (1987). *Psychosomatic Medicine and Contemporary Psychoanalysis. Stress and Health Series*, Monograph 3. Madison, CT: International Universities Press.

TAYLOR, G.J., PARKER, J.D.A. and BAGBY, R.M. (1990). A preliminary investigation of alexithymia in men with psychoactive substance dependence. *American Journal of Psychiatry* **147**, 1228–1230.

VIEDERMAN, M. and PERRY III, S.W. (1980). Use of a psychodynamic life narrative in the treatment of depression in the physically ill. *General Hospital Psychiatry* **3**, 177–185.

WINNICOTT, D.W. (1966). Psychosomatic illness in its positive and negative aspects. *International Journal of Psycho-Analysis* **47**, 510–516.

WINNICOTT, D.W. (1974). *Playing and Reality*. Harmondsworth: Penguin.

WRIGHT, K. (1991). *Vision and Separation: Between Mother and Baby*. London: Free Association Books.

Chapter 3
Psychoanalytic formulation and treatment:
chronic metabolic disturbance in insulin-dependent diabetes mellitus

Peter Fonagy and George Moran*

Childhood diabetes

This chapter aims to provide an overview of our approach to the psychological treatment of poorly controlled insulin-dependent diabetes mellitus (IDDM) in young individuals. IDDM is a relatively rare disorder. New cases of type I or insulin-dependent diabetes occur at an annual rate of approximately 14–16 per 100 000 in boys, and 12–15 per 100 000 in girls (Cahill and McDervitt, 1981; Crow, Alberti and Parkin, 1991). Epidemiological evidence from three separate British birth cohorts show that the incidence of 10 per 100 000 in 1957 rose to 13 per 100 000 in 1980 to almost 14 per 100 000 in 1986. This trend was also found in other longitudinal studies in Scandinavian countries (Bingley and Gale, 1989, 1990). The prevalence of the disease for those aged 20 years or younger is approximately 1 in 300.

The disease may be diagnosed from infancy onwards although its onset in children occurs most frequently between the ages of 8 and 12 years. The diagnosis has a sinister prognosis with an overall mortality rate of 60% within 40 years of initial diagnosis. Within the same period 21% will have suffered myocardial infarction, 16% will be blind, 12% will have gangrene or have undergone amputation and 10% will have suffered a stroke (Stiller et al., 1984).

Genetic and environmental factors both seem to contribute to the development of the disease. Infective agents, particularly viruses, seem to be the most plausible environmental triggers which set off an autoimmune process in genetically susceptible individuals. The process associated with insulin-dependent diabetes, however, encompasses immune and metabolic

*Dr Moran was Director of the Anna Freud Centre until his untimely death in January 1992.

Parts of the initial section of this chapter appeared in P. Fonagy and G. Moran (1993). Childhood diabetes. In R.M. Michels et al. (Eds), *Psychiatry*, revised edn, chap. 46, pp. 1–12. Philadelphia: J.B. Lippincott.

changes which may only sometimes progress and persist and may, in fact, remit for reasons that are as yet poorly understood (Leslie and Pyke, 1991).

There is accumulating evidence of a limited set of psychosocial factors implicated in the causation of the disease consistent with the above model. A case-control study of 161 cases of IDDM among children aged 0–17 years occurring in Montreal during a four-year period found elevated risk for children who had not been breast-fed, who attended day-care or nursery before the age of five, and who lived in a crowded household at age three years (Siemiatycki et al., 1989). A case-reference study from Sweden demonstrated that mothers of diabetic children had poorer education, fathers were more frequently manual workers, and duration of breast feeding was significantly shorter in cases than in controls (Blom et al., 1989).

Many of these associations may be linked to socio-economic status. Crow et al. (1991) dramatically illustrate the effect of deprivation on incidence – the rates in the most and least deprived areas of the region studied were 18.7 per 100 000 and 7.0 per 100 000 respectively. Stress/neuroendocrine interactions provide a potential pathway to explain the social gradient effect in the incidence of childhood diabetes. Increased psychosocial stress has been implicated in the development of IDDM (Robinson and Fuller, 1985; Siemiatycki et al., 1989) but further control studies are needed to provide definitive conclusions on this issue.

The aim of treatment is to achieve near normal levels of blood glucose by insulin therapy, attention to diet and exercise. The condition is monitored by testing urine and blood levels of glucose. As blood glucose control is achieved behaviourally through adherence to a prescribed medical regime, a psychological perspective is central to the adequate management of this chronic disease. The immediate inconvenience of poor control, as well as the possibility of long-term complications, imply that a psychological approach should focus on the stabilisation of blood glucose in IDDM patients (Bennett Johnson, 1989, 1990).

A heuristic model of diabetic control

There are two broad classes of psychological phenomena which may be considered primary determinants of blood glucose control. These are stressful events and relatively poor adherence to the medical regime (Fonagy, Moran and Higgitt, 1989).

Barglow et al. (1986) outline a bio-psychosocial model focused on the linked concepts of equilibrium and stress. Stress hormones (catecholamines, cortisol, glucagon and growth hormone) counteract the metabolic action of insulin. Diabetic patients may have a heightened endocrinological sensitivity to stress leading to hyperglycaemic response. Hyperglycaemia may provoke further metabolic derangement by decreasing the normoglycaemic effects of insulin and/or giving rise to a somatic disequilibrium provoking the release of additional quantities of stress hormones.

Clinical experience and recorded observations both suggest that life stresses are associated with glycaemic control in diabetic patients. Chase and Jackson (1981) found that scores on a schedule of stressful events covering the past three months correlated with triglyceride concentrations, glycosylated haemoglobin levels, cholesterol values and serum glucose concentrations, particularly in the adolescent age range (15–18 years) of their sample (see also Bradley, 1979; Helz and Templeton, 1990). The assumption that acute psychological stresses cause disturbances of metabolic control in IDDM patients is, however, poorly supported by the literature. Infusions of pathophysiological amounts of catecholamines cause fairly trivial rises in blood glucose in both normal and insulin-deficient subjects (Pernet et al., 1984).

In another study, Kemmer et al. (1986) subjected nine normoglycaemic and nine hyperglycaemic patients with IDDM to acute psychological stress. Marked psychophysiological (heart rate, systolic and diastolic blood pressure) and moderate endocrine (plasma adrenaline, noradrenaline and cortisol) responses reflected the stressful nature of the tasks. The stress did not lead to changed levels of glucose, ketones, free fatty acids or growth hormone.

An alternative to the stress/neuroendocrine hypothesis suggests that emotional stress leads to poor compliance or impaired decision-making with regard to diet, insulin doses or monitoring (Gill, Walford and Alberti, 1985). Adherence to the diabetic regime requires the performance of an elaborate set of procedures. Non-adherence has been shown to be common, even in studies which make no particular attempt to facilitate disclosure on the part of the diabetic patient. A sensitive report by Groen and Pelzer (1982) provides evidence in the form of personal accounts of periods in the lives of the majority of IDDM individuals when they refuse to accept the disease and neglect their insulin requirements and diet although they are aware of the nature of their disease and its dangers. Adolescence brings with it rebellion against the externally imposed regime (Goldstein and Hoeper, 1987) and a deterioration of glycaemic control (Kaar et al., 1984).

Wilson and Endes (1986) carried out a somewhat controversial investigation at the time that memory glucometers were first introduced in Europe. Children, unaware that their blood testing equipment recorded and 'remembered' the times and results of their blood tests, commonly failed to record unwelcome results (18%) and claimed tests which they did not perform (40%). Studies of children with IDDM found that the quality of adherence can account for as much as 60% of the variance of diabetic control (Kaplan, Chadwick and Schimmel, 1985; Fonagy et al., 1987). Even extreme cases of poorly controlled diabetes (see below) may be accounted for in terms of deliberate omission of insulin or other psychologically determined interference with the regime deliberately or involuntarily concealed from physicians (Gill, Walford and Alberti, 1985; Schade et al., 1985; Tattersall, 1985).

Diabetic control is the end product of a number of interactive causal factors. The distinction of a stress/neuroendocrine from a direct behavioural pathway may, however, have heuristic value in understanding the influence of psychosocial factors on glycaemic control. For example, one multivariate study (Hanson, Henggeler and Burghen, 1987), which separately measured stress, adherence and metabolic control, indicated that stress is directly associated with metabolic control *independent* of the link between adherence and glycaemic balance. Social competence buffered the effect of stress whilst family cohesion and support influenced behavioural adherence. Further, it is possible that negative life events affect glycaemic control only at particular stages of the disease. Jacobson, Rand and Hauser (1985) report a strong association of negative life events with metabolic control only in patients whose proliferative retinopathy developed within the previous two years.

'Brittle' diabetes

'Brittle' diabetes is a form of insulin-dependent diabetes mellitus (IDDM) characterised by extreme and chronic failure to maintain blood glucose control. A small group of young patients with IDDM experience long-term and severe problems in maintaining blood glucose levels near to the range for non-diabetics. The observed prevalence of such difficulties is greatly affected by clinical practice and thus varies between centres but it has been estimated at 1% of the juvenile IDDM population (Gill, Walford and Alberti, 1985; Tattersall and Walford, 1985; White and Santiago, 1985a).

The cause of brittle diabetes

The cause of brittle diabetes is not known (Gill, Walford and Alberti, 1985). As its prevalence appears to be extremely low in patients over 30 years of age, it has been suggested that the disorder is either fatal or resolves spontaneously (Williams and Pickup, 1985a,b). More recently, however, community-based studies have identified a similar clinical picture in elderly patients (Griffith and Yudkin, 1989).

Certain organic factors which may play a part in bringing about brittle diabetes are well recognised. Impaired subcutaneous insulin absorption (Dandona et al., 1978; Home et al., 1982; Williams, 1985), frank insulin resistance (Gill, Walford and Alberti, 1985; Williams et al., cited in Gill, Walford and Alberti, 1985), exaggerated response to insulin withdrawal (Madsbad et al., 1979) and hyperlactacidaemia have all been demonstrated to be more prevalent in these patients. But even when all of the known organic causes have been eliminated, there remain numerous cases whose inability to manage their diabetes is unexplained (see Pickup, 1985b).

The proportion of patients whose aetiology is unequivocally psychological has been variously estimated as one-third (Gill, Walford and Alberti, 1985), two-thirds (Williams and Pickup, 1988) and over three-quarters (Schade et al., 1985; Tattersall et al., 1991) of individuals with hyperglycaemia. They are most likely to be female, adolescent, and slightly above average in their body weight and insulin intake. They are unlikely to be helped by pumps or pens for stabilising or improving control (Brink and Stewart, 1986; Hardy, Jones and Gill, 1991). Nor are they likely to be helped by closely supervised subcutaneous infusion of insulin (Williams and Pickup, 1988). It seems likely that patients with a tendency to hypoglycaemia are in graver physical danger than those whose diabetic imbalance manifests mainly in terms of ketoacidosis (Tattersall et al., 1991).

Following the heuristic model of diabetic control outlined above, we can delineate two major pathways of psychological causation of the brittle diabetic state, the first relating to pathological biochemical functioning and the second to psychopathological functioning (see Fonagy and Moran, 1993).

It is known that the *metabolic imbalance* found in diabetic patients weakens the homoeostatic capacity of the *neuroendocrine system* of some patients who then respond to even mild psychosocial stress by excessive release of cortisol and other stress hormones (Gilbert et al., 1989). These in turn serve to counteract the normoglycaemic influence of insulin and brings about a further intensification of the stress responses. Anxiety, consequent upon continued psychosocial stress (parental psychopathology, broken homes, unhappiness at school) may thus be expected to cause chronic diabetic imbalance through its interference with the insulin regime.

The second pathway concerns the *conscious or unconscious acts of transgression* of the prescribed treatment regime. In all the cases of brittle diabetes we have treated psychotherapeutically (see Moran, 1987; Moran et al., 1991), we have found significant instances of non-adherence to the regime which could have, in and of themselves, accounted for the child's volatile blood glucose level. Non-adherence may well be associated with high levels of anxiety and stress (Fonagy, Moran and Higgitt, 1989). This formulation is consistent with the findings of a number of other specialist centres (Farberow, 1970; Schade et al., 1985; Stancin, Link and Reuter, 1989; Tattersall et al., 1991).

Whilst non-adherence to the regime is a plausible, as well as a clinically verifiable, explanation for chronic metabolic imbalance, diabetologists sometimes balk at the idea, probably because it conflicts with the common-sense model of human motivation to which they subscribe. Such a model does not readily accommodate the irrational, profoundly self-destructive nature of the behaviour of brittle diabetic youngsters. The idea that children, adolescents and young adults regularly go to extreme lengths 'deliberately' to bring about pain and ill-health is, naturally, seen as implausible if not absurd. The threat such clinical observations pose to those with an optimistic view of human nature is probably in itself sufficiently compelling to cause endocrinologists to redouble their effort to identify the biological bases of brittle diabetes in general as well as in each individual case (Keen, 1985).

A psychoanalytic formulation of brittle diabetes

From a psychoanalytic perspective there is less difficulty with the concept of self-destructiveness, inexplicable though it may seem to those who are unfamiliar with the nature of unconscious mental functioning. In our psychoanalytic assessment and treatment of a significant number of such patients, we were able to identify three patterns present in those who go on to develop brittle diabetes, and which may serve to explain their self-injurious behaviour pattern (see Fonagy and Moran, 1993, for a more detailed description). These were:

1. The regulation of the distance between the mental representation of self and the object (the mental representation of a significant other).
2. The unconscious use of diabetes for the manipulation by the child of an aspect of his or her reality situation which avoids a significant source of unpleasure.
3. The presence of irrational anxieties rooted in the unconscious personal significance of some aspect of the diabetic regime which creates the wish for avoidance and in this way leads to non-adherence.

We realise that, although presented as discrete, these categories are not independent of one another either conceptually or clinically, and we put them forward solely in terms of advice to help focus clinical intervention.

We will here restrict ourselves to the first and potentially most severely disturbed group of patients, in whom the brittle diabetic state serves what may be metaphorically referred to as a *distance-regulating function*. We maintain that the patient may be motivated by powerful feelings associated with the unconscious psychological experience of proximity (closeness or distance) vis-à-vis an internal object. Feelings of *well-being* and *safety* may be achieved through mentally distancing oneself from or achieving internal proximity to a particular internal representation of an important figure from the past. What we metaphorically refer to as 'proximity' may also be seen as the individual's readiness to undertake mental action, to think of, fantasise about or experience feelings in connection to the mental image of the other. The quality of such mental proximity may take the form of identification (to feel at one with – and this is most common), or it may involve conflict and sado-masochistic interchange (to fight, to rebel against, to be punished by some mental representation of another).

For example, one patient was chronically embattled with the medical establishment in a bitter conflict over blood glucose levels which both patient and consultant independently likened to the trench warfare of the First World War. In the course of treatment it transpired that these bloody struggles were comforting to the patient because they actualised her sense of self-criticism and self-hatred. Her mother was an ever nagging woman, quite unable to tolerate aggression in her daughter. She put her child to bed each evening with the caution that she should apologise to anyone she felt angry with in case they died during the night. Her behaviour ensured that the medical team would provide a close resemblance to the caring figure, struggling with powerfully repudiated rage, ending up as endlessly nagging.

In other patients, temporary lapses in control may have losing and recapturing as its theme (to feel abandoned in hyperglycaemia and be rescued by insulin). Indeed, probably any active mental representation of the self in *affect-laden transaction with the object* can be enacted in the 'theatre' of the diabetic body.

Many of the most seriously brittle diabetic patients appear unconsciously to experience the physical condition of chronic to metabolic imbalance as the psychic equivalent of achieving some kind of intrapsychic proximity to, or distance from, the internal mental representation of an important figure. The experiences which serve this unconscious psychological function are, however, highly variable, frequently over-determined and include symptoms such as the hyperventilation of ketoacidosis, the faintness of hypoglycaemia, the general experience of physical illness or hospitalisation, intense physical pain, infections such as boils or cystitis.

In understanding brittle diabetes in this group of patients, it is not the explication of particular symbolic links between physical state and mental representation that is of primary relevance. There is no magical cure even when such links are identified and accepted by the patient. Rather the analyst seeks to identify and interpret the source of the patient's feeling of internal danger from which the experience of diabetic imbalance, through the regulation of the closeness of the threat, affords temporary respite. The internal danger is invariably associated with the patients' representation of themselves with the object. What is feared and anticipated feels far more immediate than the remote possibility of complications or even death through diabetic mismanagement; the danger is the immediate destruction of the self in the creation of an aspect of the dreaded intolerable relationship with the object.

Through the medium of the poorly controlled diabetes, paradoxically, the diabetic individual achieves a reassurance that he or she (the self) is safe. The object may be experienced as invading the self or abandoning it. The wish to achieve separation or closeness will always be part of a profound conflict and therefore the self-destructive acts of diabetic mis-management will represent a compromise in both cases. Where the basic aim is the creation of a mental gap between dangerous objects and the self, some aspect of the physical symptoms of poor blood glucose regulation will serve to ensure closeness to the object. Alternatively, where proximity to the object is achieved mentally by chronic metabolic derangement, the patient will also seek to repudiate this closeness through the brittle diabetic state.

These patients frequently, but not invariably, fall into the category of severely disturbed, malignantly narcissistic individuals, something which has often been the subject of psychoanalytic interest. Of particular relevance is Joseph's (1982) paper describing patients who appear addicted to a mental state of being close to death. We strongly differ from this author in the general model of development we employ and diverge from her most explicitly in our speculations concerning the genesis of a mental self. Our approach utilises the developmental epistemological framework championed by Anna Freud (A. Freud, 1965) and attempts to integrate this with the perspective of modern developmental psychology and the model of psychological disturbance based upon the interrelationship of mental representations and affects (Sandler and Sandler, 1978).

The unconscious precipitant of the self-destructive behaviour patterns in patients such as these is to be found in dysfunctional self- and object-representations. The mental represntation of both self and object is incomplete as a consequence of a developmental disturbance in the establishment of the mental representation of psychological functioning. This is the result of the defensive inhibition of the capacity to conceive (create a mental representation) of the mental states of others. The inhibition of mental processes that underlie an enduring representation of the self in affective interaction with the object serves to protect against the painful awareness of violence, irrationality or vacuousness in the mind of the primary caretaker (Fonagy, 1991; Fonagy and Moran, 1991). Children with such backgrounds, in our experience, frequently defensively inhibit their capacity to think about the mental states of the other. This is most likely to occur between the ages of two and four when the child's ideas concerning the mental world undergo rapid development (Perner, Leekam and Wimmer, 1987; Harris, 1989), although there is no reason why such defensive inhibition should not take place at a later developmental stage.

Whilst in extreme cases this developmental disturbance can lead to a widespread reluctance to think about one's own, or others', mental worlds, in the cases we are concerned with here the patient's difficulties are much more limited and specific. Thus, the patients' relative incapacity to conceive of an object at a mental or psychological level causes them to seek identifications or create mental separations via bodily experiences. If the object is not represented as a thinking and feeling figure, imbued with intentionality, they may become psychically accessible only through physical experiences. This was the case for the patient described below, whose sole route to her dead mother was via the creation of a state of constant near-death within her own body.

Similarly, if the representation of the self as a thinking, feeling and experiencing figure cannot be created, an essential component of self-cohesion is absent and the child's self structure will be vulnerable to fragmentation. Thus, if the patient seeks a refuge from an overpowering internal figure, in the absence of the psychic capacity to integrate the unintegrated parts of the self into a cohesive internal picture, bodily experiences may be called upon to create an experience of psychic distance. This is evident in cases where the resource to diabetic mismanagement creates a poverty of internal object and self-representations through the dynamic inhibition of the psychic processes which underlie them.

We recognise that, in many respects, our model of the nature of this disturbance echoes the observations of McDougall (1974) and Marty and de M'Uzan (1963) of the Ecole Psychosomatique. Their concept of 'pensées operatoires' emphasises the same characteristic lack of expectable mental activity which we identify but account for differently.

The incomplete structuralisation of the self enables patients to disavow ownership of their body. This is of primary importance because the pain and discomfort they inflict upon themselves are probably only bearable as a result of the separation of their self-representation from their representation of their physical state. As their bodily states are, to a certain extent, represented outside of their self structure, the former is available as a stage upon which the nature and functioning of the mental world can be actualised or enacted. In such cases we observe a self that is not yet integrated into a bodily representation. The careless disregard of the body that characterises patients with chronic self-injurious behaviour may be rooted in a disturbed inter-subjective sense of self when the infant's identity extends beyond his or her as yet poorly organised bodily experience.

Emma: a case study

Emma at 17 was a slightly overweight adolescent, looking younger than her years. She was referred to us at the Anna Freud centre from another centre because her diabetes had been hopelessly out of control since she was first diagnosed diabetic at the age of 12. She openly admitted to manipulating her insulin to control her weight. She had been hospitalised eight times in the previous year with ketoacidosis. After her last admission her diabetologist, who is renowned for his anti-psychoanalytic sentiment, agreed to the psychoanalytic referral with the comment: 'We might as well let somebody else watch her kill herself'.

When Emma was assessed, her main concern was about her imminent failure in her Arts Foundation Course, for which she found herself unable to submit the necessary course work. She was living on her own in a tiny bedsit, spending her grant money on drugs, alcohol and vast quantities of 'bad' food. She smoked cannabis (and heroin), drank excessively and binged on crisps, chocolate, cheese and cakes. She would 'burn off' the carbohydrates by omitting insulin and abusing alcohol. The alcohol would also anaesthetise her as would the cannabis. She openly discussed her suicidal intent and readily agreed with the diagnostician when he suggested that part of her had lost all hope for herself.

Her family has been torn apart by psychiatric and physical illness. In her early years, she was cared for by her mother who had been diagnosed at various times as both schizophrenic and manic depressive. During her mother's psychotic episodes, and later during her physical illness, Emma was looked after by her three older siblings, the family's neighbours, or whoever happened to be around at the time. From her accounts it seems clear that despite being the youngest, her role in the family was a pivotal one. As the youngest child she was the person around whom the family rallied and whose survival justified the continued existence of the family unit. Soon after she turned ten the burden she had assumed as peacemaker in family arguments became even heavier when her brother and sisters and her mother began approaching her for advice. It was apparent in the way she described the interminable family conversations, sometimes reaching far into the night, that even as a relatively young girl she had a capacity to create in her mind a little space where she was able to deal with other people's confusions in a rational, even if not yet mature, way. She referred to this in a disparaging way as being 'a rubbish bin' for other people's troubles. Yet she also recalled feeling valued and appreciated.

Father's psychiatric disturbance was probably as severe as mother's. Emma recalls a very early memory of father screaming through the house, turning all the children out of their beds and making them stand outside in the garden so that the 'evil spirits' would not possess their souls. She also recalls violent battles between her parents, when they set about each other with ferocious intensity. She recalls mother giving as good as she got and stories of these battles became part of family legend. Father left the home when Emma was six, and his departure was both sudden and unexplained. He continued to live in the same provincial English town and kept up superficial contact with the children. He was, however, out of work and in and out of psychiatric hospitals, and offered the family little by way of physical or psychological support. Emma resented her father's desertion and felt that his inability to accept help was at the root of his problems. 'He was too proud to live with us in case we saw his weakness.'

Emma spoke warmly about her mother, as someone who was trying to do her best in very difficult circumstances. What united the family was their war of attrition with Social Services who repeatedly threatened to take the children into care, particularly at times when mother's illness became acute. There clearly was a very strong attachment between mother and the children. Emma recalls pretending to a social worker that her mother was out shopping when in fact her brother and sister were holding her down and trying to stop her from cutting her wrists with a razor blade. When mother was hospitalised, the children would go and visit her regularly, despite the fact that the hospital was more than an hour's journey out of town and each visit required a train journey and two buses.

Her mother became ill with a rapidly disseminating cancer when Emma was eight. She underwent a radical mastectomy and a further operation on her neck. Finally, in the last stages of the illness, Emma's mother took her own life. (Emma's siblings too have had severe psychiatric problems. The oldest brother, John, who was eight years older than Emma, was conduct-disordered and without friends at school. He found it difficult to find a job after leaving school, joined the army but was invalided out because of psychiatric illness. Her two sisters, two and four years older than her, fared little better. The oldest sister was married after becoming pregnant while still at school. The sister nearest to Emma in age was still living in the family home. Neither had success either educationally or interpersonally. The married sister is in the process of getting a divorce and Emma describes the younger one as being prone to rapid oscillations of mood like her mother.)

Emma emphatically did not want to come into treatment. Her reasons for this were both complex and telling. Having treatment was escaping, 'not facing the music'. She should be able to battle it out on her own. I said to her that I understood how hard it must be for her to contemplate receiving help when so many of her good feelings about herself were to do with being the one who could help John and her sisters and her mother. At this point she began to weep and told me that she had heard, at the Bulimics Anonymous group she had once attended, that I knew about diabetics. I said that perhaps she was concerned that I might *think* that I knew about her, whereas she knew that nobody could really know about the impossibility of her situation.

She went on to say that none of the people at the hospital understood what she was going through. 'They all think I am a naughty child, wanting to get attention, and when ignoring me doesn't work, they just don't know how to deal with me. But I really don't care about what they do, they are no use to me.' I said that perhaps she felt worried about the prospect of psychoanalysis because it might be a situation in which she would mind whether she was ignored or not. She said that she could not imagine that coming to see someone every day would do anything except make the person an addict, as food and cannabis did, 'except that food and cannabis are under my control whilst psychoanalysis is under yours'. I suggested that she might be far more worried about being out of control than she knew.

Furthermore, if she could force the doctors at the hospital to lose their tempers with her, she might also be able to force an analyst to lose control.

Many months into the analysis Emma told me how important this interview had been for her, in that she felt I was aware of her fear that she might drive me mad in treatment. Her concern for my sanity and her conviction that her open disclosure of her thoughts and feelings would lead me into confusion and perhaps madness remained the major theme of the analytic work.

In the first months of the analysis her anxieties about the potentially destructive nature of her thoughts and fantasies often caused her to be silent, sometimes to remain so for entire sessions. She would attend punctually, despite a long and complex journey, but then would just lie on the couch, make a few apparently superficial comments about the journey or about the room or even about the weather and then lapse into a state of self-imposed quarantine.

At no stage did one have the feeling, however, that she did not wish to communicate. I attended carefully to her body movements and from time to time commented on what I thought these said about her current mental state. For example, on one occasion, when she greeted me at the beginning of the session but then said nothing else, I noticed how she took out her bus pass and pressed it against her fingers until it was bent almost double under the pressure, then she released it, allowing it to snap back into its normal shape. She repeated the movement exactly five times. I said that perhaps she wanted me to know what an effort it felt to have to come and see me five times a week.

Realising that I must have been reacting to what she was doing with her bus pass, she tucked it away into her purse. The action was incomplete and the bus pass disappeared only half way, so that the part with her photograph on it was still sticking out, as if peering over the edge. I said that I understood that a frightened part was always on the look-out to make sure that nothing had been revealed inadvertently, but that there was another part of her that wanted me to understand her, and no matter how hard the frightened part might try to ensure that everything was carefully tucked away, this other communicative part of her would leave a nice clear trail for me to follow. She then said indignantly: 'What do you mean, communicative? I could no more communicate to you than I could talk to Medusa'. I said: 'You know, even Medusa could be confronted with the help of a mirror'. She turned away so that I would not be able to see her face but I could tell that she was smiling.

The moment that she decided that she wanted to talk was rather dramatic, and illustrates both the nature of her pathology and the clinical approach that we take in dealing with diabetic patients. I had been told, not by Emma but by the physician treating her, that she was about to undergo a funduscopy to check for diabetic retinopathy. Funduscopy involves instilling a mydriatic into the eye to dilate the pupil and causes a temporary blurring of vision. She came into the session directly after her investigation and uncharacteristically avoided looking at me and lay on the couch burying her head in the cushion. The silence lasted at least ten minutes. Eventually I noticed that her index finger was tracing small grooves almost imperceptibly in the texture of the couch. Fascinated, I thought the grooves she was tracing looked like rivers and their tributaries and also like the small blood vessels which are involved in diabetic retinopathy. It then struck me that Emma was tracing two rivers which sometimes seemed to be joined up by their tributaries but sometimes drifted sharply away from one another.

When I was reasonably confident of the pattern, I wondered aloud if she didn't suddenly feel that she might lose me even if she did not quite understand why she feared this. In response she buried her face even deeper in the cushion. I said that we both realised how terrified she was of losing her sight, but that perhaps what we had not up to now quite understood was that there was a part of her that felt that if she could not keep an eye on things, the analysis might break up and everything would become blurred. She remained silent but drove her fingernail deeper and deeper into the couch. Eventually she was violently criss-crossing over what had been the river pattern. I said that I knew that somewhere she felt deeply ashamed about what was happening to her body and was very angry with the analysis and with me for just standing by and watching it happen. She then broke her silence. She said, almost shouting:

> 'If you are so fucking clever, why don't you stop me from doing this before I go blind?' Reflecting on Emma's sense of helplessness and the helplessness she engendered in me, I remarked: 'I think you would like me to stop you from feeling the sadness and the rage which drive you to do this to yourself. I think you are frightened that if we come together to see the feelings that lead you to hurt yourself, it will become so unbearable that we will both be destroyed.' Emma was quite still for a moment and then said: 'I suppose it would not do if I asked what it is that you want to know?'

A limited form of therapeutic alliance evolved. Issues related to diabetes and its management were now often absent from the material for considerable periods. This turning point in Emma's analysis, and in that of numerous other diabetic patients whom we have treated, represents a spoken or unspoken realisation on the part of these patients that they are more frightened of their emotional experience and phantasies than of the immediate physical pain and the long-term consequences of their self-destructive mismanagement of their diabetes. However, Emma's preoccupation with diabetic mismanagement was to re-emerge recurrently to protect her vulnerable sense of self.

The central theme of Emma's analysis concerned the defensive fantasies which involved self-sufficient isolation. These were represented frequently, in both her free-association and dreams, as the image of a bubble or a vessel stranded in outer space. She elaborated such images mostly in tranquil terms. For example, she referred to watching lights flicker from her space capsule, imagining that each was a light from a person too far away to seem human. Sometimes anxiety would overwhelm such reflections. On one such occasion I commented on her fear that she would suffocate in her relationship with me if she abandoned her seclusion. Responding as if it was I who was terrified, she said: 'Don't worry, it's important to let things float a bit'.

Her self-esteem and grandiosity were noticeably enhanced when she inflicted pain and damage on herself through gross diabetic mis-management. She flaunted her ill-treatment of herself constantly and con-veyed her capacity calmly to damage or kill herself. She imagined me to be 'pleading' with her to take care of herself, like her relatives and the staff of the medical (endocrine) unit who had spared little effort to keep her alive. On one occasion she entered the consulting room and told me that she had just tested her blood sugar. It was so high, she boasted, that it no longer registered on the glucometer. She gave off the pungent odour of ketones, like nail-varnish remover. I replied that she seemed to feel so triumphant over pain and the fear of death that there was nothing I could offer that could compare. She said: 'When you are diabetic you have to have some-thing to feel good about.'

During the first year of the analysis there was little symptomatic improve-ment. The physicians in charge of Emma's case were alternately empathic with my struggle and derogatory about her treatment. The reality was that Emma's blood sugars remained, from a medical point of view, unacceptably high. However, in the transference a subtle but definite shift became noticeable. Over the year there was a gradual decline of positive trans-ference which gave way to more and more overt expression of aggression, provocativeness and a correspondingly intense anxiety about my well-being.

For example, one day when it was possible to smell her ketotic state several metres away from the waiting room and I could discern from her slurred speech and general vagueness that she was profoundly unwell, her conscious thoughts seemed to be taken up with my state of health. Her fantasy was that I was suffering continuously from a cold because I worked too hard. She was confident that work was my way of avoiding depression. When I put it to her that I thought she was telling me how hard she felt she had to work to protect us from *her* sadness, she responded facetiously: 'Well, one does what one can.'

In the analysis she created a shallow, half-hearted concern for her repre-sentation of others and for me in the transference. I was aware of being kept at a distance from something she felt was highly dangerous. I was also aware of the tendency to let myself drift into a state of near-complete inattentiveness. I understood this counter-transference to derive from my reluctance to allow myself to experience her terror in the face of relating to her mentally ill parents in the past. Likewise, in the transference she reacted to me with tentativeness for fear that I was unstable and could respond at any moment with mad rage.

The analysis itself at this stage came to represent that part of Emma's mind which she endeavoured to keep safe and tranquil and isolated from the incursions of the feelings and thoughts of others which constantly threatened to confuse and overwhelm her. Emma expressed this unconscious representation of her psychological state in imagery that contrasted the safe enclave of the analysis with something dangerous and ugly outside. For example, she fantasised that my garden was the only ordered, well-kept one in the area, in the middle of a veritable jungle of weeds and overgrown grass of the neighbourhood gardens. When I pointed out how frightening it must feel to be surrounded by the menace of such chaos, she shrugged: 'Well, that's your problem, isn't it?'

Her careful monitoring of my well-being was a key feature of this transference and served to pre-empt the overwhelming guilt and terror associated with her perception of my madness. These aspects were particularly vividly illustrated by the following episode. About two years into Emma's analysis I was involved in a small bicycle accident that led to quite significant bruising on my forehead as well as a sizeable cut above my right eye which required stitches. The total effect which included an extremely bloodshot eye, was as unattractive as it was dramatic. Equally striking was Emma's capacity to scotomise my injury. When I collected Emma from the waiting room she did not even glance at me. She went through the session mostly in silence. The only way of knowing that something was amiss was that the atmosphere of the session had a dreaminess about it in which it was almost impossible to sustain any kind of alertness or concentration. This gave a sense of Emma's state of mind as it tried to grapple with her fantasies about the injury through striving for a state of dissociation. At the end of the session she walked out of the room without looking at me, and again seemed to take no notice of my face at the beginning of next day's hour.

In this session, unusually, Emma reported a dream in which a number of horses had broken out of their stables. They were blind and threatened to trample all over her. She woke up just before the horses were upon her. The dream seemed to be vaguely connected to Peter Shaeffer's play, *Equus*. In her associations it was difficult to tell when she was recounting the dream and when she was giving a highly distorted account of the play. In Emma's version of the play the boy, who was in a hospital for the violently insane, developed an hysterical blindness after he had flown into a rage and blinded a horse. The focus of her account, however, was the insanity of the psychiatrist treating the boy, who was, according to her, the villain of the piece.

I said I thought that Emma was terrified in case somehow her anger might break out of the stables she created for it and make everyone in our 'analytic hospital' violent and mad. She responded that the night before she had been so anxious about not being able to see that she could not take her insulin. She found that the pain of hyperglycaemia distracted her. Nevertheless she still had to smoke herself to sleep. She went on to wonder why people talked of 'blind rage'. I said that it was so painful for her to see the manifestations of violence that being blind was almost preferable. And yesterday when she had noticed my facial injury she had suddenly felt that she was in terrible danger because she was evidently unable to keep the violence out of the room.

She now became extremely anxious and asked repeatedly what injury I was talking about. I replied that I understood how frightening it was for her to feel that there had been violence, because it made her feel both as if she might inadvertently have caused it and as if it were happening to her. She shouted that I was talking nonsense, like the psychiatrist in the play. How could I expect her to be able to see things if I could not make my meanings clear to her? I said that these thoughts were particularly frightening because if she found that I was mad I might terrify her and drive her insane.

She was silent for a while. Then slowly and very deliberately she said: 'I must have seen your eyes yesterday because I have not been able to get a picture out of my mind since then. The first time I remember visiting my mother in hospital, I could not recognise her because one of the other patients had hit her and given her a black eye.' She recalled feeling terrified of her mother and responsible for her injury. The image of the mother who was the vehicle of Emma's own aggressive wishes had to be repudiated and avoided. The anxiety-driven fusion with the mother constituted an overwhelming threat to the fragile, sane part of her self-representation that she, and all those around her, clearly valued. Emma's insane acts of self-destruction paradoxically helped her to deny her neediness in relation to her mother. Although she enacted destructive wishes on her body she did not perceive these acts to be perpetrated on herself. Rather she experienced these acts as safe and inconsequential because the body upon which they were enacted was not encompassed in her sense of self.

The experience of the self as 'bodiless' we consider to be a reactivation of a primitive stage in the evolution of the self characterised by rudimentary proprioception. This 'regression' saved her from having to own her overwhelming aggression and, just as did turning away from the Medusa and scotomising my face, it served to ward off the experience of identification and mental closeness with her mad mother.

The key to understanding Emma's self-destructive behaviour was her conflict between a fear of living and the fear of dying. It was only when conflicts surrounding the emotional investment in the object representation of her mother become the focus of the analysis that her fear of loss of love and its relation to her self-injury could be clarified. In her material, as in her actions, closeness to death (in ketoacidosis) represented the only possible way of achieving closeness to her mother. Increasingly, she feared that the ghost of her mother was in the consulting room. To illustrate this I will now describe a Monday session which turned out to be the second turning point in Emma's treatment.

She began the session by reporting a dream about a bomb-threat, described the intense fear she felt and the conflict over whether to stay in the building. In her associations she told me that she felt terrific physically, now that she had stopped eating animal products, and that when she was ketoacidotic she felt vital and somehow real. She said she had loads of life left in her. I replied: 'You seem to feel alive and real when you are on the edge of a disaster and your life is actually in danger.' I added that it was at such times that she seemed to feel most worried about herself. She said: 'How did you know that I did not take my insulin last night?'

She said angrily that she felt that there was this evil inside her, that perhaps it could only be exorcised by some 'physical means', not by talking alone. She then had an image of injecting insulin into an empty shell. This was followed by a long lecture on the way that confidence can affect your appearance. She was particularly struck by French women who, by wearing appropriate clothes, were able to make themselves almost beautiful. She wondered vaguely if there was such a thing as real beauty? I responded: 'You seem frightened that I might recognise something good in you, that I might be taken in and find you appealing as a person.'

Her voice dropped an octave. 'You despise me don't you? You must do.' She then went on the attack. When she cut her leg the other day she was terrified because she had not felt a thing. Dr Y. had looked into her eye at the clinic and shaken his head. He too must be wondering what the analysis was achieving. For two years she had been coming, and if anything, things were worse now than they had ever been. She couldn't afford another year of not getting better. I said: 'You are frightened that you are too ill ever to feel loved'.

She paused and then spoke of her Bible reading in the evenings. The previous night she had read the passage on the judgment of Solomon in which King Solomon was confronted by two women who both claimed to be the mother of the same baby. She emphasised with horror that the wrong mother had the live baby and the innocent mother had the dead baby, again emphasising that it was the wrong one. Despite reading the passage again and again, Emma could not see why, if Solomon was wise, he had said that they should cut the baby in half and divide it between the mothers. I remarked: 'You feel that "something is wrong", that the part of you which can be cared about is dead and you are terrified in case you may stop me from being able to see the difference between what is alive and what is dead and then you will be in the care of an analyst who is not capable of keeping his patients alive'. I held back the more important interpretation, that she could not understand why splitting the baby in two would be of concern, as in her phantasy, the unity of her body did not contain her mental existence and thus made no sense to her as the focus of the object's concern.

She became anxious and said that today she had thought of her mother for the first time in a long while. She had looked into the mirror and had felt for a moment that she was going crazy because she had seen her mother. She then went on to tell me how her mother had been so sad that she went to see a psychiatrist shortly before she died, but by then it was too late; how nobody had told her that she had cancer. She ended by saying: 'The poor woman, you know she stole from a shop and the local papers were going to report it. It must have been terribly humiliating for her.' I said: 'I think it is very important for you to try to hide, from me and from yourself, how ashamed and humiliated you feel because it seems as if nobody could want to look after your body, and it feels as if you've stolen whatever affection you get.'

In response Emma showed genuine emotion almost for the first time in the analysis. She said: 'I just can't listen to my body, I want to ignore it. My mind gets in the way, I can't bear to hear what it is saying to me. It's just no use for anything, it's worthless.' I said: 'I think you feel terrified by how much you need me to listen to you and talk to you. You would prefer to kill that part of yourself that wants to be liked and loved.'

She said that it hurt terribly when her senses were awake, particularly her sense of smell which she could experience when she was not acidotic. Understanding in analysis was like taking insulin. Getting nearer to being better made her feel how hopeless everything was. I responded: 'If you come back to life you feel my reason for caring for you will be gone. If you are near death I think you also feel you are near to me and somehow close to your mother.'

Towards the end of this session she revealed an important memory about her mother's double incontinence before her death and the shame and humiliation she had felt on her mother's behalf. She also remembered hating to go into the room to see her because of the smell. At the very end of the session she said: 'I suppose now I make myself smell because I am frightened you don't want to see me.'

This material enabled us to understand better Emma's extreme mismanagement of diabetes. Continuing to live by adhering to her medical regime induced anxiety and terror because of its contrast with her images of her deceased mother. Soon after the session just recounted, she vividly recalled making a forbidden entrance into the room where her mother's corpse was laid out and, after a moment's frozen observation, running from the room. She then ran to a nearby pond, saying to herself that her mother was not dead. She recalled that she went on to busy herself in catching frogs and what has recently emerged is that she was killing them.

The need to keep the object close through provocation and aggression recreated in the transference the guilt and helplessness which Emma must have felt about her intermittently crazy and dying mother. She needed to know if I was able to remain close to her despite her rageful attacks upon herself and upon me. In her attacks on her own body Emma was in part unconsciously identified with her suicidal mother. In her symptoms, she was the destroyer of her remote and mentally inaccessible mother's body, as well as the victim of its destruction.

Emma felt that she could be safe only as long as she made sure that she kept a small part of her mind clear, separate from her dangerous and chaotic feelings and ideas. In her unconscious theory of mind her active self-representation was separate, psychically distant, from the source of danger. This mode of mental functioning has a distinct pathology in which substantial aspects of her self experience were fragmented and made inaccessible for the purpose of self-representation. Elsewhere we have argued that this represents a distinct developmental disturbance originating in the second year of life, wherein the child's capacity to integrate aspects of its self-organisation are defensively inhibited to avoid psychological assault from the parent (Fonagy and Moran, 1991).

In the case of Emma, her interactions with her chaotic and crazy parents resulted in heavily invested but confusing identifications and internalisations which she could not easily integrate. Consequently she disavowed these aspects of self-structure and presented herself to herself as vulnerable but free of confusion. Because of the fragmented nature of her self-representations, she could only interact with the object in superficial and inconsequential ways. The repudiated aspects of herself which derived from identification with mad family members expressed themselves in her crazy ill-treatment of her body and in fantasies of her destructive influence on others, particularly the analyst in the transference.

Her body offered a favoured locus for such an expression because it appeared to be possible for her to exclude it from her self-representation. Her partial representation of herself implied that, experientially at least, what was happening to her body was happening to that disavowed part of herself in which was located her experience of confusion and senseless ill-treatment, which only gained mental representation outside the subjective domain of her mind. It gradually emerged that her resistance against analysis contained within it her terror that in letting down the barriers to her haven she would be confronted by the mad and unpredictable reactions of her objects. Notwithstanding her symptomatic misuse of her body, Emma's irresolvable problem was that her internalisations of her objects were inseparably interwoven with mental representations that constituted her sense of her own mental existence.

The intensity of the psychoanalytic encounter gave Emma the opportunity to extend her self-representation on the basis of differentiated perceptions of the chaotic responses of her objects. The process was a long and painstaking one. Its critical component was that Emma gradually became able to reintegrate within her self-representation the dangerous images from which she sought refuge in the pain of ketoacidosis. To give up the relative safety of her encapsulated identity, separated from the chaos that surrounded it, meant experiencing in the transference a terrifying sense of fusion with me as a psychotic object. This occurred repeatedly and sessions such as the one in which the 'Equus' dream emerged were particularly dramatic examples of a long-term process which, in our view, was critical in bringing about her limited improvement.

Discussion

The therapeutic action in brittle diabetic patients such as Emma is generated by *the reactivation of inhibited mental functions*. Although interpretations remain crucial in this context, their function is no longer limited to the lifting of repression and altering the nature of specific mental representations. Besides their capacity to present alternative views of mental events, the act of making interpretations requires the analyst to become actively involved in the mental functioning of the patient and create the possibility for the patient to become reciprocally involved with the working of the analyst's mind. Thus, they entail the active involvement of one individual in the representational world and mental functioning of another. The experience of mental involvement with another human being without the threat of overwhelming mental anguish was what ultimately led to the freeing up of the inhibition of Emma's mental functioning, and liberated her from using her body as an auxiliary to her mental representational system.

In general, in addressing disturbances deriving from the inhibition of mental processes, the patient's active mental involvement is elicited by the analyst's attention to the elaboration of the preconscious mental content of the patient. This mental involvement, combined with interpretations of the anxieties which led the patient to curtail certain mental processes, gradually brings about the reactivation of inhibited mental processes. As this occurs, slowly, the patient may become open to a gradual restructuring of distorted mental representations through further therapeutic work (see Fonagy et al., 1993).

In the case of Emma we saw how the analyst's interpretations set the patient's mind 'a challenge' to look at the working of her own mind and, in the transference, to explore her analyst's mental state. The successful engagement of the patient in trying to work out how the analyst arrives at stable constructions of the patient's subjective mental experience provides the route by which the patient's own mental processes became disinhibited. Over a prolonged time period, diverse interpretations concerning the patient's perception of the analytic relationship forced her to attempt to create a mental representation, both of herself and her analyst, as thinking and feeling. This enabled her to integrate the analyst's understanding into her own mental world. In so doing the analyst caused Emma to exercise her mental capacity for conceiving of human action in terms of beliefs and desires, to represent ideas as ideas rather than as concrete aspects of her bodily world.

This, then, in greatly simplified terms, is the technique most relevant to severely disturbed diabetic patients. Compared to changes of mental functioning which do not involve the body, the rate and extent of psychic change may often be small. Progress can be immeasurably slow. The analyst may flatter her- or himself into believing that particular episodes of insight and understanding into the problem of diabetic management were helpful in their own right only to have his or her hope cruelly dashed by the re-emergence of the same difficulty in other psychological contexts. This refractory aspect of process disturbance can lead therapists to despair about their work.

Pines (1978) described evocatively how, in patients with borderline mental structure, therapists find themselves being dragged 'unwillingly but inevitably as if by a great force into the pattern imposed by the patient so that we begin to feel provoked, hostile, persecuted and to behave exactly as the patients needs us to, becoming rejecting and hostile' (p. 115). Such confrontations may be the consequence of the therapist's failure to acknowledge the extent of the patient's impaired psychic functioning. Interpretations based on the patient's presumed mental state or other mature contributions of the analyst's intact mental function are neither real nor meaningful for these patients. Rather the primitive impulses, hostilities, persecutions and mockeries that they engender in their object feel to them genuine and real. And when interpretive attention is focused on these aspects, their experience of the therapeutic process is validated.

The patient's treatment of the therapist, his or her response to interpretations, gives clear indication of the patient's struggle with a limited mental apparatus. Our role with the patient should not be, from the patient's standpoint at least, as an interpreter of the patient's mental world or even provider of a 'containing or holding environment'. Rather, in order to enter the patient's mental world, the therapist must permit him- or herself to be a vehicle to be transformed magically and immediately by the patients' fantasies into a good or bad, protective or persecutory aspect of their internal world. If therapists are able to submit themselves to this process and tolerate the distortions to their conceptions of themselves induced by the patient's primitive projections, then they are in a position to make use of this valuable source of information about the patient's internal world and feed it back to the patient through interpretations (Sandler, 1976). If their own self-representation is insufficiently well established, or they are temperamentally unsuited to the task for some other reason, they are in danger of becoming the persecutory object for their patient and may, for example, find themselves in interminable arguments about the accuracy of the patients' judgement of them. It is a simple fact that not every clinician can work with borderline patients.

Brittle diabetic patients are able to exert total control over the therapist's mind and use it as a vehicle for their projections in order to deny the reality of the separateness of the self and the object and thus the possibility of loss. True progress may only be made when the tyranny or subjugation of the analyst's independent mental functioning is abandoned by the patient. This may be achieved by the facilitation of the process of mourning (of the loss of this control as well as the loss of the object; see Steiner, 1992) or through more confrontational tactics (see Kernberg et al., 1989). Yet both of these outstanding experts report that a critical step in the establishment of the borderline patient's sense of identity rests in the clarification of the patient's perception of the analyst's mental state.

In *The Phenomenology of the Spirit*, Hegel (1807) wrote: 'Self-consciousness exists in and for itself when, and by the fact that, it so exists for another; that is, it exists only in being acknowledged' (p. 111). In other words, in Hegel's view, the origin of self-consciousness is rooted in being known by the other and in the knowing of the other. He goes on: 'This has a twofold significance: first, it (the self) has lost itself, for it finds itself as an *other* being; secondly, in doing so it has superseded the other, for it does not see the other as an essential being, but in the other sees its own self' (p. 111). This is Hegel's rather elegant formulation of projective identification. He continues: 'First it must proceed to supersede the *other* independent being in order thereby to become certain of *itself* as the essential being; secondly in so doing it proceeds to supersede its *own* self for this other' (p. 111). This final sentence could be interpreted as elaborating the concept of the depressive position, but from an intersubjective view of the self.

This passage of Hegel's, subtitled 'Lordship and Bondage', has been interpreted as showing that man splits himself into a subject – recognising himself in another – and an object – viewed through the eyes of another. The interdependency of self-consciousness and the constructive apperception of another self is absolute (see Wilden, 1968; Butler, 1976; Kirshner, 1990).

Interpretations, particularly interpretations of the transference and counter-transference, are necessary and containing because they invite the patient to conceive of the analyst's mind even if for the moment this has to stop short of self-reflection. Interpretations of the transference–counter-transference matrix are developmentally located in the phase of inter-subjectivity when reliance on the object's capacity to reflect the infant's mental state is dominant. When the patient's psychic state is developmentally more advanced, invitation for self observation, which presupposes the mental independence of the self, becomes possible.

The failure in the capacity to recognise and attribute states of mind to self and other precludes the adequate mental separation between self and object, brings the object intolerably close to the self and forces the individual defensively to displace mental contents onto the physical self. In extreme cases, as possibly exemplified by borderline personality disorder, the patient lives in a universe populated by emotionless, inanimate objects (Bion, 1962). In less extreme cases, as exemplified by Emma, the capacity to attribute psychological qualities seems inadequate and prone to distortion.

In general, most Kleinian authors assume the patient's sense of having been understood and contained derives from the analyst's capacity to 'contain those elements he has projected into him and as a result the projected elements become more bearable' (Steiner, 1992). From a developmental standpoint we may say that the patient feels relief through his regression into a state of inter-subjectivity with the analyst, using the latter's capacity to think, feel and experience.

In the best of situations, in understanding the analyst's comments, the patient's mental work recapitulates that of the analyst, albeit within the limitations set by the patient's level of development. The reactivation of mental processes consequent on the analyst's endeavour to focus on and elaborate the mental life of the patient is seen in this context as the primary mechanism of therapeutic action, which then permits the techniques based on conflict and defence to become more effective. Hence, we view frequent and accurate interpretations of the presumed contents of the patient's mind as an essential component of successful treatment.

Psychotherapeutic endeavour in general, and psychoanalytic treatment in particular, thus brings about a general facilitation of mental functioning. Perhaps this is why all attempts at focusing on the working of the mental life of an individual have clear therapeutic effects. There is something unique about the therapeutic process that takes place between two individuals, where one person takes an interest in the mental life of another, which goes beyond the attempt to extend the limits of awareness. In a context-free way the patient's thinking is facilitated and he can conceive of his world in new, sometimes sadder and sometimes happier ways.

References

BARGLOW, P., BERNDT, D.J., BURNS, W.J. and HATCHER, R. (1986). Neuroendocrine and psychological factors in childhood diabetes mellitus. *Journal of the American Academy of Child Psychiatry* **25**, 785–793.
BENNETT JOHNSON, S. (1990). Adherence behaviors and health status in childhood

diabetes. In: C. Holmes (Ed.), *Neuropsychological and Behavioral Aspects of Insulin and Noninsulin Dependent Diabetes*, pp. 42–56. New York: Springer-Verlag.

BENNETT JOHNSON, S. (1989). Juvenile diabetes. In: T.H. Ollendeck and M. Hersen (Eds), *Handbook of Child Psychopathology*, 2nd edn, pp. 112–132. New York: Plenum.

BINGLEY, P.J. and GALE, E.A.M. (1989). Incidence of insulin-dependent diabetes in England: a study in the Oxford region, 1985–86. *British Medical Journal* **298**, 558–560.

BINGLEY, P.J. and GALE, E.A.M. (1990). The epidemiology of childhood onset diabetes: a review. *Practical Diabetes* **7**, 7–11.

BION, W.R. (1962). Learning from experience. In: *Seven Servants: Four Works by Wilfred R. Bion*. New York: Jason Aronson, 1977.

BLOM, L., DAHLQUIST, G., SANDSTROM, A. and WALL, S. (1989). The Swedish childhood diabetes study – social and perinatal determinants for diabetes in childhood. *Diabetologia* **32**, 7–13.

BRADLEY, C. (1979). Life events and the control of diabetes mellitus. *Journal of Psychosomatic Research* **23**, 159–162.

BRINK, S.J. and STEWART, C. (1986). Insulin pump treatment in insulin-dependent diabetes mellitus: children, adolescents and young adults. *Journal of the American Medical Association* **255**, 617–621.

BUTLER, C. (1976). Hegel and Freud: a comparison. *Philos. Phenomenol. Res.* **36**, 506–522.

CAHILL, G.F. and McDEVITT, H.O. (1981). Insulin dependent diabetes: the initial lesion. *New England Journal of Medicine* **304**, 1454–1465.

CHASE, J.P. and JACKSON, G.G. (1981). Stress and sugar control in children with insulin-dependent diabetes mellitus. *Journal of Pediatrics* **98**, 1011–1013.

CROW, Y.J., ALBERTI, K.G.M.M. and PARKIN, J.M. (1991). Insulin dependent diabetes in childhood and material deprivation in northern England, 1977–86. *British Medical Journal* **303**, 158–160.

DANDONA, P., FOSTER, M., HEALEY, F., GREENBURG, E. and BECKETT, A.G. (1978). Low dose insulin infusions in diabetic patients with high insulin requirements. *The Lancet* **ii**, 283–285.

FARBEROW, N.L., DARBONNE, A.R., STEIN, K. and HIRSCH, S. (1970). Self-destructive behaviour of unco-operative diabetics. *Psychological Reports* **27**, 935–946.

FONAGY, P. (1991). Thinking about thinking: Some clinical and theoretical considerations in the treatment of a borderline patient. *International Journal of Psycho-Analysis* **72**, 639–656.

FONAGY, P. and MORAN, G.S. (1991). Understanding psychic change in child psychoanalysis. *International Journal of Psycho-Analysis* **72**, 15–22.

FONAGY, P. and MORAN, G.S. (1993). A psychoanalytical approach to the treatment of brittle diabetes in children and adolescents. In: M. Hodes and S. Moorey (Eds), *Psychological Treatments in Disease and Illness*, pp. 166–192. London: Gaskell Press.

FONAGY, P., MORAN, G. and HIGGITT, A. (1989). Psychological factors in the self-management of insulin-dependent diabetes mellitus in children and adolescents. In: J. Wardle and S. Pearce (Eds), *The Practice of Behavioral Medicine*. Oxford: Oxford University Press.

FONAGY, P., MORAN, G.S., LINDSAY, M.K.M., KURTZ, A.B. and BROWN, R. (1987). Psychological adjustment and diabetic control. *Archives of Disease in Childhood* **62**, 1009–1013.

FONAGY, P., MORAN, G.S., EDGCUMBE, R., KENNEDY, H. and TARGET, M. (1993). The roles of mental representation and mental processes in therapeutic action. *Psychoanalytic Study of the Child* **48**, 9-47.

FREUD, A. (1965). *Normality and Pathology in Childhood*, Harmondsworth: Penguin Books.

GILBERT, B.O., JOHNSON, S.B., SILVERSTEIN, J. and MALONE, J. (1989). Psychological and physiological responses to acute laboratory stressors in insulin-dependent diabetes mellitus adolescents and nondiabetic controls. *Journal of Pediatric Psychology* **14**, 577-591.

GILL, G.V., WALFORD, S. and ALBERTI, K.G.M.M. (1985). Brittle diabetes – present concepts. *Diabetologia* **28**, 579-589.

GILL, G.V., HUSBAND, D.J., WALFORD, S., MARSHALL, S.M., HOME, P.D. and ALBERTI, K.G. (1985). Clinical features of brittle diabetes. In: J.C. Pickup (Ed.), *Brittle Diabetes*. Oxford: Blackwell.

GOLDSTEIN, D.E. and HOEPER, M. (1987). Management of diabetes during adolescence: mission impossible? *Clinical Diabetes* **5**, 1-10.

GRIFFITH, D.N.W. and YUDKIN, J. (1989). Brittle diabetes in the elderly. *Diabetic Medicine* **6**, 440-443.

GROEN, J.J. and PELZER, H.E. (1982). Newer concepts of teaching, learning and education and their application to the patient-donor cooperation in the treatment of diabetes mellitus. *Pediatric Adolescent Endocrinology* **10**, 168-177.

HANSON, C., HENGGELER, S. and BURGHEN, G. (1987). Social competence and parental support as mediators of the link between stress and metabolic control in adolescents with insulin-dependent diabetes mellitus. *Journal of Consulting and Clinical Psychology* **55**, 529-533.

HARDY, K.J., JONES, K.E. and GILL, G.V. (1991). Deterioration in blood glucose control in females with diabetes changed to a basal-bolus regimen using a basal-bolus regimen using a pen injector. *Diabetic Medicine* **8**, 69-71.

HARRIS, P.L. (1989). *Children and Emotion: The Development of Psychological Understanding*. Oxford: Basil Blackwell.

HEGEL, G. (1807). *The Phenomenology of Spirit*, trans. A.V. Miller. Oxford: Oxford University Press, 1977.

HELZ, J.W. and TEMPLETON, B. (1990). Evidence of the role of psychosocial factors in diabetes mellitus: a review. *American Journal of Psychiatry* **147**, 1275-1298.

HOME, P.D., MASSI-BENEDETTI, M., GILL, G.V., CAPALDO, B., SHEPHERD, G.A.A. and ALBERTI, K.G.M.M. (1982). Impaired subcutaneous absorption of insulin in 'brittle diabetes'. *Acta Endocrinologica* **101**, 414-420.

JACOBSON, A., RAND, L. and HAUSER, S. (1985). Psychologic stress and glycemic control: A comparison of patients with and without proliferative diabetic retinopathy. *Psychosomatic Medicine* **47**, 372-381.

JOSEPH, B. (1982). Addiction to near-death. *International Journal of Psycho-Analysis* **63**, 449-456.

KAAR, M.L., AKERBLOM, H.K., HUTTUNEN, N.P., KNIP. M and SAKKINEN, K. (1984). Metabolic control in children and adolescents with insulin-dependent diabetes mellitus. *Acta Paediatrica Scandinavica* **73**, 102-108.

KAPLAN, R.M., CHADWICK, M.W. and SCHIMMEL, L.E. (1985). Social learning intervention to promote metabolic control in type 1 diabetes mellitus: Pilot experiment results. *Diabetes Care* **8**, 152-155.

KEEN, H. (1985). Of mind and metabolism: An overview of brittle diabetes. In J.C. Pickup (Ed.), *Brittle Diabetes*. Oxford: Blackwell.

KEMMER, F.W., BISPING, R., STEINGRUBER, H.J. et al. (1986). Psychological stress and metabolic control in patients with type I diabetes mellitus. *New England Journal of Medicine* **314**, 1078-1084.

KERNBERG, O., SELZER, M., KOENIGSBERG, H.W., CARR, A. and APPELBAUM, A. (1989). *Psychodynamic Psychotherapy of Borderline Patients.* New York: Basic Books.

KIRSHNER, L.A. (1990). The concept of the self in psychoanalytic theory and its philosophical foundations. *Journal of the American Psychoanalytic Association* **38**, 157-182.

LESLIE, R.D.G. and PYKE, D.A. (1991). Escaping insulin dependent diabetes. *British Medical Journal* **302**, 1103-1104.

McDOUGALL, J. (1974). The psyche-soma and the psychoanalytic process. *International Review of Psycho-Analysis* **1**, 437-460.

MADSBAD, S., ALBERTI, K.G.M.M., SINDER, C., BURRIN, J.M., FABER, O.K., KRARUP, T. and REGEUR, L. (1979). Role of residual insulin secretion in protecting against keto-acidosis in insulin-dependent diabetes. *British Medical Journal* **2**, 1257-1259.

MARTY, P. and DE M'UZAN, M. (1963). La 'pensée operatoire'. *Revue Française de Psychanalyse* **27**, 1345-1536.

MORAN, G.S. (1987). De L'interaction entre troubles psychologiques et diabète infantile. *Psychiatrie de l'enfant* **30**, 35-58.

MORAN, G., FONAGY, P., KURTZ, A., BOLTON, A. and BROOK, C. (1991). A controlled study of the psychoanalytic treatment of brittle diabetes. *American Academy of Child and Adolescent Psychiatry* **30**, 926-935.

PERNER, J., LEEKAM, S.R. and WIMMER, H. (1987). Three-year-olds' difficulty with false belief: The case for a conceptual deficit. *British Journal of Developmental Psychology* **5**, 125-137.

PERNET, A., WALKER, M., GILL, G.V., ORSKOV, H., ALBERTI, K.G.M.M. and JOHNSON, D.G. (1984). Metabolic effects of adrenaline and noradrenaline in man: studies with somato-statin. *Diabete et Metabolisme* **10**, 98-105.

PICKUP, J.C. (1985b). Clinical features of patients unresponsive to continuous sub-cutaneous insulin infusion. In: J.C. Pickup (Ed.), *Brittle Diabetes.* Oxford: Blackwell.

PINES, M. (1978). Group analytic psychotherapy of the borderline patient. *Group Analysis* **11**, 115-126.

ROBINSON, N. and FULLER, J.H. (1985). Role of life events and difficulties in the onset of diabetes mellitus. *Journal of Psychosomatic Research* **29**, 583-591.

SANDLER, J. (1976). Countertransference and role-responsiveness. *International Review of Psycho-Analysis* **3**, 43-47.

SANDLER, J. AND SANDLER, A-M. (1978). On the development of object relationships and affects. *International Journal of Psycho-Analysis* **59**, 285-296.

SCHADE, D.S., DRUMM, D.A., DUCKWORTH, W.C. and EATON, R.P. (1985). The aetiology of incapacitating, brittle diabetes. *Diabetes Care* **8**, 12-20.

SIEMIATYCKI, J., COLLE, E., CAMPBELL, S., DEWAR, R. and BELMONTE, M. (1989). Case-control study of IDDM. *Diabetes Care* **12**, 209-215.

STANCIN, T., LINK, D.L. and REUTER, J.M. (1989). Binge eating and purging in young women with IDDM. *Diabetes Care* **12**, 601-603.

STEINER, J. (1992). Patient-centred and analyst-centred interpretations: Some implications of 'Containment' and 'Counter-transference'. Paper given at Conference on *The Psychoanalytic Approach to Borderline States.* London: University College London.

STILLER, C.R., DUPRE, J., GENT, M., KEOWN, J.P.A., LAUPACIS, A., MARTELL, R. et al.

(1984). Effects of cyclosporin immunosuppression in insulin dependent diabetes mellitus of recent onset. *Science* **223**, 1362-1367.

TATTERSALL, R.B. and WALFORD, S. (1985). Brittle diabetes in response to life stress: 'Cheating and manipulation'. In: J.C. Pickup (Ed.), *Brittle Diabetes*. Oxford: Blackwell.

TATTERSALL, R.B., GREGORY, R., SELBY, C., KERR, D. and HELLER, S. (1991). Course of brittle diabetes: 12 year follow-up. *British Medical Journal* **302**, 1240-1243.

WHITE, N.H. and SANTIAGO, J.V. (1985a). Clinical features and natural history of brittle diabetes in children. In J.C. Pickup (Ed.), *Brittle Diabetes*. Oxford: Blackwell.

WILDEN, A. (1968). Lacan the discourse of the other. In: *Speech and Language in Psychoanalysis*, pp. 159-311. Baltimore: Johns Hopkins University Press.

WILLIAMS, G. (1985). Blood flow at insulin injection sites. In: J.C. Pickup (Ed.), *Brittle Diabetes*. Oxford: Blackwell.

WILLIAMS, G. and PICKUP, J.C. (1985a). Continuous intravenous insulin infusion in patients unresponsive to subcutaneous insulin. In: J.C. Pickup (Ed.), *Brittle Diabetes*. Oxford: Blackwell.

WILLIAMS, G. and PICKUP, J.C. (1985b). Subcutaneous insulin degradation. In: J.C. Pickup (Ed.), *Brittle Diabetes*. Oxford: Blackwell.

WILLIAMS, G. and PICKUP, J.C. (1988). The natural history of brittle diabetes. *Diabetes Ressearch* **7**, 13-18.

WILSON, D.P. and ENDES, R.K. (1986). Compliance with blood glucose monitoring in children with type 1 diabetes mellitus. *Journal of Pediatrics* **108**, 1022-1024.

Chapter 4
Life-threatening illness as psychic trauma:
psychotherapy with adolescent patients

Dorothy Judd

> . . . the entire defence organisation of the ego is endowed with the characteristics of a protective shield and drawn into the orbit of potential traumatic onslaught. Any event for which an individual's defence measures are not sufficiently competent becomes a potentially traumatic one.   A. Freud (1967, p. 236)

> The price we pay for efficient perception is partial blindess.
> G.S. Klein (1970, p. 218)

> Emotion is essentially psychosomatic.   J. McDougall (1989, p. 95)

> I have a pain in my imagination.
> 14-year-old girl in therapy, referring to her nightmares

(Cancer constitutes the second greatest cause of death in children, after accidents. Most of the clinical examples in this chapter are based upon psychotherapeutic approaches to cancer patients, with particular emphasis on adolescents.)

Introduction

A child's unconscious phantasy life is centred primarily on the body and bodily functions, and the bodies and functions of those close to the child. (This is true of adults, too, but it is usually much closer to the surface in children and adolescents.) Phantasies of damage being done to bodies abound, as well as phantasies of damage being repaired, in both the child's internal reality and outside world. Internal reality, or the inner world, is explained by Meltzer (1981), referring to Klein: '. . . we do not live in one world, but in two . . . we live in an internal world which is as real a place to live as the outside world . . . . Psychic reality could be treated in a concrete way' (p. 178). In other words, we need to attend to this very real inner world of phantasies as they influence us as much as external events.

Receiving the diagnosis and negotiating subsequent treatment of life-threatening illness for a child or adolescent constitutes a psychic trauma. In the past the word 'trauma' has often been used loosely and the concept has had a vexed history in psychoanalytic literature. My understanding of the term is largely contained in the following definition: 'Trauma occurs when an individual is exposed to an overwhelming event that renders him or her helpless in the face of intolerable danger, anxiety, and instinctual arousal' (Pynoos and Eth, 1984). However, 'helpless' seems to be an under-statement, as the impact of trauma often leads to an inability to think, as I shall explain. It is useful to draw upon the now substantial body of literature on trauma, disasters and post-traumatic stress disorder, which includes strategies for preventive and therapeutic intervention (Krystal, 1976; O'Brien and Hughes, 1991; Laub and Auerhahn, 1993).

The diagnosis is a reminder that fatal illness can affect children as well as adults, that any one of us can be rendered helpless, subjected to extremely difficult treatment, and possibly death. Our view of the world as safe or predictable is shattered. As Freud (1915) expressed so clearly, in man there is:

> . . . an unmistakable tendency to put death on one side, to eliminate it from life . . . the civilised man will carefully avoid speaking of such a possibility in the hearing of the person under sentence. Children alone disregard this restriction; they unashamedly threaten one another with the possibility of dying . . . .   (p. 289)

The word 'trauma' (from the Greek, 'wound') implies, like a breach in the outer protective skin of the body, a piercing of the psychic protective apparatus. Freud's (1920) formulation on trauma was:

> 'We describe as "traumatic" any excitations from outside which are powerful enough to break through the protective shield . . . the concept of trauma neces-sarily implies a connection of this kind with a breach in an otherwise efficacious barrier against stimuli.'

Later (1933) he wrote about the inherent helplessness in the face of danger which indicates a traumatic state. Masud Khan (1986), drawing upon Freud, wrote about the mother's role as a protective shield against excessive stimulation for the child. This prevents the penetration of internal and external 'frights' with which the immature ego of the child cannot cope.

I prefer to think of this function as a 'protective *filter*', as this conveys something permeable, through which experiences can pass in both direct-ions, which is more appropriate than the impenetrability of a 'shield'. Not only is the parent filtering that which goes through to the child, but the child's expression of, say, distress, would be filtered back to the medical team by the mother or father processing it and then communicating it. This links with Bion's (1962) formulation of the mother's capacity for 'reverie', which is an instinctive way of containing and processing the infant's un manageable distress, and, in time, feeding it back in tolerable form. In favourable development, from birth, or before, the infant has the experi-ence of being held in his mother's mind, and, literally, in her arms, lap or gaze. From these beginnings he can take inside himself, literally, in the feeding relationship, and metaphorically in the psychic apparatus, the mother's capacity to hear, see and feel without losing the capacity to think. This will distinguish between good experiences and bad ones, and will help him to form the basis for all future coping. In this way the infant is given the formative experience of a container for his own often unmanageable feelings, and for his unintegrated or disintegrated state (Bick, 1968).

Melanie Klein (1946) describes how in the first few months of life the ego, lacking cohesion, fluctuates between integration and disintegration, 'a falling into bits' (p. 4). She continues, 'Prominent amongst . . . functions is that of dealing with anxiety. I hold that primary anxiety arises from the operation of the death instinct . . . [it] is felt as fear of annihilation [death] and takes the form of fear of persecution'. When an actual deadly threat is upon oneself or someone close, these primitive anxieties and associations may surface. It is as if one's most infantile phantasies have been realised: '. . . thought, imagining and phantasy can no longer be experienced confidently, as *distinct from the external reality*' (Garland, 1991, my italics). This seems to lead to an inability to think 'about' the situation. The ability to think symbolically about events, to distinguish them from imaginings or dreams, is a part of everyday life. When this symbolic activity becomes confused with 'a living nightmare' (to quote the familiar words of mothers of children with a life-threatening illness), symbolic functioning is impaired. This often leads to states of confusion and of not really being inside one's own body.

The eventual outcome – whether the event leads to increased disturbance for those involved, or whether it can become a focus for growth – will depend on several factors. These factors include primarily the 'pre-disaster resources' of the individual and family and friends (Menzies-Lyth, 1989), the amount of social and professional help, and the details surrounding the event. 'Pre-disaster resources' involve the impact on inner psychic reality of the external trauma, as well as, conversely, the ways in which the external trauma is coloured by internal psychic reality, including past traumas.

For example, Peter, a boy with an unusual degree of maturity which belied his insecurity, had had a childhood of living with a mother, a single parent, who had severe psychiatric problems. When, at the age of 12, he was diagnosed as having a bone tumour, he continued to take care of his mother as if she was the patient, and did not allow his own fears or needs to surface. His mother, through the support of the hospital staff, was able to find the strength to parent her son as much as possible, but he continued to perceive the situation through the eyes, feelings or unconscious phantasies of his inner world. This inner world contained an unsafe, unprotective mother who needed him to look after her. Once some trust had been built up with his psychotherapist, he could begin to explore one of his phantasies: that the illness was a reflection of inner worthlessness. Fundamental confusions between Peter's sense of inner badness, his mother's badness and the cancer were some of the major problems. It is clear in this situation that the mother's ineffectiveness as a filter for the extra stimulation was a result of his inner picture of her and not necessarily the external reality.

There is a particular group of patients who are difficult to help: those who have suffered earlier trauma, which has led to alexithymia (Krystal, 1976, 1988). This is an indicator of disturbance which manifests itself in affective and symbolic function: alexithymic patients' ability to use emotions is impaired in that they react somatically, or physiologically, with scant verbalisation. Their emotions have a vagueness and flatness, and there is thus a difficulty in distinguishing different feelings. (For further description of the affective and cognitive disturbances discovered in psychoanalytic studies of psychosomatic patients, see Marty and de M'Uzan, 1963; Marty, de M'Uzan and David, 1963; Nemiah and Sifneos, 1970; Nemiah, 1978; see also Chapter 2.)

When massive trauma threatens the illusion of unity between mother and child, or between adult and internal 'good enough' parents, the distinction between external reality and phantasy can collapse. Often, the choice then is either a repudiation of reality, which leads to psychosis, or a repudiation of fantasy, which leads to alexithymia. People can only sustain a finite amount of pain, and give it meaning, whether physical or psychological. It is not surprising, therefore, when an alexithymic response of blanking out – like an overloaded circuit – occurs. Krystal (1988) has noticed that as traumatic experiences tend to lead to the person's feeling that the event came about as a punishment, through some transgression, so the post-traumatic alexithymic individual avoids indulging in any wishing or longing. Indeed, the enjoyment of pleasure, whether fantasied or real, is blocked. (I use here the spelling 'fantasy' to denote conscious imaginings, whereas 'phantasy' is about unconscious instincts, urges or feelings.)

Krystal sees the widespread existence of alexithymia in post-traumatic survivors as a regression to infancy – in other words, their emotional response becomes pre-verbal, and physical. McDougall (1974), too, postulates that the problems of the alexithymic adult with 'psychosomatic' illness go back to very early infantile difficulties, particularly around separation. McDougall (1978) makes the important point that, as the pre-verbal infant cannot distinguish between psychic suffering and physical suffering, severe psychic trauma in infancy cannot later be reconstructed in analysis. These patients cannot use symbolic thought – cannot dream, or represent their needs.

Unable to repress their associations to emotional pain, and unable to project their feelings into other people as a means of communication, they cut themselves off altogether from a conscious awareness of the affect (McDougall, 1989). Usually, it is an *excess* of feelings – as indeed would be the case with the trauma of life-threatening illness – which cannot be contained. In other words, their feelings have remained in their bodies, or have gone back into the body if traumatised. Thus, the symptom remains concretely in the body instead of being expressed as mental pain.

Parents of children with a life-threatening illness

It is not unusual to hear parents of children who are very seriously ill talking as if they were the patient: not being able to think, feeling chaotic, developing a range of physical symptoms, losing their memory, feeling 'shell-shocked', 'going to pieces', 'walking into walls', feeling 'gone' and 'living from day to day'. Clearly they are sparing their child some of the impact by being in the 'front line of battle' themselves. The degree to which both physical and emotional resources become overwhelmed is a clear reminder that the effects of a traumatic experience cannot be separated into body and mind. A widespread reaction to stress is cognitive constriction and inhibition. Mandler's (1982) observations lead to the conclusion that memory, judgement and attention are all impaired if subject to extreme stress. Nietzsche expressed the psychological disorganisation well: 'Some situations are so bad that to remain sane is insane'.

As these parents are not able to begin to process the situation by thinking about it, because they are still living inside it, it is only when their inner world begins to be distinguishable as separate from the external catastrophe that they can begin the process of dealing with the painful events. In the parent, initial denial often gives way to a more agitated response to the sudden change in the inner and outer world, and the beginnings of an attempt at understanding it. Waves of awareness alternate with a return to avoidance. These 'doses' of pain are attempts at coping by keeping the pain in a state which is not overwhelming.

For the parents there is, possibly, a threefold aspect to the trauma: to themselves, to their child and to their other children. The initial 'acute shock trauma' of diagnosis usually gives way to 'chronic stress trauma', as they have to live daily with an injurious situation (Sandler, 1967). However, the threat of death to a child can be beyond that with which a parent can cope, so that forms of walling off emotions may be necessary. For example, Mrs F., like many parents struggling with a grim diagnosis and poor prognosis for her child, talked frequently about the vigour and health of her daughter before she became ill. Her anecdotes idealised the daughter as the strongest, tallest, cleverest in the school. English was not her first language, but her description, 'Riding her bike, shining', conveyed poetically her need to exalt the once-healthy child to shut out the impact of the diagnosis.

Some parent's responses seem to arise out of pre-existing difficulties in parenting. For example, one mother, with chronic epilepsy, said, à propos her son's bone cancer which had developed into many secondaries: 'He's all right, they can cure him, but they can't cure me'. Another mother chose the time of her daughter's brain tumour operation to undergo cosmetic breast surgery. She presented on the children's ward, asking the nurses for attention for her suppurating breast wounds. The symbolism is poignant and complex, but this serves as an example for the emotionally crippled state the mother found herself in, which was exacerbated by the child's situation. These mothers (or fathers) are often over-identified with their ill children, or the child in them feels rivalrous with the actual ill child. Some seek support from the ill child rather than supporting him or her.

Some parents respond with a powerful denial of the seriousness of the situation. For example, Mrs R. repeatedly stated that her eight-year-old son, Jason, with a very large osteosarcoma of his thigh, was 'coping fine' and resisted intervention from the hospital play specialist and child psychotherapist. When the rapid deterioration of his condition, despite chemotherapy, led to a medical decision to recommend amputation urgently, Mrs R. became like a she-wolf protecting her cub, angrily attacking the doctors, but able to talk to the non-medical members of the team. She told the psychotherapist that she could cope with the amputation, but that Jason could not. One could understand Mrs R.'s initial denial as adaptive in that it protected her from the impact of a catastrophic trauma or breakdown. It seemed she put her own difficulties and wish to deny the forthcoming operation into Jason, as she was unable to really stay with her own feelings of not coping.

These fluctuations are similar to the phases in the work of mourning (Freud, 1917; Lindemann, 1944). The themes which frequently arise in the work of mourning as well as in an attempt to master a life-threatening illness – for they both, of course, involve losses – have been listed by Krupnick and Horowitz (1981, p. 428), thus:

1. Rage at the source (of the serious life event).
2. Sadness over loss.
3. Discomfort over vulnerability.
4. Discomfort over aggressive impulses.
5. Fear of loss of control over aggressive impulses.
6. Guilt over responsibility (for inviting the event or failing to control it).
7. Fear of similarity to the victim.
8. Rage at those exempted.
9. Fear of repetition.
10. Survivor guilt.

These stress–response patterns are similar to a description of mourning, because for parents of children facing a life-threatening illness, as well as for the child her- or himself, the mourning process can start at the moment of diagnosis, as they frequently feel that life will never be the same again.

The tasks of mourning as described by Worden (1982) may be applied helpfully to the adjustment that is necessary for children (and their parents) living with a life-threatening illness, and especially with the concomitant invasive treatments, as well as surgery or amputation. Worden's tasks are listed below. (I have added in brackets the necessary implications for adjusting to a life-threatening illness.)

1. To accept the reality of the loss (of the healthy whole self).
2. To experience the pain of grief (including an awareness of earlier unresolved losses which are rekindled).
3. To adjust to an environment in which the deceased is missing (i.e. a world without the healthy self or lifestyle or expectations that preceded the illness).
4. To withdraw emotional energy and invest it in another relationship (i.e. to withdraw emotional energy from the previous 'healthy' life and to re-invest it in the new, different life).

Some degree of mourning and grieving is essential for the patient and the parents if they are not to succumb to a state of depression, or of repetitively berating or accusing themselves or others, or of total denial. Clearly they are all immensely difficult tasks to complete, and even with appropriate support and assistance may not be fully worked through.

An important factor in helping the mother or father to adapt positively to the situation is when the parent is encouraged to maintain a caring role. This can lead to greater attachment between parent and child, and increased confidence in both of the parents' abilities. The older child's ability to *verbalise* distress is crucially helpful, unlike the situation for the infant. Both adolescents and parents of terminally ill children often show a great keenness to learn as much as possible about the illness (Friedman et al., 1963). This seems to mitigate the sense of helplessness and perhaps some guilt and self-blame. Medical emergencies which do not allow time for this may well lead to unmanageable anxiety.

We need to distinguish between the parents' protective filter function for an adolescent compared with that for a young child. For an adolescent the parental function becomes more complicated. How can the parent allow the teenager to continue to struggle with adolescent goals towards independence while providing a parental protective function? The responses to this delicate situation seem to depend partly on the young person's pre-illness status: those who have already negotiated many of the tasks of adolescence towards a secure independence often continue thus, including eliciting peer support and rejecting adults' over-protectiveness. The extent to which the parent can allow the adolescent process to continue in the face of illness is inevitably influenced by the parent's own inner world and past. Those adolescents whose infantile, dependent needs are still paramount readily regress during illness to a passive, often depressed state, attempting to use the nurses to gratify their needs for mothering if parents will not oblige.

For some, the experience of a life-threatening illness is the stimulus for a premature surge towards independence. There is often a 'what the hell' attitude to both adult constraints and illness constraints, which can, of course, cause treatment problems. The self-destructiveness often seen in adolescents who abuse drugs or alcohol now has an opportunity for expression through non-compliance with treatment, or simply through inadequate self-care, when the body is at its most vulnerable with low immunity. It is difficult for the parents of these young people to remain caring and emotionally available in the face of flagrant self-destructiveness or anger which appears to attack the parents' love and care.

John, a 16 year old who had recently undergone an amputation, repeatedly went out in winter without a coat or hat. His head looked conspicuously bald from chemotherapy. His mother despaired of his repeated rejection of her attempts to encourage him to be more sensible. We can wonder if he wanted to get more ill and perhaps die, or to test and shock people with his altered body-image – making them feel some of the shock he found too difficult to deal with himself. Or was he keeping busy with this carefree life as a way of avoiding mental pain? The fact that he bought a rottweiler which accompanied him everywhere seemed to exemplify his outward defensive aggression.

Just as parents of healthy adolescents have to evolve a subtle granting of independence without abdicating ultimate control and surveillance, so parents of very ill adolescents have to attempt to continue to foster the independence and self-care of which the child is capable. A rather matter-of-fact attitude seems helpful for the physical care and more intimate nursing tasks required from parents, so that they do not infringe the normal taboos and constraints upon close physical contact, particularly with the parent of the opposite sex. Although '. . . no distinction between material and psychological can be made by the infant' (Bion, 1962, p. 29), the adolescent in the unnatural situation of serious illness can be helped in his attempts to differentiate and thus retain some privacy and autonomy.

Adolescents

I will start by briefly considering young children facing a life-threatening illness in order to better understand adolescents' reactions, for the child-within-the-adolescent will influence the older child's responses.

Younger children, like adolescents, are usually fully aware of the serious-ness of their illness but less aware of the implications of treatment plans, curtailment of activities and lifestyle. Their understanding of the deadly implications will depend on age, maturity, and previous experiences (A. Freud, 1952; Judd, 1989; Cohen, 1990; Emanuel et al., 1990; Vas Dias, 1990). Their more conscious anxiety is usually centred on separation, as expressed succinctly by a five-year-old boy, talking about death: 'The worst thing is, you don't see your mum'. Finding themselves in a strange environ-ment can be tolerable if they are accompanied by an adult who physically and psychologically acts as a buffer between them and the outside world. But if the parental protective filter is breached, the illness and the treatment may lead to the infant fearing disintegration and ultimately annihilation –

indeed, a state of trauma. Young children tend not to separate pain from painful feelings: it can all become subsumed under an undifferentiated psychic and somatic overwhelming experience.

Young children see illness as externally caused ('It was because I fell over', or 'because my friend pushed me, that I got cancer in my leg'). These thoughts are more accessible than the no less frequent idea among children (and adults) that illness is a punishment for bad thoughts or other actions leading to feelings of guilt.

With adolescents, after the widespread initial reaction of disbelief (Schmale, 1971), there is a feeling of lack of control, for their attempts to master their environment are arrested. Much more than with younger children, there is the interruption of peer friendships, which are such an important part of adolescent social support. New-found independence from parents is threatened by a renewed dependence on them. Schooling is, of course, interrupted. Sexual attractiveness, body-image and sense of intact-ness, are all threatened by the illness and by the treatment – an infantile quest for perfection, and a sense of omnipotence, having to be relinquished. Even a seemingly minor surgical incision can feel like an attack or a mutilation. The following example serves to illustrate a young ado-lescent's early reaction:

> Abigail, a 13-year-old girl with lymphoma and poor prognosis, soon after diagnosis, said, 'Some people, when they hear the word "cancer", start digging your grave immediately'. She was clearly trying to put her fears of death into others. I asked her what she thought 'cancer' meant in terms of survival? She said categorically, 'Most people have a 90% chance of success.' I said, 'What about the 10%?' 'That's the older ones,' she replied. However, she was able to explore her own shock more readily in relation to the forthcoming chemotherapy and subsequent hair loss: 'When I heard about that, people might have thought I'd fainted, I just lay there'. She talked indignantly about those who regard her illness as frightening or contagious, and who should be 'educated'. It seemed adaptive at the early stage of her adjustment for much of the problem of thinking about it to be located elsewhere.

Adolescents usually have a mature adult understanding of the concept of death, with its universality, finality and inevitability, and therefore of 'not-being'. Alongside that awareness is often a heightened sense of 'being', of existing and of a future. As we know, the adolescent is in transition between child and adult, between the old self and the new, between the loss of the dependent child and the emergence of the independent adult. No wonder, in their attempts to make sense of these polarities and to find a sense of self, they turn to poetry, or drawing, or philosophy, or good causes, or find the lyrics of pop songs meaningful. The self that emerges, struggling with life and death issues, is often one that continues to struggle, is full of doubt, has a keen sense of vulnerability and of the possibility of loss, or, conversely, is heavily defended against sadness and doubt with ebullient pseudo-confidence or aggression, or is involved with a gang of like-minded people.

Normal adolescents' goals are towards independence, sexual relationships, attractiveness; being popular, successful and adult. Their struggles towards these goals take place upon the turbulent seas of changing moods and differing viewpoints. All their hopes are jeopardised if they are to believe that they may die. If their own death becomes imminent, their normal adolescent tasks are so threatened that they have to choose between a denial of death or a giving up of the life that is left – or a middle path which encompasses both.

I have found that they generally choose the path of denial but with some areas of 'middle path': they often continue to make plans – usually un-realistic or defiant plans – for the future, but at the same time confide in one or two chosen people, or express symbolically, their awareness of the painful reality. While privately negotiating the enormous tasks of contem-plating their own death, they can continue with the ordinary tasks of working towards independence, of maintaining a sense of their own attrac-tiveness and sexuality, and of belonging to a peer group, often despite hair loss, weight loss, surgery, even amputation. Given a life-threatening illness, we see situations where adolescents are precipitated into a more mature grappling with life and death issues, including anger at their plight, and impressively move on to mourn the loss of the healthy self. If the patient has a sense that death is likely, and if the young person's earlier experi-ences have enabled him to have a belief and trust in his capacity to love, and in a secure inner world, he can live the life that is left, paradoxically by relinquishing it. He can mourn the loss of all that he loves; even, for moments, relinquish the world, with the accompanying grief and sadness, and feel gratitude and concern for others and an ability to repair relation-ships. Some of these issues are illustrated in the following example, and in the example of Anna at the end of this chapter.

Stephen

Stephen, a 17-year-old young man with a recurrence of inoperable cancer with secondaries, shared his thoughts with me as he sat up in bed making a toy for his sister's unborn baby. 'I know this may sound selfish, but it's worse for me if I die, because I lose everyone I love. They only lose one person – me. But I lose everything. I know I won't know, after I die . . . but it's hard, now.' With tears in his eyes he told me recent dreams about the death of his grandmother and sister. We could see how he was indeed already mourning *his* loss of loved ones, as well as in his dreams making them the victims in order to spare himself.

Stephen felt unable to share these thoughts with his family, although they were very close and supportive. He did not want to upset them further, he said. Already he felt that his pregnant sister's nausea was caused by worry about him. Through the experience of his half-expressed thoughts being brought more clearly into focus by me, he became prepared to talk more openly to his family about what was on all their minds.

Yet he continued to carry on his daily life as optimistically as possible, and to manage his pain control sensibly. His life conveyed a sense of meaningfulness. Unlike some dying adolescents who use manic denial and have excessively ambitious plans, he seemed to value the ordinary pleasures of family and friends, and to take a pride in his appearance. It seems that Stephen had reached a sufficient degree of maturity when he became ill; that is, he could stay with feelings of loss, of valuing life, without it all becoming exhaustingly 'over the top', or not worth bothering about, or so bad that he could only attack or feel attacked. He is an example of someone with good pre-disaster resources, or an 'internal container', to negotiate this awesome task so admirably.

Psychotherapeutic intervention

I shall consider therapeutic intervention mainly from the point of view of individual psychotherapy as one component within a multidisciplinary team, because that is the basis of my training and experience. However, family therapy and group therapy are also extremely useful approaches and will sometimes be the treatment of choice. In considering the type of treatment which is beneficial, we need to remember that these children or parents are not necessarily disturbed before the illness occurs. They have not sought psychotherapy as such, often do not know what it entails or may have negative ideas about it. But, as I have explained, their previous experience of being 'contained', as well as their belief – or otherwise – in communicating with others, is crucial to the use they would make of therapeutic help.

During the initial stage of the family's attempt to survive the shock of diagnosis, the therapist's usefulness is in being an involved witness: to feel, to hear, register, and attempt to 'contain' the immediate as well as the far-reaching implications. This early position is important to subsequent work with the family or individual, without which it is difficult for the sufferer to feel understood and believed.

As those who have had a recent or on-going trauma are not able to sustain the questioning of established patterns which is involved in the working through of chronic emotional problems in long-term intensive psychotherapy, sometimes a supportive or specially adapted therapeutic relationship is suggested – especially in the early stages after diagnosis. This need to adapt the more classical psychotherapy model is necessary if the setting and circumstances necessitate flexibility, as will be illustrated in the case of Jim which follows. This is sometimes applicable too when death is imminent. Indeed, the setting up of a short-term contract for focal work (Goldschmidt, 1986) may be the best solution. Therein, the therapeutic ingredients are empathy, attempts at understanding the confusions around the crisis (some of which might echo earlier infantile traumas) understanding the ensuing losses, giving words to feelings and the facilitation of grief. However, the more usual aims of long-term therapy, with an attempt to resolve earlier emotional patterns in the context of the present situation, can also be appropriate.

Some parents of very ill children are resistant to talking about the experience, and become more anxious when they do. This leads to their attempting to deny that it is serious, and the child may become more frightened by the parents' avoidance. It is often helpful if the worker points out to the parents that most families need help in communicating and coping when they have to live with the fact that their child has cancer. If the parents engage with a worker and recognise relief in being able to talk openly, communication between all the family members can be facilitated. The family approach then shifts from one of trying to forget about it to one of struggling to live with it (Bloch, Silber and Perry, 1956). This opening up of communication for the parents seems an essential prerequisite for working with the child, or the family as a whole, if the parents are not to block interventions.

Learning from the research of Caplan (1981) and others (Egbert et al., 1964; Skipper and Leonard, 1968; Schmale, 1971; Bordow and Porrit, 1979) we can see that high levels of appropriate social or professional support help to protect against increased physical illness in response to high levels of stress. The traumatised or highly stressed individual can become ill (Parkes, 1978; Caplan, 1981), owing to physiological changes (such as neuroendocrine changes, a reduced immune system, alterations in blood pressure and heart rate as well as in the chemical constituents of the blood). It appears that adolescents and adults who are taught about the effects of cancer and its treatments, as well as supported, are more likely to achieve a sense of coping with the situation. Narrowing our biopsychosocial view to the intrapsychic, we can understand that the support – whether pro-fessional or social – leads to the individual's ability to feel there is an external 'maternal' container (Bion, 1962) which can hold the unbearable projected infantile parts of the personality.

Alternatively, if one uses Freud's model, the patient has the opportunity to re-experience the traumatic situation in a way which is not felt to be a repetition of earlier traumas, in the presence of a therapist who can take on the function of a protective shield (or filter). This does not imply colluding with denial, but involves painstaking work at assimilating the fragments of both the internal and the external realities which are the result of the patient's attempt to render it tolerable through splitting and projection.

The therapist takes on board powerful projections, thinks about them, and in time feeds back, or reflects with the child and/or parents, until they can perform this function for themselves. In other words, the therapist tries to search for the truth in order to facilitate thought. This involves, for the therapist, surviving the emotional turbulence of a life-and-death situation: sustaining hopefulness and potency alongside vulnerability and loss. In time, for the patient, this can lead to the taking in of a capacity to transform overwhelming feelings into thoughts that can be tolerated and integrated.

Thus the therapeutic relationship provides the opportunity of re-experiencing a care-taking mother. Although this process is bound to be conflictual, the patient usually forms a positive transference with the therapist, provided there are sufficient earlier good experiences which can re-surface and link with the therapist. The patient's neediness and grief understandably often lead to a powerful maternal response on the therapist's part. The therapist may indeed be idealised, but this can have a useful function: the patient's self-esteem has recently been damaged and so the idealised parent/therapist forms a model for identification and introjection.

In undertaking the sort of work that I will describe in detail, we need to consider the particular difficulties in adapting and applying pure psychotherapy in a very unpredictable setting, such as a hospital ward. For example, the work is less private: there is often interference from without as well as implications for the effects of the work on others who may observe and hear the interaction. The patient's availability is subject to the vicissitudes of the illness, admissions and other treatments. As the work is so public, negative therapeutic reactions, or distress or depression, are often a cause of anxiety, distress or interference on the part of other professionals, or of other patients and families who witness it. Seemingly good interventions can be envied and similarly sabotaged. The therapist has to struggle to understand in the patient the interplay of physiological reactions (such as nausea) to disease or medication, and psychological disturbance manifested somatically. When is a symptom ever purely drug- or disease-related? Although elements of many of the foregoing problems are also present in most psychotherapeutic work, the difficulties for the therapist are far more extreme in managing the limitations and interference imposed by the illness and the setting. Moreover, the therapist is struggling with his or her own anguish, fear, loss, anger, despair and hopelessness, as well as the resonances in the inner world of pre-existing damage, in response to close contact with life-threatening illness in a child or adolescent. This implies the need for proper professional support in whatever form (such as supervision, analysis, peer support), in order to understand that which applies to the patient and that which may belong to the therapist.

Money-Kyrle (1956) gives a useful description of the normal aspects of the analytic experience. He describes the two basic 'drives' (in addition to scientific curiosity) which fuel the analyst's concerns with the patient's welfare, thus:

> '. . . the reparative, which counteracts the latent destructiveness in all of us . . . the patient must stand for the damaged objects of the analyst's own unconscious phantasy, which are still endangered by aggression and still in need of care and reparation,' and '. . . the parental . . . it is with the unconscious child in the patient that the analyst is most concerned . . . .'

He writes about the importance of the therapist's ability to identify with the child-in-the-patient as an early aspect of himself. He sees this reparation and parenting as part of our attempt to counteract the Death Instinct.

From the foregoing it would seem that actual psychic or physical trauma presents an acute version of those issues for the therapist. Some awareness of these inner motives, including the temptation to cure in an omnipotent way, which leads therapists and other workers into this field, are a necessary part of ongoing self-analysis and understanding. If these aspects are not understood, repeated experiences of the futility and outrage surrounding the painful treatment and possible death of a child would lead to emotional detachment or attempts at manic reparation – in other words, an omnipotent belief that one *can* repair the external and internal damage. This would be at the expense of identifying with inner parents who can only try to survive disaster and loss, and recover – though probably never completely – by eventually shifting their focus on to the next task or phase of life.

The task is made more difficult by being set against the backdrop of a society with a widespread belief that it is wrong to talk about death or cancer. The mother of a boy with cancer went to her library to obtain books on the subject, but her friends told her she was 'weird' to do so. This is a vast topic in its own right (Gorer, 1965; Cannadine, 1981; Judd, 1989) which cannot be explored here. Workers in this field have to struggle with the paradox of an acceptance of death alongside an acknowledgement of fear, outrage and loss.

Two young people's responses to life-threatening illness

Jane

Jane is a 15-year-old girl with a malignant bone tumour of her upper vertebrae. Her cancer had been detected early, there were no secondaries and her prognosis was good. When she was first admitted to the Adolescent Oncology Unit of a hospital in the south of England, there was a flurry of talk about Jane and her family among the nurses, teachers, social worker, counsellors, doctors and myself (child psychotherapist), as if there was an unbearable load which had to be shared and spread before any real thinking about the situation could begin.

Mrs A., Jane's mother, dressed in black from head to foot, hurled herself across the ward, slamming telephones and doors, wide-eyed, staring straight ahead like a hunted animal facing a rifle, not knowing whether to attack or freeze. The danger seemed tangible and threatened not only the relative calm of the other patients and their parents but also the normally extremely competent senior nurses' and sister's ability to feel that they could cope.

Mr A., who was not Jane's father (Jane's parents had separated when she was six), was a firm presence when he managed to be there. He tried to contain the situation by intervening between his wife and the doctors, telling her to wait in a side-room while he negotiated, or tried to be with his step-daughter during medical procedures. I was to learn increasingly from my contact with Jane and her mother that she had not had the experience of a mother who could contain any of her anxieties. She was overwhelmed by anxiety, trembling and calling out frantically for her mother if she was out of sight. She had not developed what we can call an 'internal container' (this links with Bion's [1962] notion of 'reverie', p. 88).

Mrs A. blocked her daughter's attempts to convey her own anxieties – for example, 'We tell Jane it's boring – yawn – when she talks about her worries. Jane, when you've had your last treatment, there's to be no mention of cancer!'. Indeed, we can see increasingly in the ensuing material that Mrs A. may have tried to project her unbearable anxieties into Jane, thus exacerbating her feeling of being intruded into now by medical interventions. Examples of this were her needle-phobia, her feelings that the chemotherapy was poison and the 'line' in her chest as damaging. This is the mother's attempt to reverse the container/contained relationship by using the child as a receptacle for her unmanageable feelings (Williams, 1993).

At the beginning of the treatment she was fused with Jane, in danger of being overwhelmed herself as Jane clung to her, limpet-like, knowing she could not provide understanding, but merely a state of sameness. A crying child on the ward echoed Jane's helpless feelings as she reacted, 'I wish that stupid baby would shut up!'.

Mrs A., meanwhile, seemed to make matters worse by continuing to off-load her panic. Whenever Jane was approached for an inject-ion, mother called out, 'She's needle-phobic, she's needle-phobic!'. She quickly told whoever came within her field of contact about her own bad back, her difficulties with her mother, about Jane's inability to cope because she was educationally 'subnormal'. She insisted that all the professionals tell Jane that she would be all right, that it wasn't serious and that she would soon be better. These are only a few of the many examples of the lack of differentiation between Mrs A. and her daughter, who was incorporated into her hysteria. She gave me a weighty folder of the correspondence relating to Jane's education since the age of four, as if to literally off-load some of the burden that she felt she was carrying. This may have carried the seed of a need to be meaningfully understood and contained, beneath the more apparent wish to get rid of something that had become unbearable.

This situation led to my seeing Jane, soon after admission, for twice-weekly regular individual psychotherapy. Mrs A. was seen regularly by the counsellor and attended the weekly support groups for parents. Jane was taught individually, daily and sometimes twice-daily, by the hospital teacher. Nurses spent time by her bedside playing games and helping with her homework. The social worker gave help to mother. The natural father, Mr D., was seen for two lengthy meetings by me. Jane's 19-year-old sister (who was estranged from both parents) was seen by various members of the team at different times. A volunteer played games with her and talked to her. Volunteers from a local cosmetic shop (who visited the patients regularly) gave massages to Jane – sometimes three at a time, all working on different parts of her body. I could mention several more interventions, as well as, inevitably, the many compli-cated and detailed medical, nursing and physiotherapy treatments, observations and interventions, during her first admission of 13 weeks. Needless to say, Jane and her mother occupied infinitely more staff meeting-time than did any other family.

Jane had more videos and electronic games around her bed than any other patient. There were many instructions, written by her mother, pinned up around her, stating when she should rest/go to sleep/what she should eat/not eat/what exercises she should do/what homework she must do/when and how she should wash out her mouth. During all this time she had to stay on her back to protect her spine from damage. Despite the foregoing attention which mother and daughter received, there was the feeling that it was never enough. Mrs A. would capture anyone who seemed at all prepared to listen, and dominated the parents' support group. Jane's refrain was that she never got as much attention as other patients.

However, the extreme tension and panic around mother and daughter did lessen within the first few weeks, and the staff managed to sustain the enormous load, possibly at times to the detriment of other patients' emotional needs, despite Jane's medical condition not being as serious as that of many other patients. The team had to provide a mothering and containing function for both mother and child, partly to protect the other patients from the otherwise pervasive panic, partly to facilitate medical interventions. Mrs A. could not carry out many of the nursing roles many mothers naturally perform, and withdrew her presence as a punishment to Jane whenever she or her husband felt that her behaviour was unreasonable. In fact, there seemed only occasional bursts of frustration and anger on Jane's part: mostly she was exceptionally compliant. Her mother was ostensibly very keen on the idea of Jane's being seen for regular psychotherapy, but always asked about the sessions and panicked if she appeared depressed afterwards. Once, at the end of a session, when I opened the cubicle curtain, Mrs A. was seated right outside it.

Her IQ had been tested previously and apparently scored at 55. Her family seemed to emphasise this low IQ by treating her as 'subnormal'. The nurses and I found this score surprisingly low, and felt that she could have scored very differently had she been treated differently. Indeed, she seemed to hide behind stupidity as an avoidance of confrontation, conflict, anger, rebellion, and many other expressions of normal development (Sinason, 1986). Her way of not using her intelligence seemed to foster a naive and disinhibited approach, which made her generally accessible. Her anxiety spilled out in the early sessions, of which this gives a flavour:

> '. . . I don't like medicines . . . I'll have to have them for nine months . . . I hate it . . . feeling sick . . . staying in bed . . . don't want to have it . . . what would happen if I didn't? Would I lie . . . die? Is it serious? Is it serious being in hospital?'

The phrases rushed out. Her questions gave me an opportunity to acknowledge and explore not only her anxieties about the unpleasant treatment and the possibility of dying, but also, through her slip of the tongue, the idea of someone 'lying'. She needed to explore, repeatedly, whether people were telling him the truth, and to sort out the confusion between her mother's insistence that it wasn't serious and that she'd soon be fine, compared with the extreme treatment, hospitalisation, and the obviously very ill young people on the ward. If she could grasp the truth – that she did have a life-threatening illness but that her particular situation was genuinely hopeful – then she would be able to begin to speak the truth, as opposed to 'living a lie', about her complex feelings.

In subsequent sessions Jane expressed her unhappy feelings

about her potential baldness: 'I don't want my Dad to see me without hair. Bald is ugly and stupid. Wearing a hat or wig isn't the same,' as she pulled at the strands of her still-thick hair. I wondered about an identification with a damaged father – her father was bald and Jane had often indicated that she felt her father was not as clever as other people. Later in the same session, 'Why can't they operate, cut it out?' as she banged the site of her tumour. 'It's his fault . . . the doctor. He's no good. He just laughs. I never thought I'd get cancer . . . . Why did I get it?'. Now the doctor and her father seemed confused, both seeming to be hopeless.

Jane's angry outburst did not seem held by me, for she went on desperately, 'I don't want it . . . , I want to go home . . . . I'm hungry . . . they don't give you enough food here . . . get me one of my yogurts . . .'. She seemed to want something much more tangible than she felt she was getting from the contact, but when I summarised this dilemma she seemed to feel understood, and said, 'Why don't you come and see me earlier? Have you a long way to come?'.

The session ended with a clear statement from me about when the next session would be, four days later, whereupon Jane returned to asking why the doctors laugh, saying '*You* take it seriously . . . but you're not a doctor'. Clearly, she was touching on the specific role of the psychotherapist: to take seriously, meaning to hear the sometimes unspoken dread, and to stay with it, whilst some members of the team cannot always do that while carrying out vital tasks in a more optimistic light. This specific role is well expressed by Sebastian Kraemer (1990), a child psychiatrist, '. . . child psychotherapy is about what people don't normally think about . . . the child psychotherapist is meant to be (intense) . . . paid to take on board worries, anxieties, on behalf of children, which most of us can hardly manage'.

As Jane felt more held by her sessions with me she was able to express her feelings of worthlessness, and her suspicion of the doctors, 'Do they give me good medicines, or just any old rubbish?'. Clearly she was splitting the staff into good and bad. Her projections of the badness, although leading to feelings of persecution, did not interfere with her cooperation with the medical treatment. In that way it seemed adaptive, because she was thus freeing me (at times) to be a source of understanding. She was interested in who had a university degree – something she felt she would never have – and felt that people with degrees should not be wasting their time seeing someone like her. She agreed that she felt like a worthless, bottom-of-the-pile baby, ignored by nurses. A young patient oppo-site was 'spoilt' and got all the attention. Although this was far from the truth, it was a true reflection of her feelings and of her inner reality, and needed to be acknowledged accordingly.

However, after a few months it became difficult for her to sustain this level of psychotherapeutic work: she would regress to an infantile state of being cocooned in her own nest, as she sucked her thumb and the sheet at the same time, uttering primordial little cries. I understood this as a withdrawal from the unbearable reality of her present life. This is an extract from a session:

> I tell her that I hear her little cry, and that it sounds like a little baby cry. She makes another more high-pitched one, thumb still in her mouth. I say, 'A little frightened cry. I wonder what you are frightened of?'. She smiles to herself, mockingly, in a way I had seen her mock me, and her father, before. I talk about it being hard for her to take her needy baby-self seriously, and to take me seriously for doing so.
>
> She then asks me to massage her palm, saying that it hurts from the computer control-stick. I say that it is easier for her to talk to me about the pain in her hand than any painful feelings.
>
> She silently opens her shirt, to show me the dressing below her chest covering the catheter into her bloodstream. I acknowledge the implications of this chest wound: the line for chemotherapy (which she detests, feeling 'it's poison going through me') and, on a deeper level, an attack on her body intactness.
>
> She snuggles closer to where I'm sitting on a chair at the side of her bed, so that her arm touches mine. I say, following a powerful counter-transference response to stroke her soft head, 'It's hard – you have to be the 15-year-old Jane most of the time, but underneath there's a baby Jane who seems to become more and more needy as she's kept in bed longer and longer and not allowed to do many of the normal 15-year-old things.'
>
> I tell her I have to go in five minutes.

(We regularly have half-hour sessions. This is a fixed factor in this usually more flexible setting if Jane is not to feel she has sent me away because she is unbearable. I had decided on this timespan because it was hard to sustain the session longer against the hubbub of a busy ward on the other side of thin curtains. Jane's torrents of anxieties within the cubicle fell onto and into me, at times like barbed wire; she also had her own difficulty in staying with the issues and not insisting that she needed a bedpan or to see one of the nurses about something that couldn't wait.)

> She says she feels she gets less than the others. She fingers my silver bracelet, and says she likes it. She asks how old it is and where did I get it.

(I wonder about the bright reflective quality of the metal evoking a baby-part of her looking into mother's eyes. Yet her mother's inability to 'absorb' any of her projections is akin to the hard, cold metal object. I do not explore these thoughts further with her as I might with a patient in long-term psychotherapy in a more sequestered setting. However, they inform my thinking and my responses to her, and are part of the essential on-going processing that any psychotherapist undertakes.)

> I say that the bracelet, and I, have to go now, but that I, and it, would be back on Thursday. She seems to watch it, not me, as I open the curtains around her bed and leave.

By the time Jane was mobilised, she was relatively confident and free of overt distress at the treatment for which she still had to return every three weeks over several months. Mrs A. seemed less despairing at her ability to take over much of Jane's care upon discharge, but took the precaution to arm herself with as much equipment from the ward as she could transport.

They returned two days later because of some leg pain Jane was having, but no cause was found. It seemed to be a useful way of temporarily returning for succour.

When Jane returned a week later for planned chemo- and radio-therapy, she was markedly depressed to be back in hospital, and felt very alienated from the nurses. This seemed to be a reflection of her difficulty in adjusting to her mother as care-taker at home and re-adjusting to the nurses, as well as an understandable depression in the light of all she had been through and all she still had to endure. Quite simply, she could not contain ambivalence: mother had become the main carer, so all the other carers were bad; home was good, hospital bad; I was bad for no longer providing regular sessions. She could not – without on-going help – remain in touch with more complex feelings, including sadness and ambivalence, in returning home and leaving a supportive network of people who had become fond of her. In parallel, Mrs A.'s inability to sustain ambivalence led to a return of her earlier denial of Jane's anxieties and depression: her repeated impatient reassurances left Jane again without someone who could hear and take in her unbearable feelings – a container. This lack seemed all the more poignant now that she had begun to know something different. The experience, albeit relatively brief, of having been believed and validated may help her to seek or use other supports later in life.

Discussion

In a malfunctioning family such as this one there seem to be potential therapeutic benefits to a child from hospitalisation, where, in time, overall treatment and support can address some of the pre-existing problems. Upon admission, Jane's unintegrated state conveyed catastrophic anxiety and total helplessness. She then had the repeated and intensive experience of being nursed in a way that encouraged her own ego development and autonomy through her involvement in decision-making, and so helped her to understand the situation she was in. In the ensuing psychotherapy her diffuse anxieties were taken seriously. Her child-self or baby-self's regression was recognised as a response to lengthy enforced inactivity, as well as a defence against a traumatic situation.

The various care-takers all met together frequently to discuss the facets of Jane's and her mother's experience and its impact on them, thus performing a parental function of thinking about the 'children' and resisting too extreme splitting or separating of the 'parents'. Our strength lay in the carrying of different functions by different team members but also in coming together to understand our functions and our difficulties. I used personal supervision at this time as a way of further having a space to sort out my own thinking. All these physical and emotional experiences (being held in my mind, in the team's mind, as well as, concretely, in the hospital bed and ward) led to Jane's feelings that her previously unintegrated state was now held together and beginning to be contained. This has as its prototype the experience for the baby of having the nipple in its mouth, or of being held in mother's mind. It is important to add that these developments could not necessarily become long term and established without a repeated working-through and a period of consolidation. Unfortunately, in Jane's case, lack of psychotherapeutic resources locally, as well as her parents' unwillingness to consider it, made this desirable ongoing treatment impossible.

I will now describe a very different adolescent who had achieved considerable maturation by the time she was to face a life-threatening illness.

Anna

She was a 17-year-old young woman who had undergone an above-knee amputation of her leg for bone cancer and successfully wore an artificial limb. She was a popular, attractive young woman who seemed to have survived her parents' divorce, her mother's emigration to Italy, and had a responsible job with an insurance company. She lived with her father and older sister.

Two years later she became terminally ill with extensive lung disease. When up against death, some people are capable of an accelerated mourning: a sense of great grief for the life that is lost, alongside an appreciation of life, a sense of understanding of others, affection, courage, even wisdom. Anna seemed capable of this rapid working-through of the 'depressive position' (Klein, 1935) because she had established internally a sufficient sense of a good-enough parental figure. If this had not been the case, she would have felt overwhelmingly persecuted and hating or hateful, and would not have been able to use me as well as she did in the short time we had available.

She wanted me to see the X-rays she had recently been shown. It was this honesty and directness that helped her (and me) to face the situation, and initially led her to try various avenues of help (help from me, the nurses, the doctors, domiciliary nurses, parents, sister, friends, healers, alternative therapies). I understood her tenacious use of help not as a denial of the reality, but as an acknowledgement of it: a young person determined to live when up against death, instinctively trying every path that may lead to help.

The help she sought was initially more towards 'cure'. As her health deteriorated rapidly and she could not walk more than a few steps because of breathlessness, she became more concerned with physical comfort, as well as proceeding to tackle any emotional problems without delay. Anna wanted to resolve her father's difficulty in facing the fact that she was dying: 'I feel angry with him for being surprised that they're not giving me more chemotherapy. I thought he knew. He's not hearing me.' I felt that this was an unconscious message to me: I had to try to be attentive to what I was not hearing. How much was I able to stay right by her, while struggling with my own wish for her to live and therefore to deny? All I could say was that her father probably found the truth too painful to acknowledge as yet and that she, or I, may be able to help him in this. I added that she probably knew about the part of her that wanted to deny the worsening situation.

I commented on my having noticed her ability to enlist help and support from those around her. She added, 'Yes, but the worst thing is when that goes wrong. Like when I'd been in pain all night and my sister was up with me, massaging my back. She was wonderful. But in the morning before she went to work I asked her for a hot-water bottle. She said, "No, I'll be late for work". I was so angry . . . had to wait for two hours 'til my Dad came home . . . . Wouldn't speak to her that night . . . but we're OK now, good friends again. And I'm going to invest in one of those electric heat pads, so I won't need hot-water bottles.'

Anna's situation, with her constant struggle for breath ('like drowning', she said) made it very hard for all those around her to bear her own intense awareness of an imminent death. Yet she herself coped in different ways: by putting faith in a different drug to ease her breathing; deciding who to approach to wheel her to the park; and by acknowledging herself as 'vain' in not feeling easy about people perceiving her as disabled. 'I had to get used to walking with a stick. Now I have to get used to being in a wheelchair. People treat you so different. They leave you miles of space all around, or they're extra nice to you. They don't treat you normal.' I thought she was talking about me as well.

I talked to her about the more extreme isolation of being so very ill, and probably dying, that makes her feel that people treat her differently. How hard it is for people to 'come close' to her, and really talk or listen. I added that perhaps she feels that I don't treat her as 'normal', and that it's hard for her to sort out her own needs versus others' motivation and fears. Anna's mother being in Italy for most of her illness must have compounded her sense of isolation at times.

She ended the session by saying that she was determined that a young man she knew would not spend Christmas alone – she was going to make sure he came to her family's house, even if he wanted to be alone. 'He can be left alone once he's there . . . but at least he'll be in our house.' This was a powerful message to me to not entirely believe her assertions of independence and of her being all right over the Christmas holidays. So I took the unusual step of giving her my home telephone number, saying that she could ring me if she wanted, and I could make a home visit. I was to see her anyway in two weeks' time when she returned to the hospital for a meeting she had requested with her mother, who would be visiting Anna from abroad, and the consultant.

Anna died two days after this meeting in January with the consultant, which brought the expected clear statement that he could not make her better. The contact we had established during her last months of life formed the foundation of a relationship between us during her last few days. She was still frightened of dying. She cried, 'I don't know what happens . . . if there's any place afterwards . . . I'm not ready to die . . . to leave everyone I love . . . there's so much I still want to do'.

I could only acknowledge what she was saying, and say that people would be with her until she died, but that dying *is* lonely. I added that there was still time to say important things to those who were important to her. A few minutes later she acknowledged her situation in her own way: 'I feel like doing something special, like going out somewhere really expensive for tea.' This simple statement conveyed so much: an awareness of the limitations to life she was up against: choosing 'tea' – not even 'dinner' or a holiday; the need for now-or-never wishes about more important things to be realised; and even a sense of self-worth in treating herself (or being treated) to something special.

The next day she died. She seemed to allow herself to let go only after she had permitted her mother to appease some of her guilt for having been away by nursing Anna and talking with her. Anna, even in the most extreme moments of being up against death, and without a religious or spiritual approach, seemed to be able to use me appropriately as someone who could try to contain some of her terror, speak truthfully and be with her until the final goodbye.

She brought a capacity to hold onto her traumatic situation and to try to make sense of it. I had only to facilitate this, and, at times, act as an auxiliary ego for her. Thus her state of psychic trauma was short-lived: not only cut short by death but by her own impressive capacity for accelerated mourning, encompassing an appreciation of life and of people.

Just when I was feeling most helpless at being able to do so little in the face of the immensity of her task in facing death, I felt that she was implicitly forgiving me, and indeed, containing me:

> I like Dr R. . . . he apologised to me twice . . . for not being able to cure me . . . but I said that it was alright, that it wasn't his fault.

This illustrates one dying young woman's struggle to overcome terror and depression. It is a last-minute struggle to make something of dying: to name unnamed terrors, to repair damaged relationships, to create something whole out of fragments. Awe-inspiring feelings are aroused in the onlooker: feelings of sadness, but also of hopefulness and a kind of joy, as the work of overcoming depression is wrought before one's eyes.

Acknowledgements

I would like to thank the following people for reading drafts of this chapter or for discussions around it: Aleda Erskine, Caroline Garland, Sebastian Kraemer, Gianna Williams and Juliet Hopkins.

References and bibliography

BICK, E. (1968). The experience of the skin in early object-relations. *International Journal of Psychoanalysis* **49**, 484–486.

BION, W. (1962). Learning from experience. In: *Seven Servants*. New York: Jason Aronson.

BION, W. (1967). *Second Thoughts*. London: Maresfield Reprints, 1984.

BLOCH, D., SILBER, E. and PERRY, S. (1956). Some factors in the emotional reaction of children to disaster. *American Journal of Psychiatry* **113**, 416–422.

BLUEBOND-LANGNER, M. (1978). *The Private Worlds of Dying Children*. Princeton, NJ: Princeton University Press.

BORDOW, S. and PORRITT, D. (1979). An experimental evaluation of crisis intervention. *Social Science and Medicine* **13A**, 251–256.

BOWLBY, J. (1961). Processes of mourning. *International Journal of Psycho-Analysis* **42**, 317–340.

BOWLBY, J. (1991). *Attachment and Loss*. Vol. III, *Loss: Sadness and Depression*. London: Penguin.

CANNADINE, D. (1981). War and death, grief and mourning in modern Britain. In: J. Whaley (Ed.), *Mirrors of Mortality: Studies in the Social History of Death*. London: Europa.

CAPLAN, G. (1981). Mastery of stress. *American Journal of Psychiatry* **138** (4), 413–420.

COHEN, P. (1990). Coping processes in well adjusted chronically ill patients on a paediatric ward. *Journal of Child Psychotherapy* **16** (2), 39–48.

EGBERT, L.D., BATTIT, G., WELCH, C. et al. (1964). Reduction of postoperative pain by encouragement and instruction of patients. *New England Journal of Medicine* **270**, 825-827.

EMANUEL, R., COLLOMS, A., MENDELSOHN, A. et al. (1990). Psychotherapy with hospitalised children with leukaemia: is it possible? *Journal of Child Psychotherapy* **16** (2), 21-37.

FREUD, A. (1952). The role of bodily illness in the mental life of children. *The Psychoanalytic Study of the Child*, vol. 7. Colorado: International Universities Press.

FREUD, A. (1967). Comments on trauma. In: S.S. Furst (Ed.), *Psychic Trauma*, p. 236. New York: Basic Books..

FREUD, S. (1915). Our attitude towards death. *The Complete Psychological Works of Sigmund Freud*, Standard Edition, Vol. 14, pp. 289-300. London: Hogarth Press.

FREUD, S. (1917). Mourning and melancholia. *The Complete Psychological Works of Sigmund Freud*, Standard Edition, Vol. 14, pp. 239-258. London: Hogarth Press.

FREUD, S. (1920). Beyond the pleasure principle. *The Complete Psychological Works of Sigmund Freud*, Standard Edition, Vol. 18. London: Hogarth Press.

FREUD, S. (1926). Inhibitions, symptoms and anxiety. *The Complete Psychological Works of Sigmund Freud*, Standard Edition, Vol. 20. London: Hogarth Press.

FREUD, S. (1933). Anxiety and instinctual life. *The Complete Psychological Works of Sigmund Freud*, Standard Edition, Vol. 22. London: Hogarth Press.

FRIEDMAN, S., CHODOFF, P. et al. (1963). Behavioural observations on parents anticipating the death of a child. *Pediatrics* **32**, 610-625.

GARLAND, C. (1991). External disasters and the internal world: an approach to understanding survivors. In: J. Holmes (Ed.), *Handbook of Psychotherapy for Psychiatrists*. London: Churchill Livingstone.

GOLDIE, L. (1985). Psychoanalysis in the NHS General Hospital. *Psychoanalytic Psychotherapy* **1** (2), 23-34.

GOLDSCHMIDT, O. (1986). A contribution to the subject of 'psychic trauma' based on the course of a psychoanalytic short therapy. *International Review of Psycho-Analysis* **13**, 181-199.

GORER, G. (1965). *Death, Grief and Mourning in Contemporary Britain*. London: Cresset Press.

HOXTER, S. (1986). The significance of trauma in the difficulties encountered by physically disabled children. *Journal of Child Psychotherapy* **12** (1), 87-102.

JUDD, D. (1989). *Give Sorrow Words – Working with a Dying Child*. London: Free Association Books.

KHAN, M. (1986). The concept of cumulative trauma. In: G. Kohon (Ed.), *The British School of Psychoanalysis – The Independent Tradition*. London: Free Association Books.

KLEIN, G.S. (1970). *Perception, Motives, and Personality*, p. 218. New York: Knopf.

KLEIN, M. (1935). A contribution to the psychogenesis of manic depressive states. In: *Love, Guilt, and Reparation*. London: Hogarth, 1975.

KLEIN, M. (1946). Notes on some schizoid mechanisms. In: *Envy and Gratitude*. London: Hogarth, 1975.

KRAEMER, S. (1990). *Won't they just grow out of it?* Film on child psychotherapy, Producer: Hannah Lowy. Child Psychotherapy Trust.

KRUPNICK, J. and HOROWITZ, M. (1981). Stress response syndromes: Recurrent themes. *Archives of General Psychiatry* **38**, 428-435.

KRYSTAL, H. (Ed.) (1976). *Massive Psychic Trauma*. New York: International Universities Press.

KRYSTAL, H. (1988). *Integration and Self-healing - Affect, Trauma, Alexithymia*. Hillsdale, NJ: The Analytic Press.

LAUB, D. and AUERHAHN, N. (1993). Knowing and not knowing massive psychic trauma: forms of traumatic memory. *International Journal of Psycho-Analysis* 74, 287-302.

LINDEMANN, E. (1944). The symptomatology and management of acute grief. *American Journal of Psychiatry* 101, 141.

McDOUGALL, J. (1974). The psychosoma and psychoanalytic process. *International Review of Psycho-Analysis* 1, 437-454.

McDOUGALL, J. (1978). Primitive communications and the use of countertransference. *Contemporary Psychoanalysis* 14, 173-209.

McDOUGALL, J. (1989). *Theatres of the Body*. London: Free Association Books.

MANDLER, G. (1982). The generation of emotion. In: R. Plutchik and H. Kellerman (Eds), *Emotion Theory, Research and Experience*. New York: Academic Press.

MARTY, P. and DE M'UZAN, M. (1963). La 'pensée operatoire'. *Revue Française de Psychoanalyse*. 27, 1345-1356.

MARTY, P. and DAVID, C. (1963). *L'investigation Psychosomatique*. Paris: Presses Universitaires.

MELTZER, D. (1981). The Kleinian expansion of Freudian metapsychology. *International Journal of Psycho-Analysis* 62, 177-185.

MENZIES-LYTH, I. (1989). The aftermath of disaster. In: *The Dynamics of the Social*. London: Free Association Books.

MONEY-KYRLE, R. (1956). Normal counter-transference and some of its deviations. In: *The Collected Papers*. Perthshire: Clunie Press, 1978.

NEMIAH, J. (1978). Alexithymia and psychosomatic illness. *Journal of Continuing Education in Psychiatry*, 39 25-37.

NEMIAH, J. and SIFNEOS, P. (1970). Affect and fantasy in patients with psychosomatic disorders. In: O.W. Hill (Ed.), *Modern Trends in Psychosomatic Medicine*, Vol. 2. London: Butterworth.

O'BRIEN, L. and HUGHES, J. (1991). Symptoms of post-traumatic stress disorder in Falklands Veterans five years after the conflict. *British Journal of Psychiatry* 159, 135-141.

PARKES, C.M. (1978). *Bereavement - Studies of Grief in Adult Life*. London: Pelican.

PYNOOS, R. and ETH, S. (1984). The child as witness to homocide. *Journal of Social Issues* 40 (2), 87-108.

SANDLER, J. (1967). Trauma, strain and development. In: S.S. Furst (Ed.), *Psychic Trauma*. New York: Basic Books.

SCHMALE, A. (1971). Psychic trauma during bereavement. In: H. Krystal and W. Niederland (Eds), *Psychic Traumatization*. Boston: Little, Brown & Co.

SKIPPER, J.K. and LEONARD, R.C. (1968). Children, stress, hospitalisation: a field experiment. *Journal of Health and Social Behavior* 9, 275-287.

SINASON, V. (1986). Secondary mental handicap and its relationship to trauma. *Psychoanaytical Psychotherapy* 2 (2), 131-154.

VAS DIAS, S. (1990). Paediatric psychotherapy: the development of a service in a general paediatric out patient clinic. *Journal of Child Psychotherapy* 16 (2), 7-20.

WILLIAMS, G. (1993). Dolorosi Legami ('Painful Links'). Italian Association of Psychoanalytic Child Psychotherapists Conference, Rome. Rome: Borla Publications.

WORDEN, J.W. (1982). *Grief Counselling and Grief Therapy: A Handbook for the Mental Health Practitioner*. New York: Springer.

YORKE, C. (1986). Reflections on the problem of psychic trauma. *Psychoanalytical Study of the Child*, vol. 14, pp. 221-236. New Haven: Yale University Press.

Chapter 5
Reflections of self:
the use of drawings in evaluating and treating physically ill children

Mary Sue Moore

Introduction

What use can we make of the drawings of children suffering from physical illness? How can we consider treatment issues in the light of this rich form of communication, without relying either on our own (often fallible) intuition or the child's (often limited) verbal capacity to explain his or her experience? Let us consider two examples, where a child's drawing revealed an understanding of his or her inner psychic and physical experience, and life history, to the benefit of those working with the child.

Stephen, a 10-year-old boy referred to an outpatient clinic for school problems – including extreme fatigue, muscle weakness and lack of ability to concentrate – was asked to draw a tree by his psychotherapist. His carefully constructed tree was rather bleak; it had branches but no leaves, and had a large knot-hole about a third of the way up the trunk. Asked about the tree, Stephen stated that it was 'about ten or twelve years old' and it 'got the knot-hole when a branch was sawed off when the tree was just four years old'. The therapist was aware that 90% of children draw live trees, with leaves and often fruit, and that this child's depiction was unusual (DiLeo, 1983). She was also aware that Stephen's father had died when he was four, and that knot-holes in trees are often thought to represent 'loss', so she was not surprised to hear the boy's story of his tree. What made the drawing most meaningful was the fact that the child was completely unaware of the parallel in his own life, and had no conscious intent to portray the traumatic impact of that aspect of his history and his experience.

Elizabeth, a 12-year-old girl under medical investigation for severe, re-current headaches, repeatedly drew a picture of a female face as a way of distracting herself from her physical distress. In each picture she added a bright red mark, in the hair, on one side of the head. Asked about it, she said: 'It's my hair clip'. This was the only use of bright colour in the drawing, and a careful observer might notice that despite this sincere explanation, Elizabeth never wore anything in her short hair. During testing in hospital, physicians administered a CT scan, and found a brain tumour growing in the spot where the 'red hair clip' had been drawn in each of the child's self-portraits.

These clinical vignettes touch on some of the most important aspects of drawings when used in clinical settings. There is a developmental order to drawings which can serve as an aid in considering points of trauma or conflict in the child's experience. The observer can learn from a drawing without the child having to be conscious of the communication being made. Equally true, an observer can never 'know' exactly what a child is representing or depicting in a drawing, in any absolutely objective sense. Drawings evoke the observer's projections, as surely as they reflect the artist's experience or intention. Drawings communicate both conscious and unconscious experience of self and the environment (which includes significant people in relationships with the artist) – sometimes with graphic accuracy, sometimes in symbolic form.

Useful texts are available which address the general topic of the drawings of individuals who have chronic or terminal illness (see Bibliography). Adding to that literature, this chapter will primarily consider children's depictions of the *human figure* and of *trees*, as these contain especially rich reflections of an individual's conscious and unconscious experience of illness. Two important areas will be mentioned only briefly, because they are well described elsewhere: ill children's use of colour in drawings, and the interpretation of spontaneous drawings done by children with chronic or terminal illness (Bach, 1969; Furth, 1988).

As a framework for the chapter, relevant aspects of child development theory will be considered, along with recent research describing multiple, differentiated human memory functions. Each constitutes an important parameter of an individual's potential capacity for expression of experience – both conscious and unconscious – through drawings. Meaning given to experiences of illness and medical interventions will be reflected in an individual's body memories, psychological defences and coping strategies, all of which are consciously and/or unconsciously expressed in the projective quality of drawings (Burgess and Hartman, 1993). Although the dynamics of self experience and the projective aspects of drawings are equally valid for adults and children alike, children's drawings will be given special attention here.

A combined focus on drawings of the *tree* and the *human figure* may seem an unlikely one, but in fact, since the original publication of the House–Tree–Person test in 1948 (Buck), it has been recognised that drawings of persons and trees share many projective aspects of the self (Hammer 1955, 1980, 1985; Mortensen, 1991). In addition, studies have shown drawings of trees and the human figure to be reliably robust and stable in presentation and re-testing (Vane and Kessler, 1964; Bolander, 1977; DiLeo,

1983), and to reflect powerful aspects of personality organisation which are particularly relevant in a study of the drawings of those suffering from chronic or acute illness (Furth, 1988).

As examples, I have selected particular drawings of a person or a tree, done by children who have a history of illness or medical interventions of a serious or chronic nature. Some examples will be from clinical case material, some will be based on empirical studies analysing and comparing a larger number of drawings to determine 'group norms'. When empirical studies were done, the drawings were collected in a standardised manner, scored on standardised scales, and rated by individuals who were unaware of the purpose of the study. I find that both clinical reports and statistical analysis provide important knowledge about the use of drawings in any setting, and I believe both have real value in our work with patients who have physical illness. The originals of all the drawings were done on A4 paper, and the representations here are often considerably smaller (up to one-third the size).

Finally, I close the chapter with practical suggestions concerning the collection of drawings.

Cognitive development and drawings

Given access to paper and drawing materials, once children have the hand–eye coordination and fine motor control needed to draw, they progress through an ordered sequence of developmental stages in drawing: from scribbles of various types which children begin around the age of two and two and a half, to more representational drawings, which adults can generally recognise, around the age of four or five (Goodnow, 1977; Gardner, 1980; Levick, 1983). These universal stages provide a firm basis for the use of drawings in studies which seek to understand children's growth and development (Mortensen, 1991). Drawings continue to reflect an increasing capacity to depict detail and perspective until and beyond adolescence. Specific, identifiable, developmental stages in the drawing of the human figure are evident in all children's artwork, regardless of the child's country or culture (Kellogg, 1969). This is so, because drawing capacity is a direct reflection of brain development, with cognitive capacity, emotional experience and motor control mediating the resulting production on paper (Hammer, 1980).

Due to the universal nature of the development of human figure drawing capacity in children, the drawing of a person has been used for many years as a measure of non-verbal cognitive or conceptual maturity. Goodenough developed a reliable method of scoring a human figure drawing, using a standardised scale to give credit for specific details and proportional aspects of the figure, which results in a 'developmental age' being derived for the human figure drawing (Vane and Kessler, 1964). In 1963, Harris revised Goodenough's scale (published originally in 1926), developing what has become the best known and most widely used scale for evaluating human figure drawings: the Goodenough–Harris Draw-A-Person Test (Harris, 1963). Recognising that the rate of development was different for boys and girls, and that drawings of women differ in the amount of detail typically depicted, Goodenough and Harris derived separate scales for drawings of men and women, by boys and girls. Other developmental scales used to assess children's human figure drawings have been devised following the general conceptual model of Goodenough–Harris (Koppitz, 1968, 1983; Naglieri, 1988), each validating the universal aspects of the stages of development in the drawing of the human figure (see Mortensen, 1991, for review).

Traditionally, the Goodenough–Harris scales have been used to calculate a 'non-verbal IQ score' by comparing a child's chronological age to the developmental age achieved on his or her drawing of a human figure. A drawing with a *developmental score* equal to the *chronological age* of the child will produce a ratio equal to 1, equivalent to a non-verbal IQ of 100, the average IQ expected for a child of that age. Although this use of the child's human figure drawing as a measure of intellectual and cognitive capacity was the primary focus in the early phase of drawing research, it has been apparent to many clinicians that personality factors were also elicited by the projective task (Hammer, 1980). Goodenough herself felt that a child draws what he or she *knows*, not simply what is seen. What has been experienced is projected onto the drawn human figure, house or tree (Burgess and Hartman, 1993).

Koppitz, in 1968, added another scale to the assessment tools available for use with children's human figure drawings. Her work took into account the child's age and sex, building on the Goodenough–Harris findings, but she added a clinical dimension, by determining 30 aspects or features in children's drawings which may indicate an unusual level of emotional distress. These items comprise the Emotional Indicators Scale (Koppitz, 1966, 1968), and have been shown to be reliable in test–re-test standardisations since that time (Ogdon, 1978; Moore, 1981; Koppitz, 1983).

In recent years, I have found the developmental age of a child's drawing also to be a possible indicator of a period in the child's life when there was traumatic stress which may have disrupted normal developmental patterns in some way (Moore, 1990). This has been shown to be a useful assessment tool in cases where a child has encountered emotional distress and/or trauma due to the experience of a medical diagnosis and/or treatment, or any type of abuse. The case accompanying Figure 5.1 illustrates one way in which a drawing's developmental age score can inform case workers about traumatic events that are still psychologically unresolved for a child.

Mark was five years old when he drew this 'person' as part of an evaluation for aggressive and tantrum behaviour in school. His human figure has no nose, and was drawn without a chest (or body). The giant 'mouth' is

Figure 5.1   Human figure drawing by Mark, a 5-year-old asthmatic boy.

filled with numerous vertical lines, and its boundaries coincide with the outline of the face in such a way that it covers the entire lower half of the face – giving the impression that it is not a mouth at all, but rather something which is solid and covers the area where a mouth would be. These features suggested the experiences of many asthmatic children – terribly constricted chest, mouth and nose covered or unable to get air.

Taking a history from Mark's mother, the psychotherapist learned that Mark had had physical and emotional difficulties from birth. Asthma was diagnosed at one year, and he had had several acute attacks leading to emergency hospitalisations. The physical experience of asthma, including traumatic hospitalisations, was thus communicated in the specific features and omissions of normal body parts that would be expected in a human figure drawing of a boy his age (see Koppitz, 1968, 'Expected Items').

Mark's psychotherapist also realised that the developmental level of Mark's tiny human figure drawing would be approximately that of a two and a half to three-year-old child. Keeping this in mind, at the end of the interview, the therapist asked whether there were any particular events that might have been especially traumatic for him or the family, when Mark was two or three years old. At that point, Mark's mother became very tearful, saying she had placed him in day-care when he was two, while she went back to work. He was there every weekday for several months before she found out from another parent that he (and other children) were being gagged as a punishment for screaming, and at times shut in a cupboard. Once this information came to light, Mark's mother joined the other parents in bringing legal action which resulted in the closure of the day-care centre. Nonetheless, she had been unable to resolve the intense guilt she felt for having placed him in such an abusive environment. She had not discussed her feelings with him, having been told by other parents that the children were 'really too young to remember, and if they weren't reminded, they would get over it a lot sooner'. (I will return to Mark's case when discussing drawings which reflect multiple traumas, especially chronic illness and abuse experiences, later in the chapter.)

Procedural memory and drawings

In this section I deal with conscious and unconscious, declarative and non-declarative memory. Drawings of the human figure, and symbolic self-representations such as trees, reflect both conscious self-perception and/or self-knowledge, and an unconscious, historical record of the actual experiences one has had – especially those of a traumatic nature, the memory of which may be totally beyond awareness (Hammer, 1955, 1980; Ogdon, 1978; Klepsch and Logie, 1982; Levick, 1983). An illustration of this aspect of drawings was produced by a young diabetic boy who, when asked to draw a person, drew a male human figure looking very distressed, with six heavily drawn 'pockets' on the otherwise only outlined clothing. A tiny dot or circle was drawn in each pocket. Looking at the drawing, it was striking that these pockets corresponded exactly to the areas on his body where he received repeated insulin injections. Realising that both actual experience and constructed meaning (including defences and copying strategies) are potentially being expressed in a drawing allows the psychotherapist to vary interpretive content appropriately, recognising that non-symbolic representations may reflect memories which cannot be verbalised at present.

As the observer of a drawing, it is never possible to identify *definitively* which aspects in a drawn human figure are conscious and reflectively created, and which are an unconscious representation of actual experience. Our role as subjective observer keeps the *interpretation* of drawings a joint communicative process involving both the viewer and the artist, rather than an objective science. However, we are increasingly able to understand the potential levels of representation in a drawing, with the aid of our patients and some very important new knowledge available to us from the areas of cognitive and neuropsychological science (Cohen and Squire, 1980; Grigsby, Schneiders and Kaye, 1991; Nadel, 1992; Schacter, 1992). These authors, and others, have articulated the idea that we hold memories in separate and not always verbally accessible parts of our mind (Johnson, 1985).

Recent neurocognitive research has introduced the idea of a multi-modular memory system in the brain (Grigsby, Schneiders and Kaye, 1991). A modular memory system allows certain aspects of experience to be recorded in interactive patterns as 'procedural' knowledge or memory. *Procedural memory* is one type of *non-declarative memory*, which records habit-forming and skill-learning experiences, but is generally not accessible to verbal recall. By contrast, knowledge held in *declarative memory* can be verbalised (Cohen and Squire, 1980; Grigsby, Schneiders and Kaye, 1991; Squire, 1992). In some instances, procedural and declarative memory are linked (for example, knowing *that* you know how to play draughts, *being able to tell someone else how to play* – including how you move each piece on the board and strategies for winning – versus *playing a game*, intent on winning), but various circumstances can result in a complete dissociation of the two memory capacities.

In a review of the literature on declarative and non-declarative memory systems, Squire (1992) offers the following definitions: '*Declarative* (or *explicit*) *memory* refers to memory for words, scenes, faces and stories. It is assessed by conventional tests of recall and recognition. It is a memory for facts and events.' (p. 232). In effect, '*It can be brought to mind and content can be declared*' (Cohen and Square, 1980, my emphasis).

By contrast, '*Nondeclarative* (including *procedural*, and *implicit*) *memory* is utilised in "nonconscious" abilities. This type of knowledge is grouped under several subsystems in the brain – the subgroups only having in common the fact that the memories cannot be consciously accessed and verbalised' (Squire, 1992, p. 233, my emphasis). Examples of the types of learning which might be considered 'non-declarative' are (1) the knowledge acquired during skill learning: motor skills, perceptual and cognitive skills; (2) habit formation; and (3) emotional learning or classical conditioning. In other words, *this knowledge is expressed through performance*, rather than recollection (Squire, 1992).

This has obvious relevance for human personality organisation, conscious and unconscious self-perception, and projectively, for the levels of self-knowledge reflected in drawings. Traumatic experience that is held in declarative memory can be consciously recalled, verbalised and represented in a drawing – whether related to illness, abuse or other events (Goodwin, 1982; Naitove, 1982; Kelley, 1985; Terr, 1988; Udwin, 1993). In some cases, knowledge of what occurred may be repressed or dissociated – *not* retrievable from declarative memory – due to its traumatic impact. The interactive process or body memories of traumatic experience *will be held in non-declarative memory* – in procedural form – *whether there is a declarative memory that is available or not*. These non-declarative, procedural memories *cannot be articulated* verbally but will be reflected in *behaviour* in specific ways, such as in habit formation.

A key feature of the various non-conscious mental processes is that 'nondeclarative memory can support *long-lasting changes in* performance *following a single encounter*' (Squire, 1992, my emphasis). A single near-death experience such as almost drowning, or the experience of a serious car accident, can alter our sense of self and behaviour for years – whether accessible to declarative memory or not. In most cases the experience of the event will be part of one's procedural, non-declarative memory for a lifetime (Terr, 1990).

Recent studies have shown that procedural memory is fully functional even in early infancy (Nadel, 1992; Hartman and Burgess, 1993). A child of

Figure 5.2   Human figure drawing by Maria, a 7-year-old girl born with an open skull.

four or five years, without conscious memory of a traumatic or life-threatening experience in the first year of his or her life, can accurately recreate the dynamic situation in play materials, when allowed the unstructured time to do so (Gaensbauer, 1993). A tendency to enact (Terr, 1988) or portray in drawings (Burgess and Hartman, 1993) 'unremembered' as well as remembered early traumatic experiences is well documented in research studying the behaviour and physiological sequelae of child survivors of traumatic events (Eth and Pynoos, 1985; review of literature in Udwin, 1993). A child's drawing *process*, as well as the drawing itself, may reflect *specific procedural memories* of early childhood trauma, as illustrated in Figure 5.2.

Maria's human figure was drawn beginning with an initial 'U' shape for the head, rather than the expected circle. After adding facial details and curved lines along the side of the head for hair, she drew a curling spring-like line connecting the top points of the 'U'. She placed a heart in one hand. Maria's unusual drawing process and choice of added features in her drawing took on communicative value later when the psychotherapist took a history from Maria's mother. She learned that Maria had been born with an 'open skull' which seriously endangered her life. Concerned physicians believed that surgery to repair the skull was necessary to save her life, but Maria's mother felt she would rather take her daughter to a 'faith healer' whom she trusted. Maria was in an extremely vulnerable state for many months, with the family in a state of high anxiety, but her mother reported with pride to the psychotherapist that Maria's skull did eventually become closed.

Self experience and human figure drawings

In a different vein, with equal applicability to the study of drawings and illness, Bollas (1992) has described two separate but complementary self experiences we regularly encounter in dreams. One is the experiential 'simple self', capable of deep experience but unable to view it other than unconsciously from within the (subjective) dream actor's position. The other is the 'complex self', capable of observing the actions of the simple self, reflecting upon that experience and interpreting events to give a logic and meaning to the experience. In Bollas's words, 'dream life mirrors an important feature of self experience, particularly that essential split between two subjective locations: the place of the *initiating subject who reflects upon the self*, and the position of *that subject who is reflected upon*, turned in a brief moment into *an object of thought*' (my italics) (p. 13).

The key to this 'dynamic reflexivity' is that as 'observed object' the experiencing self exists in an unconscious mode of being, fully unaware of any observed aspect of self. This loss of consciousness allows what Bollas refers to as the 'simple self' to be present, and as such – without the consciousness of reflective process about the self – this self experience is capable of certain self experiences that are meaningful, but escape full knowing. 'When we are "in" the dream, although as a simple self we do perceive dream objects, it is more to the point to say that *we endure deep experiences there*' (my italics). 'Recollection and interpretation of the dream's meaning do not necessarily address the essence of self experience gained by the simple self's movement through the events of the dream' (Bollas, 1992, p. 15). Full knowing is provided by the activity of the reflective or 'complex self' where an observing function is activated. Bollas believes we oscillate between these two psychic positions.

Some qualities of dreams are extremely similar to aspects of drawings, and undoubtedly utilise some of the same cognitive and affective memory systems in the brain (Moore, 1991). We might, in this context, substitute the word *drawing* for *dream* in the above paragraphs, and reach an important understanding of the rich texture of a human figure drawing. There will be reflections of a 'simple self experience', experiences which involved intense affect and proprioceptive knowledge of our body state (procedural) which may not be accessible to our 'complex, observing' self process – the declarative process by which we seek to verbalise and represent our experiences.

In the drawing of a human figure, the process of projection allows for both types of self experience to be reflected and both conscious and non-conscious memories to be accessed in the creation of the drawing. Although these two aspects of self are reflected in the drawing, we should hold in mind that the simple self experience *may not be symbolic* in nature. Body and simple self experiences held in non-declarative memory may be depicted graphically, placed physically on the body where the physical experience is held 'procedurally'. Aspects of the drawing held in declarative memory will represent the reflective self, an interpretive, symbolic expression of the meaning we have given to non-conscious, simple self and body

Figure 5.3   Human figure drawing by Carl, a 7-year-old boy with severe motor coordination and language difficulties.

experiences. Thus, a rich tapestry of self experience is interwoven in the final product, however sketchily it may be manifested.

Two examples of this dynamic interweaving of complex and simple self experience are shown in the drawings below. Carl's birth was difficult, and there was a brief period of asphyxia during which time he was reported to have 'turned blue'. At the time he was assessed for cognitive delays and/or mental handicap at the age of seven and a half, he showed severe gross motor control problems, and pronounced speech and language difficulties. His drawing of a human figure (Figure 5.3) was 'loosely' drawn; however, his facial expression reflected intense concentration during the task. Without words he produced this eloquent expression of the experience of living with major physical and language handicaps, feeling within himself a kind of double existence: a deeper self inside a physical self which is not coordinated or integrated with inner experience or intention. In the fist and punching arm, we might understand some of his anger that those on the outside respond to him and treat him as though that 'outer armour' were all of him!

A second example of simple and complex self-representation is a human figure drawing (Figure 5.4) by an eight-year-old asthmatic boy using a simple line across the chest as the only 'clothing detail'. The added detail to the face 'complicates' the nose, whereas the line across the chest may represent the physical experience of tightening of the muscles, and constriction, a hallmark of an asthma attack. Here we may see representations of the experience of constricted breathing and loss of air in a frightening asthma attack, held as non-declarative procedural memories. In addition, the line across the chest is reminiscent of the 'crossing warden' who protects children as they cross the road. Perhaps there is a symbolic representation of the wish to protect his life when it is endangered by a severe asthma attack?

I am suggesting here that the communicative quality reflected in young children's 'enactments' and 're-creation of the events' in play materials is in part an expression of the procedural, non-declarative memory of the child, and is equally represented in the projective drawings of the child. Simple and complex self experience are simultaneously reflected, as they might be in a dream. Life experience and self-perceptions are expressed on conscious and unconscious levels. This understanding of the complexity of communication in drawings allows many interpretations of specific features of the drawings of chronically or seriously ill children, as their physical, procedural memories will be represented – at times graphically, at times symbolically – alongside the symbolic representations communicating a more complex intrapsychic and interpersonal experience.

It is extremely important to remember that, as outside observers, we have no accurate way to determine which features of a drawing represent various levels of communication, and cannot claim to be able to differentiate aspects which reflect simple self experience, procedural memories or complex, declarative self-perceptions. We do know that some representations in a drawing will not be symbolic in nature, but will accurately reflect some body experience that is held without reflection in nondeclarative, procedural memory. Although we cannot know for sure which features are non-symbolic, we can hypothesise about the child's experiences, and can do further non-intrusive investigations along the lines of our hypotheses.

Trauma and illness

The impact of trauma on a child has been documented widely (Eth and Pynoos, 1985; Nir, 1985; Terr, 1990; Udwin, 1993), and both traumatic medical procedures and traumatic abuse experiences will be reflected in

Figure 5.4 Human figure drawing by a 7-year-old asthmatic boy.

children's drawings (Burgess and Hartman, 1993). There are similar representations in drawings of children who have a history of chronic medical difficulties and interventions, and those who have had a history of physical or sexual abuse (Goodwin, 1982; Wohl and Kaufman, 1985; Moore, 1990; Kaufman and Wohl, 1991; Burgess and Hartman, 1993). It is important to note that although we see identifiable evidence of traumatisation in drawings, *we cannot determine from a drawing alone* whether the cause was a medical intervention or procedure, or abuse experiences of one type or another. Simply recognising that the child has been traumatised will be of help in treatment planning in either case, while we obtain more information regarding the exact detail of the child's experience(s).

One of the experiences that will vary among children and, as a result, will be shown in various ways in their drawings, is the degree to which the child is traumatised by specific medical procedures. The number and type of 'anxiety indicators' on a drawing serve as one measure of the child's level of distress. Chronic heightened anxiety is commonly seen in children and adults who have traumatic histories (Eth and Pynoos, 1985; Udwin, 1993). Many sources confirm the finding that anxiety is commonly reflected by one or more of the following drawing features: excessive shading, small figures, rigidity in the drawing process, over-worked or heavily drawn lines in drawings (Koppitz, 1968; Hammer, 1980; Klepsch and Logie, 1982; Furth, 1988; Burgess and Hartman, 1993). As anxiety is reduced, the process of drawing becomes more spontaneous, excess shading is reduced and overworking of lines during the drawing process decreases.

The usefulness of drawings in evaluating and treating children in hospital has become more widely acknowledged in recent years. Nurses have found communication with children in oncology units to be enhanced by the use of drawings (Johnson and Berendts, 1986), and therapists can document shifts in a dying child's self experience with sensitive interpretation of a child's communication in drawings (Judd, 1989). Children's experience of hospitalisation is effectively reflected and communicated to care-givers through drawings (Allen, 1978; Broeder, 1985, cited in Wilson and Ratekin, 1990). Communication is enhanced when certain key qualities of a drawing can be discerned and utilised. One indicator that knowledge is held in declarative memory and can be verbalised is symbolic depiction in a drawing. Where experience is depicted graphically, verbal memories may not be available, and questioning or probing about traumatic experiences may be experienced by the child as intrusive and anxiety-provoking, if not re-traumatising. In such cases, interpretation of the child's affect and longing for protection in a frightening environment, will be more appropriate as an initial focus. When children initiate conversation about their experience – indicating that they are able to access declarative memory, either directly or by relating the story that accompanies a drawing – discussion of actual experience and more traditional psychoanalytic interpretation of events, and the symbolic meanings given to experience, become the goal of therapeutic treatment.

Repeated medical treatments for an allergy of unknown origin were ineffective in curing Christina's hives, which covered her limbs and trunk. Referred by her general practitioner to a psychotherapist at age five, she stated that 'she knew where her pain was, because she could see it in her skin'. A history revealed that the hives began when Christina was placed in nursery school at the age of four, a year after her father had died of congenital heart failure. He died in hospital very suddenly having gone in for what he and his family had considered a routine check-up. Christina was told that he 'had not felt pain' and 'he was sorry he did not come again to see her, as he'd promised he would'. Christina's mother experienced extreme but unconscious anger at her young husband for leaving her with three young children, and when Christina showed extreme distress whenever her mother left her, mother felt intense guilt. Christina's drawing (Figure 5.5), at referral, would have been appropriate for a child of about four, and revealed her bodily preoccupation, especially with marks on her skin, and a diffuse, non-differentiated, body-image.

Work began around her experience of fear and terror at separation from her mother, and her need to 'know she will come back for me'. Christina vehemently denied any links made to her feelings about her father's sudden death two years earlier. Work with the mother took place in traditional psychotherapy, where her complex feelings about her children and her unresolved mourning for her husband were explored. As mother's unconscious rage and guilt became conscious, her ambivalence about her children's post-traumatic heightened dependency needs was reduced, and she was able to comfort Christina at times of separation during the day and at night.

Figure 5.5 Human figure drawing by Christina, 5 years, with hives.

Figure 5.6   Human figure drawing by Christina, 5 ½ years; hives have disappeared.

When Christina found she could ask for and receive comfort from her mother, the hives disappeared. She began to move in her own therapy to work on feelings of guilt and responsibility for her father's death. This included confusion about his having died when he had 'not felt pain'. She was able to ask how her father 'got the hole in his heart'. She wondered very anxiously whether she herself 'had shot him one time'. At this point, her human figure drawings changed dramatically, and showed age-appropriate body awareness and identity (Figure 5.6).

Christina's second human figure clearly indicates that she still experienced anxiety about her skin (heavily shaded arms and legs), and her defences against feelings of abandonment raised fears about her aggressive impulses ('muscles' and 'big arms'). We might speculate that the inclusion of flowers on her dress is a symbolic expression of her oedipal fears and wishes regarding her relationship with her father and mother prior to her father's death (when she was three). These unconscious feelings may have been masked, initially, by more graphic, concrete (and age-appropriate for a four year old) concerns about illness and death, as her original undifferentiated human figure drawing masked the body and gender of the figure.

Multiple traumas: illness and abuse

In some cases, a child has a severe illness and has experienced some other type of trauma – perhaps physical or sexual abuse – which is also reflected in the characteristics of the drawing. Many aspects of a drawing may be multi-determined. One particular feature may represent both a graphic level of non-declarative memory or experience, and symbolise complex meaning given to declarative knowledge. When we see something that appears to be symbolic to us, it may be more than that – it may be a graphic re-presentation of an unconscious procedural memory from early childhood and/or a repressed memory about something which the child is denying, in order to reduce the current state of anxiety.

Earlier I discussed the drawing of five-year-old Mark, shown in Figure 5.1. Using the developmental level of the drawing as a clue, his psychotherapist helped his mother to discuss very traumatic abuse experiences he had had at the age represented in the drawing. Mark's psychotherapist knew that his abuse history included having been gagged and locked in a cupboard, and she quickly saw that his drawing graphically reflected this experience – both procedurally and declaratively. It was also expressive of his experience of asthma since infancy.

It is crucial that we do not assume to 'know' all that or 'exactly what' a drawing 'means' even when one hypothesis has been confirmed by other sources of information. What a loss it would have been for Mark and his mother, if his therapist, receiving this particular drawing, knowing his referral problem had been tantrums and aggressive behaviour, had simply interpreted the 'large mouth' and 'big teeth' as symbols of his aggressive impulses. (Which they may very well have been, *in addition to* the other non-symbolic levels of expression we have discussed.) We do ourselves and our patients a disservice when we bring closure to our exploration of meanings in a drawing relying on any one particular theory rather than a knowledge of the multiple levels of human communication.

David's case provides us with another poignant example of the complexity of cases where chronic illness and abuse are both part of the child's history. This child was seen in a family therapy setting within a child guidance clinic. David was the identified patient, brought because of aggressive acting out at school and at home, including uncontrolled fits of rage. He was nine years old, and very small in stature. His impulsive, restless behaviour seemed to reflect extreme anxiety. Asked to make a drawing of a person, he drew a tiny (under 2 inches) outline of a human shape, with eyes, but no mouth or nose (Figure 5.7a). He put a hat on it. Asked to draw a figure of the opposite sex, on a separate paper, he drew an almost identical figure with eyes but no nose or mouth; however, this one was twice the size of the first, without a hat, but with eyelashes (Figure 5.7b). He said that 'that was the best he could do'.

Initial interviews with David's mother revealed that he and his brother had a rare genetic disease that they had inherited from their mother: a progressive degenerative disease of the teeth and gums, which is carried by females but only manifested in males. The disease would cause all David's teeth to decay, necessitating surgery and replacement with false teeth by the time he reached adolescence. He had already had several traumatic trips

Figure 5.7   Male and female human figure drawings by David, 9 years, with gum disease.

to the dentist, and was well aware of his illness and the painful aspects of his future tooth loss. Mother was aware of feeling extreme guilt for passing on the disease to her sons, as she had known she would do so if she had male children.

This in itself would be a rather straightforward explanation of David's highly unusual depictions of human figures without mouths. However, it turned out to be only part of the story conveyed in this child's drawings. On-going psychotherapeutic work with the family later revealed that David's father, a high ranking member in a fundamentalist religious sect, habitually battered his wife and children, and had threatened each of them with terrible retribution *if any one of them were ever to talk about* the physical abuse they experienced. When this information came to light, it made clear a second powerful determinant of the highly unusual lack of a mouth on this child's drawings. If he had no mouth (and mother had no mouth) neither could run the risk of saying something which would bring destruction on the entire family.

Developmental stages in children's human figure drawings

Although there are no validated scales that can be used to evaluate the developmental age of human figure drawings of children under the age of five, many authors have described the earliest stages in the development of drawings of the human figure in very similar terms (Kellogg, 1969; Goodnow, 1977; Thornburg, 1977; Gardner, 1980; Levick, 1983; Moore,

1990; Mortensen, 1991). Between the ages of two to two and a half and five, all children progress through three or four more or less universal stages in the development of the drawing of a person. In part, the reason that no more specific, standardised scale exists is that children's development in those years is so varied, with lags and spurts in various skills and sensory modalities, with a great diversity in what is considered normal for boys and girls at any particular age. By the age of five, differences in rates of normal development have become stabilised within narrower parameters – particularly in the areas of fine motor skills, language and cognition, and capacity to use and reproduce written symbols – making standardisation of assessment scales more feasible. A general overview of the major shifts in capacity to draw a person, in children between the ages of two and five, is given below.

Children's earliest graphic expressions are *scribbles*; innate pleasure in movement is one motivation, although children are obviously pleased that their efforts leave a visible mark on the environment. Between the ages of two and three years, scribbles become more skilful, and designs of whirls, zigzags and lines are produced. However, it is still pure play with little accommodation to reality and little control over what the pencil might produce.

Some time after the age of three, children begin to label their scribbles. This transitional stage falls between scribbling and representation proper. Representation is verbal in character during this stage, until motor development catches up. Hilary, who, at the age of three and a half years, responded to the request to draw a person with a scribble picture extending over the whole page, gives us an example of this 'transitional' phase. She comments on her drawing: 'It's a person with a lot of hair – he is having a shampoo' (Thornburg, 1977, p. 5).

Soon after the child begins naming his drawings, he establishes greater control over his pencil and begins to create simple but *intentional representations of forms*. The straight line and circle or ellipse start to appear, freed from the whirls and scribbles that surrounded them before. In the circle the child finds an effective tool to create figures and objects. The circle can be the sun, a face, eyes, mouth, bellybutton, etc. The child has moved to the discovery of similarities and develops his first representational concepts. Of course, still hampered by immature motor control, he cannot coordinate the medium with his intentions. These early phases of development are followed by sequential stages in the drawing of a human figure, which continue into childhood and early adolescence.

Children's first and most frequent representation of a person is a large circle. During the next stage of development (usually between two and a half to three years of age), two vertical lines sprout downward from the circle, creating the 'tadpole human'. The child intends the two lines as an outline of the body as well as legs; the area between the lines is not perceived as empty space. Thus the bellybutton frequently found between these lines is not 'floating' there but is appropriately placed in the centre of the trunk from the child's point of view. Some time after the appearance of legs, arms are drawn at right angles to the circle or torso/legs. (An example of a 'tadpole person with arms' is seen on p. 117.)

An enclosed trunk appears on drawings of children who are approximately between four and a half years and five and a half years, creating the first 'complete person'. A horizontal line connecting the two verticals may show where the tummy ends. The square trunk arrived at by this method and the round trunk – where a second circle is placed under the head – are equally typical.

Once the trunk is enclosed, the human figure becomes increasingly sophisticated as limbs are drawn with two lines (rather than as 'sticks'), and clothing items, hair, feet and eventually a neck are added. The arms drop closer to the body, hands and later fingers are added, along with pupils in the eyes and nostrils in the nose. Details and proportions become refined and increasingly reality-oriented (Thornburg, 1977).

It is widely recognised that this ordered developmental sequence in the drawing of the human figure allows a child's intellectual maturity to be estimated when his or her drawings are studied. Long, widespread use of the developmental scales evaluating children's human figure drawings has confirmed the reliability and validity of the human figure drawing as a universal measure of cognitive abilities in children from 5 to 12 (Goodenough, 1926; Harris, 1963; Koppitz, 1968; Moore, 1978, 1981, 1990; Naglieri, 1988) or 15 years of age (Koppitz, 1983).

Trees and human figure drawings

Due to the universality of the development of the capacity to draw the human figure, the study of person-drawings in particular has been fruitful in understanding how our self-perception is or may be projected onto paper. The traditional definition of a projective device is an ambiguous or unstructured stimulus or series of stimuli which necessitate the subject being prompted by his or her own perceptions in order to give meaning to the stimuli. 'Symbolically, potent concepts such as house, tree, and person are saturated with the emotional an ideational experiences associated with the personality's development, and the drawing of these images compel projection on the part of the drawer' (Hammer, 1985).

With increasing maturity, the request to draw a person or draw the self is likely to evoke increasingly complex defences, produced by self-consciousness and increasing awareness of how the self is viewed by others. In adolescence and adulthood these defences are very well established, and result in increased conscious 'disguising' of the material being produced.

For this reason, the drawing of a tree becomes more and more important as a second source of a more symbolic projected self-image in older children, adolescents and adults. Few of us have well-developed defences regarding the drawing of a tree!

Clinical experience suggests that it is easier for a person to attribute more conflicting or emotionally disturbing negative feelings to a drawn tree than to a drawn person, because the former feels less close to a self-portrait (Hammer, 1955, 1985; Bolander, 1977). Although there have been no studies showing 'developmental stages' in children's tree drawings, several authors refer to 'commonly seen' characteristics in trees drawn by children of various ages. Koppitz (1968) refers to the 'apple or fruit bearing tree' which is common among five- to six-year-old children, and DiLeo (1983) interprets the drawing of an animal in a hole in a tree as a reflection of impulses which are within the conscious awareness of the child, but are being kept under control. Children draw a live (as opposed to a dead) tree 85–90% of the time (DiLeo, 1983). Hammer (1985) articulates the similarities and differences in communication of self-perceptions in adult drawings of trees:

> As to the tree and the person, both these concepts touch that core of the personality which theorists, notably Paul Schilder (1935) have labeled the body image and the self-concept. The drawing of the tree appears to reflect the subjects' relatively deeper and more unconscious feelings about themselves whereas the drawn person becomes the vehicle for conveying the subjects' closer-to-conscious views of themselves and their relationship with the environment . . . . The tree, a more basic, natural entity has been found to be a more suitable symbol to project the deeper personal feelings, feelings about the self residing at a more primitive personality level than what is considered the norm. The subject's methods of dealing with others and feelings toward them, are more apt to be projected onto the drawn person.   (p. 138)

Trees provide us with a powerful 'container' for our projections of self experience and defensive organisation. Data from normal children's drawings show that trees are not only usually drawn as live, but are also drawn with leaves and fruit, birds' nests, animals living inside, etc. Children who have had experiences with rejecting or abusive parents or who have been in other abusive environments, may draw pine trees with sharp needles, or palm trees with their spiky branches and sharp, thickly armoured trunks. Violet, a seven-year-old child from an abusive family, diagnosed with a dissociative disorder, drew a simple house and stick figure, next to a large tree with deep horizontal gashes across the trunk between the ground and the leafy top (Figure 5.8). She labelled the heavy marks on the tree trunk 'scars'. She spontaneously added that she had 'made the scars into places where she would put her feet' when she was climbing the tree, 'to get into the top, where I can hide for a long time, and no one can find me'.

Figure 5.8   House-tree-person drawing by Violet, 7 years, dissociative disorder.

This drawing illustrates Hammer's statement (1985) describing the portrayal of emotional (and I would add physical, actual) trauma 'by scarring the drawn tree's trunk, and truncating its branches'. Hammer believes that such a depiction is much more likely than the 'mutilation of the drawn person's face and body and similar damaging of the drawn person's arms' (p. 138). It is my belief that the child's heavy shading of the person's clothing – especially the heavy pencil pressure used in drawing lines across the shirt – may represent repressed memories of physical abuse, reflected without conscious awareness, from the child's procedural memory.

Findings from studies of children with chronic illness also shed light on the use of the tree as a projective measure. Drawings of trees were collected from diabetic children in a London teaching hospital. The trees drawn by these children had several surprising features in common, and differed from what one would expect of normal children: the trees consistently bore broken branches, showed leaves or branches falling, or were described by the child as 'dead or dying' (Figure 5.9).

The striking and highly unusual commonality of these children's trees reflected what appeared to be a shared experience of the traumatic impact of receiving the diagnosis of diabetes, and beginning the anxiety-provoking and painful insulin treatment process. One child told the evaluator, 'This is a live tree, but it has just been told it has Dutch Elm disease and it will be cut down at the base tomorrow'. Perhaps the characteristics of the tree draw-ings reflect something of the 'shortened life-span expectation' that has been documented in traumatised children (Eth and Pynoos, 1985; Terr, 1988, 1990; Udwin, 1993).

Cindy: a diabetic case study

In 1992, a child psychotherapist in Melbourne, Australia, contacted me to relate the following story of the use of drawings in the

Figure 5.9   Tree drawing by a 13-year-old diabetic boy.

treatment of a diabetic girl. The child was already in psychotherapy when her therapist learned of the unusual characteristics seen in the London diabetic children's tree drawings. Cindy was a 10-year-old diabetic girl referred to a large Australian paediatric hospital, due to her endocrinologist's concerns about her severe and prolonged grief reaction to the diagnosis of diabetes. Her symptoms were the most extreme he had seen.

A history revealed that Cindy was seven years old at the time of diagnosis, which came just a few months after the sudden and unexpected death of her maternal grandfather. Her mother's family were very close both emotionally and geographically, living a mile apart on the same farm property. From the family's description, the maternal grandmother's reaction to her husband's death had also been severe. Maternal grandmother was still significanty depressed – in a state of 'learned helplessness' – remaining very dependent on Cindy's mother for emotional support and day-to-day care. During the three years post-diagnosis, Cindy had become more and more reluctant to go to school. She emphatically wailed that she was dumb and, in order to stay at home, claimed daily that she suffered numerous aches and pains. In the few months preceding referral, she had attended school on only two occasions.

Cindy presented as a solid, but immature girl. On reflection, she seemed much more like a seven year old (her age at diagnosis and family crisis) than a ten year old. She was friendly and talkative throughout the assessment with a clinical psychologist on the hospital staff, who continued to work with her in a combination of individual and family therapy. Due to the long distance the family needed to travel to the hospital, short-term, time-limited psychotherapy was planned.

Coinciding with Cindy's time in psychotherapy, her psychotherapist attended a workshop on the use of drawings in assessment
of children with physical illness. Although past the assessment
phase, she wondered whether she could use the technique therapeutically as part of the psychotherapy. In the next individual
therapy session, she suggested that Cindy draw a tree. As a large
majority of the diabetic children in the London sample had drawn
dead or dying trees with broken branches, Cindy's psychotherapist
found herself 'expecting' to see a dead tree drawn. Instead, Cindy
drew what appeared to be a live tree.

When asked if there were a story about the tree, Cindy related the
following: 'It's the tree in our front yard. It's half broken. The big
storm knocked half of it over. Now, Mum and Dad are fighting
about what to do with it. Mum wants to cut it down, and Dad wants
to let it live.' Cindy's psychotherapist reflected: 'I wonder if it's a bit
like the battle inside you. One part feels dead and the other parts
want to be allowed to live and start growing again.' Cindy quietly
nodded.

Following this session, Cindy seemed less internally conflicted
and anxious and started going to school without difficulty. It was as
if the intervention, while highlighting her dilemma, acted as a
freeing device. In the following family session, all members were
happier about Cindy, but they informed the psychotherapist that
Cindy's brother James had hurt his leg so *he* was now at home. This
information was used to help the family think about the need for
one family member to stay at home to look after mother and
grandmother. In response to the psychotherapist commenting out
loud on how worried the family seemed to be about Cindy's
mother, everyone began to cry. Another family session followed,
focusing on how the mother could convince the family she was OK.
Focus had shifted from Cindy to her mother. Follow-up three
months later found Cindy settled back at school, her brother's leg
healed and her mother starting part-time work.

A sun in human figure or tree drawings

Along with trees and houses, drawings of the *sun* are apt to be clinically
significant in children's drawings. At the age of five or six they are very
normal: most children include a sun in one upper corner or the other of a
house or person drawing. After that age, suns are not as common, and by
the age of nine or ten, they are considered 'uncommon' in children's
drawings. Clinically, drawings of the sun are thought to represent a protective figure – most often a parent – or an emotionally significant figure in
the life of a child. At the age children start school, they may be leaving home

for the first time and spending a substantial amount of time in the company of other non-parental authority figures. In this context, the drawing of a sun in the corner of a picture can reflect the child's sense of being 'watched over and protected' by the internal parental object, who replaces the actual object in the child's experience away from home.

Later, in latency, a smaller, whole (round) sun is more common than the 'part object' sun drawn in the corner of the page. Due to this developmental progression in sun drawings, the larger a sun is drawn, or when in the corner of the page (partial view) rather than a circle, the greater the likelihood that a tendency toward dependency on the parent – of the kind that would be considered normal in a five- or six-year-old child – is being expressed. In some cases the drawing of an inappropriately large sun over a house, tree or person can be a reflection of an overprotective parent in the child's life.

Figure 5.10   House-tree-person drawing with sun, by Richard, an 8-year-old boy born prematurely.

Obviously, a child who is ill from infancy, or who has a chronic or terminal illness, is likely to be more dependent on his or her parents for help in managing the illness, or coping with medical procedures. Here we might expect to see a larger sun drawn, especially if the medical diagnosis occurred when the child was five or six years old. In other cases, parents whose child is ill from infancy may have difficulty letting the child become less dependent as he or she matures, and an enmeshed or overprotective parent–child relationship may result. I believe Richard's drawing illustrates just such a case (Figure 5.10).

Richard
During assessment in a mental health clinic, Richard, a frail-looking boy of eight, drew a picture of a house, a person and a tree. He added a sun with rays that filled almost half the page. Scribbling heavy pencil lines on both sides of the tree trunk, he commented:

'This green stuff is moss and algae'. He went on, spontaneously:
'What happens is, it's always raining around there but with that sun,
that green stuff grows all over the tree'. The 'person' in Richard's
drawing was only half an inch tall, but a 'flower' (slightly larger than
the person), grew out of the algae-covered side of the tree. He
placed a small 'animal' in a large knot-hole on the tree. He commented that he didn't know 'what kind of animal it was, but it had a
home there, and was protected from the rain'. I felt these were
hopeful signs.

When I met Richard's parents I learned that he had had many
physical difficulties from the time of his premature birth. He had
respiratory and eating difficulties as an infant, was colicky, allergic
'to most foods' and slow to learn to speak. His mother stated
immediately that she had inadvertently become pregnant at the
point when the couple had finally decided to separate, after three
years in a very unhappy marriage. Each parent felt so guilty about
his difficult birth and on-going physical difficulties that they felt
obligated 'for Richard's sake' to stay together. When I met them
eight years later, they had no remaining personal or intimate
relationship as a couple, and were both extremely depressed.
Richard's mother cried much of each day, and his father adopted a
rigid 'Let's always look on the bright side!' attitude to cope with his
own internal despair. Richard's experience was of being simultaneously smothered and drowned and inappropriately restricted
physically.

His tiny 'person' – a conscious self-portrayal – was a direct
contrast to his unconscious self expression reflected in the large
tree, almost centre-stage on the paper. Here we see his procedural
self-knowledge, as the object of constant physical and medical
attention from each of his parents and many doctors. During
psychotherapy sessions with Richard and his family I learned that
he had 'never smiled until his little sister was born'. Five years
younger, his sister was an active and affectionate child, his closest
companion, and his 'best friend'. We might wonder about that
'flower' growing out of the algae on the tree!

Suns and unmourned loss, or bereavement

An additional meaning may be ascribed to a small, circular sun when it is
placed directly above a specific person in a drawing: it may represent the
unmourned loss or bereavement of a significant person – often a parent – in
that person's or the child's life. An example of this special use of 'sun'
depictions is the drawing of a sun over one parent in a kinetic family
drawing. An eight-year-old girl drew her family in a psychotherapy session

after the resolution of an acrimonious divorce where mother was granted sole custody, and father was not allowed access. She asked to draw two pictures of her 'families'. In one picture, she drew herself standing outside her home, with a large sun (quarter circle) placed across the upper corner of the page, over the house. On the second page, she drew her father, naming him as 'my dad who I can't see any more'. Above her drawing of her father, she carefully placed a small round sun. The content of the session was directly connected to the child's sense of loss of her father – 'almost like he died'.

An elaboration of this theme in work with children with physical illness is seen in the placing of a small circular sun over a self drawing done by a child with a terminal illness (Judd, 1989). In this situation (as in the case of a girl with a serious congenital heart defect who habitually drew herself with a small sun over her head), we might consider the 'personal sun' as a representation of anticipatory mourning by the child who is aware that he or she will not live much longer, and, simultaneously, a representation of the child's expected loss of her parents who will be 'gone' when she has died.

Spontaneous drawings and the use of colour

Formal cognitive and developmental scales require a standard administration procedure to ensure comparability of drawings obtained across time and in various settings. Drawings must be done in lead pencil in order to allow a high degree of detail in the child's portrayal, as the scale scores are based on the number and quality of details included in the human figure drawing. Coloured pencils or felt tipped pens, due to the flow of ink or the softness of the coloured pencil leads, may obscure drawn elements or features which are essential scoring details. These requirements in administration are well documented in basic texts on the use of drawings (Harris, 1963; Koppitz, 1968, 1983; Ogdon, 1978; Naglieri, 1988).

However, children's *spontaneous* drawings almost always use colour, and are potent projective communications of the child's affective state, fears, joys, concerns about physical health, relationships with family members, and so forth, with an intended receiver in mind. In this way, the creation of spontaneous drawings in psychotherapy is very similar to the creation of dreams. Dreams inhabit the 'intermediate area' (Winnicott, 1971), a third area, reflecting both experiential and reflective self states, that paradoxically allows a psychic sense of actual space and is composed of objects that have actuality but which also signify aspects of the subject's inner world (Bollas, 1992). I am suggesting that drawings, like dream material, co-habit this paradoxical area.

Thus, such drawings have a very different purpose from those produced in compliance with the request from a therapist or other person. As in a dream, unconscious expression utilises every mental resource available to create meaning, and form, content, colour are intertwined and manipulated 'ruthlessly' – to use Winnicott's term for the use of the transitional object (Winnicott, 1971). In the service of communicating self experience, ill children's drawings may include brightly coloured blue or red trees, or flowers may become black, taller than houses and people, or embedded in other objects (Bach, 1969; Furth, 1988).

This material needs to be utilised by the child and psychotherapist, just as the communication of a dream might be – personally, intimately, searching for the unique meaning given a form or colour by the individual child. In this way, the somatic experience of the child is provided symbolic expression – something which may not have been possible previously. McDougall calls some somatic expressions 'dreams which are not dreamt' (McDougall, 1989). Spontaneous drawings can projectively bridge the gap between the world of somatic experience and the dream.

Two authors have produced substantial texts based on years of sensitive work with individuals who are chronically or terminally ill. Their thorough analyses of spontaneous drawings and use of colour by children with physical illness are extremely valuable resources (Bach, 1969; Furth, 1988). Others have written with fresh insight about various aspects of work with children with cancer, and issues around the experience of hospitalisation (Allen, 1978; Broeder, 1985; Johnson and Berendts, 1986; Wilson and Ratekin, 1990). Psychotherapy with children who are ill would be enriched by the use of drawings as illuminated by these authors.

An example of a spontaneous drawing which was a powerful communication arising out of material in a psychotherapy session is shown in Figure 5.11. The drawing was created using coloured felt tip pens, but is reproduced here in black and white.

Figure 5.1 Kinetic family drawing with rainbow by Betty, a 10-year-old girl with panic attacks and multiple food allergies.

Betty

Betty, while talking to her therapist about her family, drew four people in a row. They are careful likenesses of her two sisters, her mother and herself. She is the second from the left, and drew herself with a 'heart-shaped hole' on her chest, then added many 'freckles' within which the dot for her nose became obscured. She has a 'rip' in one leg of her trousers. At this point in her drawing, Betty's mother entered the therapy room. Greeting her mother, Betty quickly added 'ground' for the figures to stand on, and a rainbow which encloses the entire family. The rainbow ended underground in a circle of gold.

Betty's history included severe croup and bronchial infection from infancy, with food allergies developing and increasing as she matured. At the time of therapy she was being treated for a mild school phobia which had developed when mother and father were divorced the previous year. Mother was agoraphobic, and severely depressed (with suicidal ideation) after the divorce. She commented that Betty had always been the child who took care of her, 'made things better'.

Particularly striking to an observer, I think is the tightly enclosed space inside the rainbow. There is no room for growth or development. One wonders whether aspects of Betty's panic attacks – possibly 'air hunger', inability to breathe and a pounding heart – are portrayed in her figure with 'covered nose' and a 'heart-shaped hole in the chest'.

Procedure in collecting drawings

If at all possible, it is best to be present when the child is doing the drawing. It is only in this way that one can be certain *where* on the human figure, house or tree, the child *starts* the drawing. Very frequently a child will start with a part of the body (or the symbolically equivalent part of a house or tree) which has psychic significance for him or her. It is possible to use this as a reliable guide to unconscious meaning in a child's drawing, precisely because there is a universal standard not only for what is 'typically' drawn by a child of a certain sex and age, but also for the process of creating a human figure drawing. Approximately 85% of human figure drawings are begun with the head and face, and completed from the head down (Koppitz, 1968, 1983). If a child starts his or her drawing with the feet or the genital area, or with one hand, he or she is telling us something about the importance of that part of his or her body, and is sharing something of his or her experience in relation to it.

When watching a child draw a person, the *direction that lines are drawn* is also significant. In one case, a young boy drew a figure with stick legs and both of the legs were drawn from the ground up into the figure. The figure was drawn 'floating' above the ground, and then the legs were drawn, heavily and overworked, repeatedly upward, as though the act of drawing the 'legs' up into the figure already on the page were a *re-enactment* of something having been 'stuck, or pushed' into the lower half of the boy's body. This becomes significant because we know that most children (and adults) draw the details of the human figure from the head down and draw each limb starting from the body which has already been created, directing the lines of the limbs away from the body.

Of course, seeing this, we are not able to tell *why* the child has started with an unusual part of the body, or reversed the expected direction of the lines drawn. There can be many reasons for this. The fact that it happens so rarely in the children's drawings tells us that it is *unusual* – not that it is pathological – and that it very probably does have some meaning for the child, perhaps a totally unconscious one. Very young children (four years and under), just beginning to draw or write, may alternate directions while learning the fine motor skills involved in the use of paper and pencil. It is the habitual and emphasised reversal of the 'usual' direction in drawing that takes on significance for the evaluator.

In the case of the boy above, obtaining a history from the parents revealed the fact that he had had a chronic problem with constipation, and daily enemas had been prescribed by his paediatrician. This procedure, which the child resisted and which involved significant physical and emotional distress for the boy and his parents, had continued for many weeks. This information allows us to consider one *possible meaning* which can accompany the reversal of direction in lines drawn on a human figure: the child may be reflecting a 'procedural' memory which involved physical penetration of the body. We can see the possible implications for other 'unusual directionality' in lines drawn on the human figures of children who have experienced multiple medical interventions, as well as physical or sexual abuse.

Appendix: using children's drawings for assessment purposes

The following guidelines cover those articulated in the standard texts (Harris, 1963; Koppitz, 1968, 1983; Ogdon, 1978; Naglieri, 1988):

1. When having a human figure drawn, encourage the child to do the 'best' drawing he or she can, but if the child seems anxious about lack of drawing skill, reassure him or her that you are interested in all drawings, not because they are 'art' but because only that child can do his or her drawing . . . no one else could create it! Creating a drawing for another (in this case for the evaluator) is giving that person a gift no one else can give.

2. Do not give any 'suggestions' for the drawing, even if the child asks for help. When they are drawing a person, just encourage them to 'do the best drawing of a person they can'. Whichever task they are attempting – drawing a person, house, tree or their family (a kinetic family drawing) – any way they choose to do it is fine.

3. Often children ask to draw a favourite picture they 'like to draw' – such as a car, or spaceship, or gun, or an animal. If you are planning to use one of the scoring systems to evaluate their drawings, it is best to have them draw a person first – let them know that 'after this' you'd like to have them do their 'favourite drawing' for you.

4. When a child has drawn something, you can talk to him or her about it to learn what they might be communicating to you in the drawing, such as, 'What's the story that goes with the drawing?'.

   However, questions *not* to ask are 'Why did you draw this thing?' or 'What is this thing?', 'Where are the (*missing body parts*)?'. These questions sound like a judgement about the quality of the drawing, and frequently make children feel self-conscious. When this happens, they often stop communicating about the drawing, because they are afraid of not giving the 'right' answer.

   Some questions you might ask are: 'Can you tell me about your picture?', 'I'm interested in this picture – can you tell me what is happening here?'. You can also ask about specific people or things in the picture by asking how the figure might be thinking or feeling, how old the person (or tree, or animal) is, what might happen next in the picture, when the person (or animal) feels happiest, and/or saddest.

5. Never criticise children's drawings or their answers to your questions. Statements like 'Shouldn't this person have arms?' are shaming to the child. Remember they are telling you about their experience of them-selves as well as the drawing.

Acknowledgements

Many thanks to my colleagues from the USA, UK and Australia who have shared with me the drawings of children with physical illness. They are: Gail Arnold, Children's Hospital, Melbourne; George Moran, who collected the London diabetic children's tree drawings (and whose untimely death sadly preceded the publication of this chapter); Sue Jeter, Boulder County Mental Health Center, Colorado; Charlene Slover, Adams County Mental Health Center, Colorado; Lorna Gillio, Children's Health Council, Stanford, California; and Mia Beaumont, Educational Therapist, London.

Bibliography

ALLEN, J.M. (1978). Influencing school-age children's concept of hospitalization. *Pediatric Nursing* **5** (2), 26–28.

BACH, S. (1969). *Acta Psychosomatica: Spontaneous Paintings of Severely Ill Patients*. Switzerland: Geigy S.A.

BOLANDER, K. (1977). *Assessing Personality Through Tree Drawings*. New York: Basic Books.

BOLLAS, C. (1992). Aspects of self experiencing. In: *Being a Character: Psychoanalysis and Self Experience*. London: Routledge.

BROEDER, J.L. (1985). School-age children's perceptions of isolation after hospital discharge. *Maternal–Child Nursing Journal* **14** (3), 153–174.

BUCK, J.N. (1948). The H-T-P Technique: A quantitative and qualitative scoring manual. *Clinical Psychology Monographs* **5**, 1–20.

BURGESS, A. and HARTMAN, C. (1993). Children's drawings. *Child Abuse and Neglect* **17**, 161–168.

COHEN, N.J. and SQUIRE, L. (1980). Preserved learning and retention of pattern-analysing skill in amnesia: Dissociation of knowing how and knowing that. *Science* **210**, 207–209.

DILEO, J. (1983). *Interpreting Children's Drawings*. New York: Brunner/Mazel.

ETH, S. and PYNOOS, R. (Eds) (1985). *Post-Traumatic Stress Disorder in Children*. Washington DC: American Psychiatric Press.

FINKELHOR, D. and BROWNE, A. (1985). The traumatic impact of child sexual abuse: a conceptualization. *American Journal of Orthopsychiatry* **55**, 530–541.

FURTH, G. (1988). *The Secret World of Drawings: Healing through Art*. Boston, MA: Sigo Press.

GAENSBAUER, E. (1993). Memories of Trauma in Infancy. A paper given at Vail, CO, Jan. 1993. Colorado Psychiatric Society Conference on Post-Traumatic Stress Disorder.

GARDNER, H. (1980). *Artful Scribbles*. New York: Basic Books.

GOODENOUGH, F. (1926). *Measurement of Intelligence by Drawing*. New York: Harcourt, Brace & World.

GOODNOW, J. (1977). Children drawing. In: J. Bruner, M. Cole and B. Lloyd (Eds), *The Developing Child Series*. Cambridge: Harvard University Press.

GOODWIN, J. (1982). Use of drawings in evaluating children who may be incest victims. *Children and Youth Review* **4**, 269–278.

GRIGSBY, J., SCHNEIDERS, J. and KAYE, K. (1991). Reality testing, the self and the brain as modular distributed systems. *Psychiatry* **54**, 39–54.

HAMMER, E. (1955). A comparison of H-T-P's of rapists and pedophiles: The dead tree as an index of psychopathology. *Journal of Clinical Psychology* **11**, 67–69.

HAMMER, E. (1980). *The Clinical Application of Projective Drawings*. Springfield, IL: C.C. Thomas.

HAMMER, E. (1985). The House-Tree-Person Test. In: *Major Psychological Assessment Instruments* pp. 135–165. Needham Heights, MA: Allyn & Bacon.

HARRIS, D.B. (1963). *Children's Drawings as Measures of Intellectual Maturity*. New York: Harcourt, Brace & World.

HARTMAN, C. and BURGESS, A. (1993). Information processing of trauma. *Child Abuse and Neglect* **17**, 47–58.

JOHNSON, J.L. and BERENDTS, C.A. (1986). The "We Can" weekend. *American Journal of Nursing* **86** (2), 164–166.

JOHNSON, M.K. (1985). The origin of memories. In P.C. Kendall (Ed.), *Advances in Cognitive-Behavioral Research and Therapy,* Vol. 4, pp. 1–26. New York: Academic Press.

JUDD, D. (1989). *Give Sorrow Words: Working with a Dying Child*. London: Free Association Books.

KAUFMAN, B. and WOHL, A. (1991). *Casualties of Childhood*. New York: Brunner/ Mazel.

KELLEY, S. (1985). Drawings: Critical communications for sexually abused children. *Pediatric Nursing* 11, 421-426.

KELLOGG, R. (1969). *Analyzing Children's Art*. Palo Altos, CA: Mayfield.

KLEPSCH, M. and LOGIE, L. (1982). *Children Draw and Tell: An Introduction to the Projective Uses of Children's Human Figure Drawings*. New York: Bruner/ Mazel.

KOPPITZ, E.M. (1966). Emotional indicators on human figure drawings of children: A validation study. *Journal of Clinical Psychology* 22, 313-315.

KOPPITZ, E.M. (1968). *Psychological Evaluation of Children's Human Figure Drawings (Ages 5-12)*. Orlando, FL: Academic Press.

KOPPITZ, H. (1983). *Human Figure Drawings of Middle School Pupils (Ages 11-14)*. Orlando, FL: Academic Press.

LEVICK, M. (1983). *They Could Not Talk and So They Drew*. Springfield, IL: C.C. Thomas.

McDOUGALL, J. (1989). *Theatres of the Body*. London: Free Association Books.

MOORE, M.S. (1978). *Frequency and distribution of Koppitz' emotional indicators on the human figure drawings of learning disabled children*. Unpublished Master's Thesis, California State University at Hayward.

MOORE, M.S. (1981). *Diagnostic implications in the human figure drawings of learning disabled children, aged 6-12*. US: Dissertation Abstracts International.

MOORE, M.S. (1990). Understanding children's drawings: Developmental and emotional indicators in children's human figure drawings. *Journal of Educational Therapy* 3 (2), 35-47.

MOORE, M.S. (1991). Dreams and drawings after trauma. Poster presented at Developmental Psychobiology Research Group meeting, May, Estes Park, Colorado.

MORTENSEN, K.V. (1991). *Form and Content in Children's Human Figure Drawings: Development, Sex Differences, and Body Experience*. New York: New York University Press.

NADEL, L. (1992). Multiple memory systems: What and why. *Journal of Cognitive Neuroscience* 4 (3), 179-188.

NAGLIERI, J. (1988) *Draw A Person: A Quantitative Scoring System*. Orlando, FL: The Psychological Corporation, Harcourt, Brace Jovanovich.

NAITOVE, C.E. (1982). Arts therapy with sexually abused children. In: S. Segroi (Ed.), *Handbook of Clinical Intervention in Child Sexual Abuse*. New York: Lexington Books.

NIR, Y. (1985). Post-traumatic stress disorder in children with cancer. In: S. Eth and R. Pynoos (Eds), *Post-Traumatic Stress Disorder in Children*. Washington, DC: American Psychiatric Press.

OGDON, D. (1978). *Psychodiagnostics and Personality Assessment: A Handbook*, 2nd edn. Los Angeles, CA: Western Psychological Services.

SCHACTER, D. (1992). Priming and multiple memory systems: Perceptual mechanisms of implicit memory. *Journal of Cognitive Neuroscience* 4 (3), 244-256.

SCHILDER, P. (1935). *Image and Appearance of the Human Body*. London: Kegan Paul.

STEMBER, J. (1980). Art therapy: A new use in the diagnosis and treatment of sexually abused children. In K. MacFarlane (Ed.), *Sexual Abuse of Children: Selected Readings*. National Center on Child Abuse and Neglect, US Government Publications.

SQUIRE, L. (1992). Declarative and nondeclarative memory: Multiple brain systems supporting learning and memory. *Journal of Cognitive Neuroscience* 4 (3), 232-243.

TERR, L. (1988). What happens to early memories of trauma? A study of twenty children under age five at the time of documented traumatic events. *Journal of the American Academy of Child and Adolescent Psychiatry* 27, 96–104.

TERR, L. (1990). *Too Scared to Cry: Psychic Trauma in Childhood*. New York: Harper & Row.

THORNBURG, S. (1977). Emotional indicators on the human figure drawings of public school children. Unpublished Master's Thesis, California State University at Hayward.

UDWIN, O. (1993). Annotation: Children's reactions to traumatic events. *Journal of Child Psychology, Psychiatry and Allied Discplines* 34 (2), 115–127.

VANE, J.R. and KESSLER, R. (1964) The Draw-A-Man-Test: Long-term reliability and validity. *Journal of Clinical Psychology* 20, 487–488.

WILSON, D. and RATEKIN, C. (1990). An introduction for using children's drawings as an assessment tool. *Nurse Practitioner* 15 (3), 23–25.

WINNICOTT, D.W. (1971). The location of cultural experience. In: *Playing and Reality*. London: Tavistock Publications.

WOHL, A. and KAUFMAN, B. (1985). *Silent Screams and Hidden Cries: An Interpretation of Artwork by Children from Violent Homes*. New York: Brunner/Mazel.

Chapter 6
The psychotherapeutic application of a dysregulation model of illness

Graeme J. Taylor

Introduction

Despite the historically important tie between psychoanalysis and psychosomatic medicine, very few clinicians nowadays choose to treat somatically ill patients with psychoanalysis or analytical psychotherapy. This disinterest may be attributed to the generally disappointing results of treatment outcome studies (Karush, Flood and O'Connor, 1977; Karasu, 1979), and to the theoretical limitations of Alexander's specificity theory (1950) and other early psychosomatic disease models on which the psychoanalytic approach has been largely based (Mendelson et al., 1956; Gitelson, 1959; L. Deutsch, 1980).

Although several psychoanalysts have proposed important and useful revisions to the psychoanalytic understanding of psychosomatic illness (see, for example, Marty, de M'Uzan and David, 1963; Nemiah and Sifneos, 1970; McDougall, 1974, 1989; Gaddini, 1977), they failed to integrate their concepts with advances in the biomedical sciences. During recent years, however, psychosomatic theorists and researchers have made considerable progress in devising a new integrative model which conceptualises many illnesses and diseases as disorders of psychobiological regulation (Taylor, 1987; Schwartz, 1989; Weiner, 1989). This dysregulation model offers the opportunity for a renewed involvement of psychoanalysis with somatically ill patients.

As I have described the development of the new model and reviewed the scientific data on which it is based in several earlier contributions (Taylor, 1987, 1992a,b), my aim in this chapter is to demonstrate the clinical application of the model. First, however, I will outline briefly how the dysregulation model differs from earlier psychosomatic disease models.

Earlier models were applied primarily to the 'classical' psychosomatic diseases and were derived largely from instinct theory and Freud's concep-

---

145

tualisation of psychoneurotic symptom formation (Alexander, 1950; F. Deutsch, 1959). Although these are multi-factor models that include important roles for biological and environmental variables, they employ a linear conception of causality (the so-called 'mysterious leap from the mind to the body') and promote the therapeutic technique of attempting to identify and resolve unconscious drive-related conflicts. In contrast, the dysregulation model is derived from general systems theory and a synthesis of convergent findings from developmental biology and the biomedical sciences (Weiner, 1975, 1989; Schwartz, 1983, 1989; Hofer, 1984, 1987; Pert et al., 1985; Blalock, 1989). Although at its inception the model encompassed the concept of intrapsychic conflict, I later extended the psychological dimension (Taylor, 1986, 1987, 1992a,b) by incorporating into the model recent theoretical developments in psychoanalysis and findings from infant-observational studies, in particular those pertaining to affects, object relations and the development of the self.

The essence of the new model is its conception of human beings as self-regulating cybernetic systems, each person being comprised of a hierarchy of subsystems that interface via the brain with the larger social system. The psyche is conceptualised not merely as the origin of conflicts that might produce prolonged states of emotional arousal with pathogenic effects on the body, but also as one component within the hierarchical arrangement of reciprocally regulating subsystems (Sander, 1987; Ciompi, 1991). A transition from health to illness or disease is likely to occur within this self-regulating system when there are perturbations in one or more components of the feedback loops, which lead to changes over time in the rhythmic functioning of one or more of the subsystems (Schwartz, 1983, 1989; Weiner, 1989). Perturbations can arise at any level in the system, from the cellular or subcellular level (as with viral infections, and variations in the expression of genes) to the psychological and social level (as with intrapsychic conflicts, attachment disruptions, affect arousal and loss of self-esteem) (Taylor, 1992b). Because the affected subsystem interacts with other subsystems, several physiological functions may become dysregulated and lead to somatic symptoms and, in some instances, also to changes in bodily structure.

Consistent with recent psychoanalytic opinions that somatically ill patients need a different approach from that required to understand and treat neurotic parts of the personality (McDougall, 1974, 1989; Krystal, 1982), the dysregulation model emphasises a psychoanalytic approach aimed at overcoming psychological deficits involving affect regulation and the maintenance of a stable sense of self. Such deficits are presumed to stem from early developmental deficiencies which are reflected in the patient's inner self and object representations, in the quality of current interpersonal relationships, and by impaired ego functioning. According to the model, psychoanalytic interventions may favourably influence health not only by enhancing the regulatory capacities of the patient's psyche, but also by modifying the reciprocal feedback which it has with other subsystems.

The dysregulation model obviously surmounts the outmoded distinction between 'functional' and 'organic' disorders (Weiner, 1989; Reynolds, 1990), and has a much sounder scientific foundation and wider clinical application than the earlier psychosomatic disease models. I will demonstrate the application of the model by describing the analytic treatment of a patient with spasmodic torticollis.

A case of spasmodic torticollis

The patient, whom I will call Tom, was 31 years of age when he first consulted me. Tom indicated that for almost seven months he had experienced involuntary spasms of his neck muscles that had resulted in sustained torsion of his head. This symptom was first noticed by some of Tom's friends, and he had initially attributed it to a minor head injury that he had received while playing football. Tom had consulted three neurologists and a specialist in physical medicine, who all made the diagnosis of spasmodic torticollis.

Although much of the early literature attempted to distinguish between 'organic' and 'psychogenic' forms of this disorder (Murphy and Chasen, 1956; Meares, 1971), the current consensus is that spasmodic torticollis is a *focal dystonia* caused by an abnormality in the basal ganglia which probably involves a dysregulation in dopaminergic and/or cholinergic pathways to the pre-motor and ultimately motor cortex (Besson et al., 1988; Owens, 1990). Indeed, while torticollis can be aggravated by emotional distress, empirical research has provided no evidence that the disorder is a form of conversion hysteria or that it is associated with any particular pre-morbid personality (Cockburn, 1971; Duane, 1988; Naber et al., 1988; Owens, 1990).

Tom's doctors had all given a poor prognosis, advising him that he had an incurable disease and should not have children because of probable genetic transmission of the disorder. These opinions were not entirely justified because, as with many other medical diseases (e.g. multiple sclerosis, ulcerative colitis), spontaneous remissions of torticollis sometimes occur, although relapses are usual (Friedman and Fahn, 1986). Tom had been treated medically with various combinations of muscle relaxant drugs and a beta-adrenergic blocking agent, but he had obtained minimal improvement. He had also failed to benefit from electromyographic biofeedback, which is sometimes of considerable help to patients with spasmodic torticollis (Korein and Brudny, 1976). Consequently, Tom became increasingly depressed and seriously considered committing suicide.

Upon his insistence that he needed psychiatric help, Tom was referred to me by one of his physicians with the request that I improve the patient's ability to cope emotionally and 'teach him to accept the illness'. We agreed to meet once weekly for psychoanalytic psychotherapy and see what we could accomplish. The entire treatment lasted for six years and was conducted with Tom seated diagonally across from me, a position I selected so that the patient needed to turn his head against the direction of the torticollis if he wished to face me directly.

In the early assessment sessions, I learned that Tom was the first-born child of lower middle-class parents who had married in their teens – mother was only 16 and father 18. He had two brothers and two sisters; there was no family history of dystonia or of major psychiatric disorder. Tom had been raised in a small country town, and at the age of 18 he decided to leave home and move to the city to pursue a career in journalism. He was currently working as a junior news reporter for a major daily newspaper, but had aspirations to do more creative writing. Although Tom described himself as a shy person, he had a steady relationship with a girlfriend, who was very supportive about his illness, as well as many male friends with whom he spent much time drinking beer.

Like many patients with spasmodic torticollis (Lal et al., 1979), Tom had discovered that alcohol produced transient improvement of his neck spasms. In the assessment sessions, I observed also that Tom had an essential tremor of his hands, a benign neurological symptom that often accompanies torticollis (Lal et al., 1979; Duane, 1988), and that he had developed a moderate scoliosis, suggesting that his dystonia might progress and produce more severe disability. Prior to becoming ill, Tom had been an avid baseball player and had won a trophy for his skills. He could no longer play sports, and felt extremely frustrated over his disability and by the embarrassment it caused him at work and in social situations.

The psychobiological–dysregulation model of disease incorporates the contemporary psychoanalytic view of the self as a complex open system (Sutherland, 1983; Grotstein, 1986), as well as the recent discovery that relationships can function as external regulators of biological as well as psychological processes (Hofer, 1984; Pipp and Harmon, 1987; Taylor, 1992b). Conceptualising Tom's illness within the framework of this model, I initially began (1) to assess the nature of his social relationships and their regulatory functions; and (2) to search for areas of primitive mental functioning that might signify disturbances in self-regulation (Sander, 1987).

The first lead in my psychoanalytic approach came from learning that Tom's closest male friend had been killed in a motor vehicle accident just one month before the onset of the torticollis. Although this sequence of events paralleled Engel and Schmale's (1967) findings with many physically ill patients, Tom's response to his friend's death had been primarily one of shock and grief rather than the classic 'giving up/given up' complex that these analysts conceptualised as the psychobiological state intervening between object-loss and the onset of disease. Nonetheless, I decided to analyse Tom's pre-existing relationship with his friend to determine the extent to which the friend may have functioned as an external regulator, helping to maintain narcissistic equilibrium in Tom.

It gradually became apparent that the friend had indeed been an important selfobject for Tom; he had been an *alter ego* figure with a much more confident and outgoing personality than Tom. In his presence, Tom was transformed from a self-doubting and somewhat insecure person into a rather confident individual who could express his feelings, assert his opinions, and even entertain other friends as he and his buddy sang duets at parties. At other times this aspect of Tom's personality was usually inaccessible. Tom could perceive certain desirable characteristics in his friend, and then, presumably via a merging fantasy and affirmative interactional feedback, achieve union with this seemingly 'split-off' dimension. He would then joyfully experience a sense of completeness, which was manifested through his wider repertoire of behaviours. Here then was evidence of a defect in Tom's self-organisation which, according to the conceptualisations of Kohut (1977), could be temporarily repaired by the experience of selfobject functions within an interpersonal relationship. When Tom began treatment with me, he was no longer grieving the loss of his friend, but he had been unable to overcome the loss of the self-enhancing function formerly provided by that friend.

Exploration of Tom's other relationships revealed that he was extremely sensitive to criticism, especially from his supervisors at work. While his defensive style included a contemptuous attitude towards his superiors, as well as passive–aggressive and acting-out behaviours (such as frequent lateness for work), Tom's response to unfavourable criticism was now almost entirely at the somatic level, with an intensification of spasm of his neck muscles, and no awareness of any underlying fantasies.

This tendency to respond somatically to perceived threats to the achieved harmony in important relationships is not necessarily a defence against unacceptable affects, but, as several authors have suggested (Rodin, 1984, 1991; Gedo, 1988; Stolorow and Atwood, 1991), often signifies an unstable self-organisation and an arrest in affect development. In addition to an excessive vulnerability to experiencing narcissistic injury, Tom appeared limited in his ability to identify, contain and modulate the distressing affects associated with such injuries; the resulting perturbation in his self-organisation and its neurological substrate presumably triggered further dysregulation of the neurotransmitter systems involved in his dystonia. Such changes in cerebral activity in response to negative social input are consistent with new insights into information processing between the environment and the hierarchically organised brain (Hadley, 1983; Ciompi, 1991; Levin, 1991) which had been incorporated into the dysregulation model (Schwartz, 1979; Weiner, 1989) and also led to a reconceptualisation of many neurological disorders as 'dynamic disorders of function' (Reynolds, 1990).

Further evidence of deficits in self-regulation stemmed from my observations of Tom's communicative style. Although he had little difficulty in remembering and reporting past experiences, the first six months of treatment were extremely trying for both of us. Tom remained depressed and potentially suicidal, and we had many sessions during which he complained incessantly about his torticollis and/or the failure of the various medical therapies, thereby engendering in me his own sense of hopelessness and the belief that his condition would not improve. While I endeavoured to remain interested in the content of Tom's verbal communications, there were many sessions in which his preoccupation with somatic symptoms evoked in me intense feelings of boredom and/or sleepiness. As I have elaborated previously (Taylor, 1977, 1984), and as McDougall (1978, 1982) has also observed, such counter-transference responses are often indicative of an alexithymic dimension in a patient's mental functioning. While Tom was not globally alexithymic, I will show later how certain primitive emotions and terrors had not been fully elaborated psychically by him and appeared to play a significant role in the pathogenesis of his torticollis.

Tom's self pathology could be traced easily to deficiencies in his early object relationships. His parents not only lacked a capacity for warmth and empathic attunement, but had also subjected him to active humiliating attacks. The father had ridiculed and belittled Tom during childhood by constantly teasing and picking on him. He had also failed to teach Tom certain boyhood skills, including how to swim and to use carpentry tools, and he had called Tom a 'stupid dummy' whenever his ineptness was evident during his teenage years. During late adolescence, when Tom proudly gave him a copy of a short story that he had written, his father never bothered to read it. As Tom grew older, he had defensively adopted a similar style whereby he teasingly mocked his father's accomplishments, especially when his father scoffed that Tom was lacking in manliness.

Tom's mother had been equally poorly attuned to her son's emotional states and to the impact of her behaviour on his developing sense of self. She had breast-fed Tom during his infancy, but later told him that the experience had been unpleasant and for this reason she had bottle-fed her subsequent children. Tom's mother also frequently reminded him that he had cried constantly as a baby, suggesting a deficiency in her capacity to soothe her infant son as well as her tendency to blame him. She showed little spontaneous affection and when they now met Tom experienced her greetings as completely lacking in warmth.

Among Tom's painful memories were occasions when his mother had ridiculed his interest in Shakespeare and accused him of shaming her when he grew his hair long during adolescence. Even when Tom became ill with torticollis, his mother showed no empathy for her son's embarrassing disability. Completely unattuned to his emotional distress, she mocked and teased him whenever she found him looking in a mirror, just as she had done during his adolescence when she accused him of constantly admiring himself before the mirror. During his adolescence, Tom had suffered from terrible acne on his face, chest and back, and had experienced severe embarrassment when forced to attend school gymnasium classes. Although there was no significant scarring on his body, he still found it difficult to appear in public without a shirt or wearing short pants, for fear of ridicule. Also, unless he was accompanied by a female friend who could offer advice, he was unable to shop for suits or other clothing that had to be tried on for size before a store mirror and in the presence of a salesperson.

The patient's shame sensitivity over his body-self was evident in some of the initial dreams he reported, in which he was naked and feeling humiliated and embarrassed either because his body was being scrutinised, or because he was sexually aroused and fearful that women would consider his erect penis shorter than the penises of other men. While there were undoubtedly exhibitionistic wishes underlying the manifest content of these dreams, I quickly discovered that interpreting such wishes during the early phase of treatment evoked little response from Tom and certainly had no impact on his torticollis. Similarly, attempts to identify conflicts over libidinal or aggressive drives, and to interpret phallic or other symbolic meaning to the torticollis were fruitless, thus demonstrating that conversion was unlikely to be a principal mechanism in the pathogenesis of the symptom.

Such interpretations would be consistent with earlier psychosomatic models of disease, which emphasised neurotic conflict as a pathogenic factor. Guided instead by the dysregulation model and by my awareness of an emerging selfobject transference, I decided to restrict my comments mainly to acknowledging Tom's narcissistic needs and vulnerabilities, and to questions aimed at identifying painful affective states and their association with specific experiences within his current and previous relationships. This approach led gradually to a delineation of Tom's inner object world and to a further understanding of his deficits in self and affect regulation and of his difficulties in establishing mature interpersonal relationships. I will now elaborate these issues.

The failure of Tom's mother to establish a close bond of understanding and enjoyment of her child had left Tom deprived of a maternal introject with soothing and protective functions. Instead, the maternal image was split into a cold and persecutory representation that threatened psychic or even physical death, along with an idealised part-object that offered comfort and love. This split was demonstrated in the first dream Tom reported, in which he and a young woman he loved were held captive in a Nazi prisoner-of-war camp. He begged for their release but only the woman was set free and Tom was tortured. He felt devastated and wept profusely. Eventually the woman returned and Tom was reunited with her family.

The faulty mirroring of the maternal selfobject was captured in the manifest content of another early dream, in which Tom was looking in a mirror and trying to improve his appearance by trimming and combing his beard. His mother appeared and taunted him with comments that he was behaving like a vain woman. When Tom protested, his mother declared that she did not mean what she had said and gave him a hug. Tom felt that he was hugging a cold mannequin. The coldness of his mother, as well as Tom's retaliatory homicidal rage, were captured in several other dreams in which Tom deliberately smashed a glass sculpture of a woman or some other glass object.

My initial tentative interpretations of this rage evoked further psycho-biological dysregulation in Tom with symptoms of depersonalisation and complaints that his torticollis was 'killing' him. Acknowledging my awareness of his psychic pain, and linking it to the deficiencies in his family relationships, were more constructive interventions which restored a stabilising positive transference and helped activate memories of pleasant childhood experiences with an aunt, who had openly admired Tom and shown him some genuine warmth and affection. While this aunt was a rather plain and grossly overweight woman, she had a 'heart of gold' and had been internalised to partly constitute the idealised maternal image with which Tom yearned to be united. The idealised internal object also appeared to be derived from pin-ups of attractive nude or semi-clad women, which Tom's father had hung on the walls of the family's lakeside cottage. The favourite aunt appeared in some of Tom's early dreams either as a woman from whom he sought help for his torticollis, or as a second wife for his father.

Tom's associations to these dreams led not only to memories of important childhood experiences, but also to clarification of the relationships with his current girlfriend and a former girlfriend with whom he had lived for one year. While the former girlfriend was extremely beautiful, Tom had experienced her as emotionally cold and, in that respect, he thought she resembled his mother. His current girlfriend was physically less attractive, but manifested a more genuine concern for him. Nevertheless, Tom was deeply anxious about becoming too attached to her; consequently, for a long time he was deprived of the solacing and other self-regulating benefits that are a part of mature love-relationships.

There were also many occasions when the internal sado-masochistic relationship involving split self- and object-representations was reversed and externalised into the relationship with his girlfriend. Like his parents, Tom would inflict psychic pain by magnifying and criticising his girlfriend's minor flaws and by mocking her in the presence of friends. This pattern of relating gradually changed following the analysis of Tom's own vulnerability to shame and his defensive splitting and identification with the sadistic part-object. With the experiencing of ruth and guilt, Tom developed a greater appreciation of his girlfriend and, as I describe later, he expressed increasing admiration for her and gradually fell in love.

As I indicated earlier, Tom's proneness to self-fragmentation and the existence of a subself with exhibitionistic aims were suggested by the selfobject relationship that he had previously had with his male friend, and by the content of several of his early dreams. The association of his subself-organisation with unmet or rejected needs for affirmation and approval, and the shame for having such needs, were made clearer in the third year of treatment as Tom acquired sufficient confidence in the therapeutic relationship to reveal some of his secret thoughts and fantasies.

As a teenager, Tom had wanted to be successful and famous, to be a star like Elvis Presley, John Lennon, Leonard Cohen or Neil Simon, and to be recognised and admired as he walked down the street. He felt intense shame over these 'egotistical fantasies', as he referred to them. During his adolescence, he would sometimes stand in front of his sister's bedroom mirror with a fake microphone and imagine that he was a famous rock singer; he felt that he would be great, one of the 'chosen' ones. In real life, however, Tom regarded himself as a failure in his career; he was shy and inhibited about speaking to groups, and had been unable even to prepare a résumé and apply for jobs that might provide a higher salary.

In addition to Tom's ambitious and exhibitionistic subself, which was usually concealed by the dominant identity of an ineffectual person, analysis revealed another subself which was more readily available, based on an identification with his father. The patient's father was a charismatic man who had deliberately cultivated a 'larger-than-life' persona, including a reputation for being able to consume large quantities of alcohol. In need of an idealising selfobject as well as his father's affirmation that he was a 'real man', Tom had learned to admire many of his father's pathological behaviours; like his father, Tom had become a heavy drinker and acquired a large group of male friends who shared his enthusiasm for getting drunk and deriding the establishment.

The gradual relinquishment of this subself-organisation, following interpretations of its origin and meaning (i.e. its basis in an identification with a father whose love the patient desired and whom he wished to admire), evoked considerable guilt in Tom, as he experienced a strong sense of being disloyal both to his father and to his drinking buddies when he attempted to distance himself from their behaviours. In addition, he experienced shame over an increasing desire to strengthen his skills and use his talents as a creative writer, an activity that failed to interest either his parents or most of his friends. There was one close friend, however, who shared Tom's interest in writing; during the course of treatment, they became a strong writing team and have subsequently attracted favourable responses to their creative work.

As I will show later, the analysis of Tom's intrapsychic experience of his object-relationships gradually led to a more integrated and cohesive self and to more stable and satisfying interpersonal relationships that undoubtedly contributed to the resolution of his torticollis. However, essential to the achievement of this result were my parallel efforts to resolve the encapsulated area of alexithymic mental functioning and thereby advance Tom's affect development and capacity for affect regulation.

During the seventh month of treatment Tom had reported some bizarre dreams consisting mainly of disturbing images including guns pointed at him, people chasing him and ugly, threatening faces. These dream images were interspersed with comforting images of beautiful and naked women. Although the disturbing dream images soon subsided, they reappeared towards the end of the second year of treatment. Now they generally awakened Tom and were described by him as 'brutal and nasty' and as 'the closet of a horror show'. As though to protect me, but perhaps also to test my ability to tolerate sharing his terrifying experiences, Tom stated that 'they are not the kind of images one would want to see ... they are pornographic and involve killings and death'. He eventually told me that they included images of people being murdered, of women being whipped, of bleeding and gaping vaginas, of men performing oral or anal sex on each other, and of men sexually abusing children. In some of these dreams it was Tom himself who was stabbed or shot. Images of guns and knives were now also popping into Tom's mind during his waking hours. He feared that he might be a latent child molester, a rapist or a homosexual.

While I indicated some interest in the content of these concrete, psychotic-type images and dreams, I thought that they signified a failure of the defensive and regulatory functions of Tom's ego, in particular a defective alpha function (Bion, 1962), and I made no attempt to interpret repressed wishes. Such dreams, as Segal (1981) has indicated, cannot be analysed according to the classical theory of dreams; they generally have an 'evacuative' function and indicate a need for attention to the patient's impaired ego functioning, in particular to the capacity for symbolisation.

The acts of violence and perverse sexuality in Tom's dreams closely resembled the themes recorded by Levitan (1989) in his studies of the dreams of patients with 'classical' psychosomatic diseases. They also reflected the primitive emotions and psychotic anxieties that are associated with early psychic trauma and that generally underlie encapsulated areas of alexithymic mental functioning (Krystal, 1978, 1988; McDougall, 1982; Taylor, 1987). However, the appearance of these primitive dream and fantasy elements, at this stage of the treatment, signalled that Tom had developed a sufficient sense of safety and relatedness to me that he could now risk the activation and exposure of archiac instinctual impulses and primitive emotional states that were experienced as dangerous and overwhelming. These primitive impulses and emotions had not been encoded hitherto in any symbolic form and had remained as unregulated somatic states (de M'Uzan, 1974; H.A. Rosenfeld, 1978, unpublished paper).

Such arrests in affect development are considered a consequence of faulty early object-relationships, in particular a lack of attunement and failure of the parents to fulfil their 'containing' and validating functions whereby the child learns to elevate emotions from the sensorimotor enactive mode of experience to an awareness of subjective feelings (Emde, 1984; Krystal, 1988). Indeed, recent observational studies of infant–mother interactions suggest that problems in affect development, and the associated failure to develop a stable positive sense of self, can be linked to an absence from infancy of on-going positive affective exchanges with a caregiver who recognises that the infant's emotions are signals communicating needs and satisfactions (Stern, 1985; Beebe and Lachmann, 1988; Osofsky and Eberhart-Wright, 1988).

If the caregiver ignores these signals and fails to prevent the infant's primitive affects from reaching an unbearable intensity, states of psychic trauma may develop which result in faulty psychic structure and an arrest in the genetic development of affects, as Krystal (1978, 1988) has elaborated. The emotional unavailability of my patient's mother, and the absence of sustained pleasure, smiling and other positive mirroring from her, constituted cumulative traumatisation that may well have arisen during Tom's infancy, when his mother was an adolescent and presumably still dealing with her own developmental issues. As noted earlier, the mother had not enjoyed breast-feeding and appeared to have had difficulty soothing her infant son.

In a manner echoing the relation between an attuned parent and a young child (Edgcumbe, 1984; Stern, 1985; Beebe and Lachmann, 1988), I tolerated and remained receptive to my patient's disturbing dream and fantasy images, and employed an educational and mediating approach in an attempt to correct the deficit in his emotional functioning.* Consistent with contemporary theories of affect development (Krystal, 1982, 1988; Lane and Schwartz, 1987; Kopp, 1989; Ciompi, 1991), I conveyed to Tom that his primitive dream and fantasy images signified the emergence of a mental (i.e. cognitive) component to profoundly disturbing emotions and impulses that were manifest mostly through his somatic symptom. Reflecting the subjective feeling component of the various emotional states suggested by the dream images and by the patient's facial expressions and bodily postures (especially states of intense rage, anxiety, sadness or profound shame), and teaching him to identify and accurately label these feelings for himself, gradually provided Tom with a greater capacity to use the symbolic system of language to modulate distressing emotions.

---

* The need to part company with the strictly interpretive method and to institute educational approaches was first recommended for torticollis patients by Clark (1917), who regarded deficits in affect development as the primary fault. Ruesch (1948) subsequently described affect deficits among patients with many other types of somatic illness and advised similar modifications in technique.

There was considerable psychic pain for Tom during this phase of treatment, as the dreams sometimes generated a fear that he was going mad. McDougall (1974) has reported similar observations from the analysis of somatically ill patients, whom she found 'may have to recreate their psychotic monsters, and live with them even in projected form for a while, until such time as they can be contained and integrated' (p. 450). Such 'monsters' are to be regarded not as a return of thoughts and wishes that have been rejected from the conscious mind, but, as McDougall (1974, 1989) proposed, as the initial mental representations of disturbing emotions and experiences that were foreclosed from the mind and consequently could not be managed through psychic fantasy activity and the development of neurotic symptoms.

According to Cohen and Kinston (1984; Kinston and Cohen, 1986) these isolated images and undifferentiated emotions signify the re-emergence of unmet needs and traumatic states from infancy and childhood that characterise primal repression (as distinct from repression proper), and which now require the mediating function of the analyst to enable the representation of needs and the growth of psychic structure. 'The process of repair', as Kinston and Cohen (1986) indicate, 'involves having certain experiences *for the first time*' (p. 347).

This viewpoint obviously differs from the pregenital conversion theory of psychosomatic symptom formation (F. Deutsch, 1959; Sperling, 1978), which is based on Freud's conception of hysteria and attributes the symptoms of somatic disease to the symbolic expression of repressed fantasies and affects. It is consistent, however, with MacAlpine's argument (1952) that psychosomatic symptoms are rudimentary and partly expressed emotions, and not a defence against neurotic conflict.

The progressive desomatisation and attachment of primitive impulses and emotions to words and to mental representations of object-relations, and Tom's increasing ability to report and think about these images and affects in the treatment setting, led to important insights and psychic growth that were followed by a gradual but steady improvement of his torticollis. Initially, he became more aware of the connection between sudden spasms of his neck muscles and abrupt states of intense emotional arousal that were evoked by various situational experiences. Tom discovered, for example, that intensifications of his torticollis prior to attending important meetings at work were associated with an anticipatory anxiety that he might say or do something that would be judged negatively by his colleagues and trigger a sudden self-fragmentation as he was flooded with unregulated shame.

Clarification and interpretation enabled him to link such fears with reconstructions of childhood situations in which he had experienced disappointment and painful humiliation and shame (rather than pleasurable pride), when his mother or father had responded critically or indifferently (rather than joyfully) to his achievements and attempts to share his interests and excitement with them. Tom subsequently also developed an understanding of how these frequent misattuned affect transactions during childhood had been internalised and still contributed to his sense of incompetence and to his proneness to states of narcissistic depletion and problems with unregulated narcissistic rage.

The patient's deepening conviction that he was accepted and genuinely valued by me, despite his 'pornographic and violent dreams', enabled me to initiate periods of playful dialogue that promoted further symbolisation and helped transform some of the narcissistic rage associated with his torticollis to wish-based psychic structure. I suggested jokingly, for example, that perhaps he wished at times to get revenge on his critical colleagues at work by 'twisting their necks to resemble pretzels'. Such comments now evoked amusement in Tom and obvious enjoyment of the analytic sessions.

As Tom's capacity to imagine the hitherto unimaginable increased, he became more accepting of his own primitive drives and emotions, which were then revealed in more elaborate and meaningful fantasies and dreams and gradually integrated into his self structure. This in turn permitted some modification of his internal object-relations, in particular those involving the double image of the mother. Initially, there was a transformation from the bewildering panic attacks and neck muscle spasms, which Tom sometimes experienced while his mother was visiting and making belittling comments, to a realisation that he felt angry with his mother as well as guilty for not wanting to see her.

Then, at the beginning of the fourth year of treatment, Tom reported a dream in which he felt a compelling desire to lie down in a pool of water that was collecting alongside a large melting block of ice. As he did so, an extremely powerful force, which he associated with his mother, suddenly pulled him up and told him that he must not lie there.

In a later dream, which was reported when the patient was conflicted over whether to send his mother a card for Mother's Day, Tom was lying on a couch cuddling with a woman he loved. He then slowly pushed the woman into the couch until she was sucked in and had disappeared completely. While these dreams expressed Tom's underlying fantasy of being fused with an idealised mother, they also reflected an increasing ability to own and control the destructive part of himself which previously had been projectively identified with the dangerous and omnipotent maternal image.

Further evidence of an increasing tolerance for his destructive rage was provided a few weeks later when the patient reported a dream in which a man resembling himself had used a golf club as a weapon and brutally murdered a person. In his associations to this dream, Tom recalled a recent telephone conversation during which his boastful father had threatened to 'kill' him by beating him in a golf game they were planning to play on Father's Day. These commemorative Father's Day and Mother's Day dreams contrasted with several dreams from the first year of treatment in which Tom was the helpless victim of his parents' primitive aggression.

While Tom's sense of helplessness and the shortcomings of his parents were evident early in treatment, it was important, as Steiner (1982) has advised, not to collude with that part of the patient that viewed himself as an innocent victim now caught in the grip of a malevolent internal organisation. The analytic treatment approach helped Tom to identify and accept his own destructive self, and then to stand up to the persecutory internal part-objects. He indicated that in his dreams he could now experience himself both as the 'brutaliser' and as the 'victim'. This insight was paralleled in his waking life by an increasing ability to challenge his parents over issues with which he disagreed, and by the disappearance of the intense anxiety which he had experienced previously when he anticipated telephoning or seeing them. Similar changes also occurred in the way Tom interacted with his colleagues and supervisors at work.

By the end of the third year of treatment Tom had achieved an almost complete recovery from his torticollis. He was able to resume playing baseball and squash, and he began to devote considerable time to improving his skills at golf. The development of a more cohesive self and an increasing ability to experience pride in himself, rather than the affect of shame, also enabled Tom to begin to shop alone for suits and to admire his image as reflected in the mirrors of menswear stores.

At work, Tom was far less sensitive to criticism from his supervisors; his increased commitment to the job was rewarded by greatly improved semiannual evaluations. He still suffered occasional attacks of torticollis, however, which were invariably linked to situational experiences that evoked narcissistic rage or overwhelming feelings of humiliation or shame. These occasional attacks of the somatic disorder eventually ceased, as the continuation of analytic treatment led to further stabilisation of Tom's self-regulating capacities (including an ability to use the affects of rage and shame as signals for action or reflection), and to the establishment of mature interpersonal relationships that provided age-appropriate mirroring and other interactional regulations.

Tom's difficulty in relinquishing the archaic aims of his grandiose/exhibitionistic self, and the association of this subself-organisation with defective mirroring by the parental selfobjects and with a regressive yearning for closeness with an idealised object, were illustrated in numerous fantasies and dreams during the final three years of treatment. In one dream, which followed recovery from the torticollis, even death was idealised in an attempt to win approval from the parents. Not surprisingly, the patient's self–selfobject experiences in such dreams (Tolpin, 1983) paralleled his everyday experience with his parents, who gave minimal attention to their son's recovery from the torticollis; they merely attributed his improvement to a trivial head blow which he had received in a minor snowmobile accident during the third year of treatment. His mother also continued to make shaming comments, including telling Tom that she hoped that his first-born child would embarrass him as much as he had embarrassed her by not getting married and having children.

Despite the on-going traumatic encounters with his parents, Tom was able gradually to transform his desire for uniqueness and specialness into more realistic goals and ambitions as well as a set of ideals that fostered the maturation and expression of his pre-existing talents. This transformation was apparent in a dream in which the patient was initially observing a group of people who were organising a parade. As the band began to play, he decided to march with the people and then discovered that the parade was in honour of Elvis Presley. They all smiled and waved to the crowd that had gathered. While this dream suggested that Tom had relinquished his wish to be as famous as Elvis Presley, I offered the interpretation that the patient was able partially to gratify his exhibitionistic wishes and need for acknowledgement by participating in the parade.

Listening to Elvis or other pop singers on his transistor radio late at night had been an important source of solace for Tom during his childhood years. He recalled that 'the song "Love me tender" felt so warm, [he] could crawl right up into the womb'. Much work in the final phase of treatment enabled Tom to find similar solace within a mature loving relationship with his girlfriend. He had surmounted most of his earlier anxiety and decided to live with her during the fourth year of treatment.

About a year later, he reported a dream in which he had awakened from a deep sleep to find himself looking admiringly at the genitals of a woman who had a beautifully sculptured body. However, he was unable to see the woman's face. As he tried to get closer to her, an enormously fat naked man entered the room. Gradually more and more naked men and women arrived for a party. The patient felt anxious and embarrassed because he was the only person wearing clothes and was unable to recall the name of the fat slob. After awakening from the dream, Tom remembered that the man had the same name as his creative writing partner. In his associations, Tom recalled his earlier disturbing dream images of gaping vaginas, as well as a memory from age 11 when he had caught a glimpse of his mother's bruised and swollen genitals soon after she had given birth to a younger sibling. He remembered the horror and shame he had felt at that young age and how he had struggled to suppress the frightening image.

During the first year of analysis, Tom had reported a dream in which he was amputating the leg of a hockey player who was screaming as he lay on the operating table. While that dream seemed to be a vivid and barely disguised portrayal of castration anxiety, I had concluded at the time that it expressed Tom's much deeper anxieties about survival as well as the intensity of his psychic pain. My conclusion was now supported by his dream of a beautiful but faceless woman who, as Kohut (1979) proposed in his analysis of a dream of Mr Z., represented a more dreadful experience than castration, namely, 'the mother whose face does not light up at the sight of her child' (Kohut, 1984, p. 21). The 'fat slob' in the dream, whom Tom saw instead of the face of the beautiful woman, seemed to represent his mother whose body was distorted by multiple pregnancies. Given that the 'fat slob' had the same name as one of Tom's current twinship self-objects, I interpreted that he might also be a representation of Tom himself which was based on an identification with his mother's 'ugly, deformed genital', which Tom had viewed as a boy and unconsciously linked with his perception of her view of him. Amputation of the leg in the earlier dream could now be interpreted as an attempt to escape from the entrapment with the horrifying image of the mother. Yet, like the hockey player who 'lived for the game and would prefer to die than lose a leg', Tom's survival at the beginning of treatment was just as much dependent on, as it was threatened by, his internal link with the omnipotent and persecutory image of the mother.

The patient's attempt to dissociate himself from the perverse relation with the dreaded and compelling internal image of the mother was evident in much of the subsequent analytic material. In one of his later dreams, for example, the patient was preparing to show a soft-porn video to his girlfriend. As she entered the room, her face suddenly changed into his mother's face. The woman then exposed her breasts and demanded that the patient make love to her. As he tried to resist her insistent demands, the patient realised that he had a legitimate reason for refusing – it would be incest and therefore a crime if they made love. Rather than interpreting conflict over unconscious incestuous desires, I commented on Tom's use of the incest barrier in this dream to combat a greater danger to the self, namely, a threatened disruption of his link to an appropriately responsive internal object.

Gradually, there was a strengthening of the patient's internal relation with a warm and appropriately affectionate maternal image, which emerged increasingly in his dreams as well as in memories, including further recollections of pleasant encounters with the favourite aunt and with his former girlfriend's mother, who was described as the 'ideal mother'. Over the next few months Tom reported a deepening love for his current girlfriend; it was 'a remarkable and extremely satisfying feeling', one that he had not previously experienced.

While the relationship with his girlfriend now fulfilled Tom's need for a mature, loving attachment with a woman, and clearly functioned also as an important external psychic regulator, the interpretation and working through of his pathological internal object-relations had resulted also in greater self-reliance, including more reliable self-esteem regulation and an ability to modulate distressing affects. These personality changes should not only protect him from a recurrence of spasmodic torticollis, but also render him more resilient to other somatic illnesses and diseases.

Summary

The case of spasmodic torticollis described demonstrates the clinical useful-ness of a new theoretical model of somatic illness and disease. Based on a conception of the living organism as a self-regulating system, the model attributes somatic disorders to a variety of regulatory disturbances including deficits in affect regulation and in the ability to maintain a stable and cohesive self. Throughout the analytical treatment, attention was given to repairing deficits in the patient's self-organisation, and to elevating chaotic impulses and inchoate emotions from a primitive sensorimotor level of experience to a mature representational level where they could be valued for their signal function and modulated through imaginal activity and communication with others. Analysis of the patient's pathological internal object-relations modified his self-organisation, and enabled him to establish regulatory interpersonal relationships that complemented his enhanced self-regulatory capacities. These changes were accompanied by a gradual resolution of the patient's torticollis.

References

ALEXANDER, F. (1950). *Psychosomatic Medicine*. New York: Norton.

BEEBE, B. and LACHMANN, F.M. (1988). The contribution of mother-infant mutual influence to the origins of self- and object-representations. *Psychoanalytic Psychol-ogy* **5**, 305-337.

BESSON, J.A.O. et al (1988). Brain imaging and treatment response in spasmodic torticollis. *British Journal of Psychiatry* **153**, 399-402.

BION, W.R. (1962). *Learning from Experience*. London: Heinemann.

BLALOCK, J.E. (1989). A molecular basis for bidirectional communication between the immune and neuroendocrine systmes. *Physiology Reviews* **69**, 1-32.

CIOMPI, L. (1991). Affects as central organising and integrating factors: A new psycho-social/biological model of the psyche. *British Journal of Psychiatry* **159**, 97-105.

CLARK, L.P. (1917). A discussion of the mechanism of mental torticollis. *Journal of Abnormal Psychology* **12**, 257-259.

COCKBURN, J.J. (1971). Spasmodic torticollis: A psychogenic condition? *Journal of Psychosomatic Research* **15**, 471-477.

COHEN, J. and KINSTON, W. (1984). Repression theory: A new look at the cornerstone. *International Journal of Psycho-Analysis* **65**, 411-422.

DE M'UZAN, M. (1974). Psychodynamic mechanisms in psychosomatic symptom for-mation. *Psychotherapy and Psychosomatics* **23**, 103-110.

DEUTSCH, F. (1959). *On the Mysterious Leap from the Mind to the Body*. New York: International Universities Press.

DEUTSCH, L. (1980). Psychosomatic medicine from a psychoanalytic viewpoint. *Journal of the American Psychoanalytic Association* **28**, 653-702.

DUANE, D.D. (1988). Spasmodic torticollis. *Advances in Neurology* **49**, 135-150.

EDGCUMBE, R.M. (1984). Modes of communication: The differentiation of somatic and verbal expression. *Psychoanalytic Study of the Child* **39**, 137-154.

EMDE, R.N. (1984). The affective self: Continuities and transformations from infancy. In J.D. Call, E. Galenson and R.L. Tyson (Eds), *Frontiers of Infant Psychiatry*, pp. 38-54. New York: Basic Books.

ENGEL, G.L. and SCHMALE, A.H. (1967). Psychoanalytic theory of somatic disorder: Conversion, specificity and disease onset situation. *Journal of the American Psychoanalytic Association* **15**, 344–365.

FRIEDMAN, A. and FAHN, S. (1986). Spontaneous remissions in spasmodic torticollis. *Neurology* **36**, 398–400.

GADDINI, R. (1977). The pathology of the self as a basis of psychosomatic disorders. *Psychotherapy and Psychosomatics* **28**, 260–271.

GEDO, J.E. (1988). *The Mind in Disorder: Psychoanalytic Models of Pathology*. Hillsdale, NJ: Analytic Press.

GITELSON, M. (1959). A critique of current concepts in psychosomatic medicine. *Bulletin of the Menninger Clinic* **23**, 165–178.

GROTSTEIN, J.S. (1986). The psychology of powerlessness: Disorders of self-regulation and interactional regulation as a newer paradigm for psychopathology. *Psychoanalytic Inquiry* **6**, 93–118.

HADLEY, J.L. (1983). The representational system: A bridging concept for psychoanalysis and neurophysiology. *International Review of Psychoanalysis* **10**, 13–30.

HOFER, M.A. (1984). Relationships as regulators: A psychobiologic perspective on bereavement. *Psychosomatic Medicine* **46**, 183–197.

HOFER, M. A., (1987). Early social relationships: A psychobiologist's view. *Child Development* **58**, 633–647.

JAMES, M. (1979). The non-symbolic nature of psychosomatic disorder: A test case of both Klein and classical theory. *International Review of Psychoanalysis* **6**, 413–422.

KARUSH, A., FLOOD, C. and O'CONNOR, J.F. (1977). *Psychotherapy in Ulcerative Colitis*. Philadelphia: Saunders.

KARASU, T.B. (1979). Psychotherapy of the medically ill. *American Journal of Psychiatry* **136**, 1–11.

KINSTON, W. and COHEN, J. (1986). Primal repression: Clinical and theoretical aspects. *International Journal of Psychoanalysis* **67**, 337–355.

KOHUT, H. (1977). *The Restoration of the Self*. New York: International Universities Press.

KOHUT, H. (1979). The two analyses of Mr Z. *International Journal of Psycho-Analysis* **60**, 3–27.

KOHUT, H. (1984). *How Does Analysis Cure?* Chicago: University of Chicago Press.

KOPP, C.B. (1989). Regulation of distress and negative emotions: a developmental view. *Developmental Psychology* **25**, 343–354.

KOREIN, J. and BRUDNY, J. (1976). Integrated EMG feedback in the management of spasmodic torticollis and focal dystonia: a prospective study of 80 patients. In: M.D. Yahn (Ed.), *The Basal Ganglia*, pp. 385–424. New York: Raven.

KRYSTAL, H. (1978). Trauma and affects. *Psychoanalytic Study of the Child* **33**, 81–115.

KRYSTAL, H. (1982). Alexithymia and the effectiveness of psychoanalytic treatment. *International Journal of Psychoanalytic Psychotherapy* **9**, 353–378.

KRYSTAL, H. (1988). *Integration and Self-Healing: Affect, Trauma, Alexithymia*. Hillsdale, NJ: Analytic Press.

LAL, S. et al. (1979). Neuropharmacological investigation and treatment of spasmodic torticollis. *Advances in Neurology* **24**, 335–351.

LANE, R.D. and SCHWARTZ, G.E. (1987). Levels of emotional awareness: a cognitive-developmental theory and its application to psychopathology. *American Journal of Psychiatry* **144**, 133–143.

LEVIN, F.M. (1991). *Mapping the Mind: The Intersection of Psychoanalysis and Neuroscience*. Hillsdale, NJ: Analytic Press.

LEVITAN, H. (1989). Failure of the defensive functions of the ego in psychosomatic patients. In: S. Cheren (Ed.), *Psychosomatic Medicine: Theory, Physiology, and Practice*, Vol. 1, pp. 135-157. Madison, CT: International Universities Press.

MacALPINE, I. (1954). Psychosomatic symptom formation. *The Lancet* **i**, 278-282.

McDOUGALL, J. (1974). The psychosoma and the psychoanalytic process. *International Review of Psychoanalysis* **1**, 437-459.

McDOUGALL, J. (1978). Primitive communication and the use of the countertransference. *Contemporary Psychoanalysis* **14**, 173-209.

McDOUGALL, J. (1982). Alexithymia, psychosomatosis, and psychosis. *International Journal of Psychoanalytic Psychotherapy* **9**, 379-388.

McDOUGALL, J. (1989). *Theaters of the Body: A Psychoanalytic Approach to Psychosomatic Illness*. New York: Norton.

MARTY, P., DE M'UZAN, M. and DAVID, C. (1963). *L'investigation psychosomatique*. Paris: Presses Universitaire, France.

MEARES, R. (1971). Features which distinguish groups of spasmodic torticollis. *Journal of Psychosomatic Research* **5**, 1-11.

MENDELSON, M., HIRSCH, S. and WEBBER, C. S. et al. (1956). A critical examination of some recent theoretical models in psychosomatic medicine. *Psychsomatic Medicine* **18**, 363-373.

MURPHY, W.F. and CHASEN, M. (1956). Spasmodic torticollis. *Psychoanalytic Reviews* **43**, 18-30.

NABER, D. et al. (1988). Personality variables, neurological and psychopathological symptoms in patients suffering from spasmodic torticollis. *Comprehensive Psychiatry* **29**, 182-187.

NEMIAH, J.C. and SIFNEOS, P.E. (1970). Affect and fantasy in patients with psychosomatic disorders. In: D.W. Hill (Ed.), *Modern Trends in Psychosomatic Medicine*, Vol. 2, pp. 26-34. London: Butterworths.

OSOFSKY, J.D. and EBERHART-WRIGHT, A. (1988). Affective exchanges between high risk mothers and infants. *International Journal of Psycho-Analysis* **69**, 221-231.

OWENS, D.G.C. (1990). Dystonia - a potential psychiatric pitfall. *British Journal of Psychiatry* **156**, 620-634.

PERT, C.B. et al. (1985). Neuropeptides and their receptors: a psychosomatic network. I. *Immunology* **135** (Suppl.), 820-826.

PIPP, S. and HARMON, R.J. (1987). Attachment as regulation: a commentary. *Child Development* **58**, 648-652.

REYNOLDS, E.H. (1990). Structure and function in neurology and psychiatry. *British Journal of Psychiatry* **157**, 481-490.

RODIN, G. (1984). Somatization and the self: psychotherapeutic issues. *American Journal of Psychotherapy* **38**, 257-263.

RODIN, G. (1991). Somatization: A perspective from self psychology. *Journal of the American Academy of Psychoanalysis* **19**, 367-384.

RUESCH, J. (1948). The infantile personality: The core problem in psychosomatic medicine. *Psychosomatic Medicine* **10**, 134-144.

SANDLER, L.W. (1987). Awareness of inner experience: a systems perspective on self-regulatory process in early development. *Child Abuse and Neglect* **11**, 339-346.

SCHWARTZ, G.E. (1979). The brain as a health care system. In: G.C. Stone, F. Cohen and N.E. Adler (Eds), *Health Psychology: A Handbook*. San Francisco: Jossey-Bass.

SCHWARTZ, G.E. (1983). Disregulation theory and disease: Applications to the repression/cerebral disconnection/cardiovascular disorder hypothesis. *International Review of Applied Psychology* **32**, 95-118.

SCHWARTZ, G.E. (1989). Disregulation theory and disease. Toward a general model for psychosomatic medicine. In: S. Cheren (Ed.), *Psychosomatic Medicine: Theory, Physiology, and Practice*, Vol. 1, pp. 91-117. Madison, CT: International Universities Press.

SEGAL, H. (1981). The function of dreams. In: J.S. Grotstein (Ed.), *Do I Dare Disturb the Universe*, pp. 580-587. Beverly Hills, CA: Caesura Press.

SPERLING, M. (1978). *Psychosomatic Disorders in Childhood*. New York: Aronson.

STEINER, J. (1982). Perverse relationships between parts of the self: a clinical illustration. *International Journal of Psycho-Analysis* **63**, 241-251.

STERN, D.N. (1985). *The Interpersonal World of the Infant: A View from Psychoanalysis and Developmental Psychology*. New York: Basic Books.

STOLOROW, R.D. and ATWOOD, G.E. (1991). The mind and the body. *Psychoanalytic Dialogues* **1**, 181-195.

SUTHERLAND, J.D. (1983). The self and object relations. *Bulletin of the Menninger Clinic* **47**, 525-541.

TAYLOR, G.J. (1977). Alexithymia and the countertransference. *Psychotherapy and Psychosomatics* **28**, 141-147.

TAYLOR, G.J. (1984). Psychotherapy with the boring patient. *Canadian Journal of Psychiatry* **29**, 217-222.

TAYLOR, G.J. (1986). Object relations theory, self psychology and psychosomatic medicine. In: J.H. Lacey and D. Sturgeon (Eds), *Proceedings of the 15th European Conference on Psychosomatic Research*, pp. 22-26. London: Libbey.

TAYLOR, G.J. (1987). *Psychosomatic Medicine and Contemporary Psychoanalysis*. Madison, CT: International Universities Press.

TAYLOR, G.J. (1992a). Psychoanalysis and psychosomatics: A synthesis. *Journal of the American Academy of Psychoanalysis* **20**, 251-275.

TAYLOR, G.J. (1992b). Psychosomatics and self-regulation. In: J.W. Barron, M.N. Eagle and D.L. Wolitzky (Eds), *Interface of Psychoanalysis and Psychology*. Washington DC: American Psychological Association.

TOLPIN, P. (1983). Self psychology and the interpretation of dreams. In: A. Goldberg (Ed.), *The Future of Psychoanalysis*, pp. 255-271. New York: International Universities Press.

WEINER, H. (1975). Are 'psychosomatic' diseases diseases of regulation? *Psychosomatic Medicine* **37**, 289-291.

WEINER, H. (1989). The dynamics of the organism: Implications of recent biological thought for psychomatic theory and research. *Psychosomatic Medicine* **51**, 608-635.

Chapter 7
Working with the false body

Susie Orbach

In the course of my work with women who have eating and body-image problems* (Orbach 1978, 1982, 1986), I have been grappling with theoretical aspects of an endemic clinical problem: the problem of the body. The body for the woman with a distorted body image is not only the site of an expressive symptom but it is also the principal medium through which she negotiates her psychosocial existence. In the course of therapy the anorectic, the bulimic, the (obese) compulsive eater or the woman with an unstable body size describes her body in distinctive ways which we need to understand. We are forced to take heed of the issues of corporealisation, a person's sense of his or her physicality and the ways in which somatic development dovetails with psychological development.

The treatment of women with eating problems brings to our attention two interrelated theoretical questions: the first centres on the conundrum of how to understand psyche–somatic development and the taking up of a corporeal sense of self; the second centres around the notion of what I shall call the false body. In stating the project in this way I realise that I am perhaps raising many questions. The very words 'self' and 'corporeal' hide a multiplicity of concepts that are in themselves problematic. I am inclined to think that they are problematic precisely because the notion of the body as distinct from the psyche is in itself an unworkable proposition. And yet we are here in a dilemma for this is indeed how the patient with an eating problem experiences her body. Indeed her vision of this may be so compelling as to incline the psychotherapist to conceptualise her problems in a bifurcated manner.

---

* Women who are clinically obese and women with anorexia share a version of this distorted body sense although in the opposite direction, i.e. it is the case that some obese patients see themselves as considerably smaller than they are: they represent themselves in pictures as above the norm but not obese.

The corporeal sense of self

The relationship between physical and psychological development poses a conundrum because this is a somewhat unworked out and under-theorised area of developmental psychology. The issue of how the self becomes a subject and how the self recognises the physical boundaries of subjectivity is to an extent a tautological exericise, for implicit within it is the notion that it is possible to conceive of a psyche-self and a soma-self.

In his metapsychology Freud has drawn us a visual/hydraulic image of development by using metaphors from nineteenth century newtonian mechanics to describe libidinal growth. But at an intrapsychic level, while the body and the unfolding of instinctual aims are clearly essential to his schema, we are left with the rather undeveloped notion of the body ego.

Spitz (1965), working within an object-relations framework, proposes the existence of two systems: the co-anaesthetic, which is the bodily, and the diacritic, which is the emotional. For him, the co-anaesthetic is eventually fused with the diacritic as the latter becomes more highly developed within the context of the infant's relationship with its mother. As Spitz has shown, babies who are only the recipients of adequate *physical* care can fail to thrive. They suffer anaclitic depression and even die. For the meeting of physical needs to be of any use to the neonate it needs to be imbued with an emotional resonance. In other words, the details of being attended to physically take on meaning and aliveness within the context of an emotional relationship.

Mahler, Pines and Bergman (1975) link the development of body awareness with the psychological birth of the human infant during the process of separation–individuation. As the baby develops increased motor activity and interest in its physicality, mother names the body parts and mirrors the baby's interest in its body. The baby becomes a toddler and uses its body to differentiate self from non-self. Mother's responses legitimate the body and its capabilities, helping the child to build a sense of body awareness. Rycroft (1985) speaks of the psyche's capacity to 'convert meaningless physiological sensations into significant psychological experiences . . . the psyche transforms sensations, which are discrete and passively received, into experiences, which form part of a continuum and are actively created'.

Winnicott (1965) sees subjectivity and the sense of selfhood firmly linked with the physical. 'The live body, with its limits, and with an inside and outside, is felt by the individual to form the core for the imaginative self' (p. 244).

McDougall (1989) sees the body as the mode of expression before symbolisation is developed. Before language can contain the intolerable or uncontainable feelings that infants experience, the body becomes the theatre in which distress is played out. For these theorists, then, the acquisition or attainment of a corporeal sense of self is entwined with psychological notions of the self.

These ideas suggest that, from a clinical point of view, difficulties in early object-relations may be manifest not only in the individual's psychical sense of self but in her physical sense of self as well. The capacity to somatise – to put onto the body – symptoms of psychic distress is clearly part of this. The phenomenon of a patient's feeling that she does not live in her body, that she *is* only her body, has 'out of body experiences', or is alienated from it in some fundamental way, is not a bizarre symptom or developmental lesion of a different order; rather, it may be an expression of physical and psychic mismatching in the earliest of relationships.

When working with women who appear to have gross misperceptions of their bodies, in that they perceive them to be either significantly larger or smaller than is demonstrably the case, one is led to look at the meaning and symbolisation of the body. More accurately, one is led to look at the way in which the individual creates a split between what she describes as 'herself' and what she describes as 'her body'. Such a patient experiences a distinct cleavage between a mental, thinking, sometimes feeling self and a physical self that is an unwanted or deviant part. The body is felt to be an *acquisition*, rather than an *attribution*, of the self. In Palazzoli's (1974) view, this disjuncture in the anorectic can be understood as her attempt to control the still-much-needed but felt-to-be-rejecting object.

The attempt to control the body and its appetites corresponds to the desire to control the object. Similarly one might argue that the bulimic's or the compulsive eater's disavowal of regulatory mechanisms in the body which signal satiety and hunger is an attempt to blot out or disempower the still-much-needed but felt-to-be rejecting object.

Using Palazzoli's framework one can see how the body becomes a powerful arena for the attempted externalisation of internal conflict. The disclaimed, disassociated body becomes both the site and the source for the enactment and re-enactment of painful affect towards the object representation. In the case of anorexia, the anorectic's wish to be free of encasement in or encumbrance by the body can be interpreted as a desire to do away with the internal objects and to create a distance between the negative or destructive feelings towards the object. In this way, the (still much-needed) object is protected from what the anorectic experiences as her dangerous or poisonous self.

In the large compulsive eater, the felt greed or insatiability of the woman overwhelms the need for the object, thus rendering (in fantasy) the person as autistic, need-free or unattached. The physical manifestation of apparently feeding oneself gives the appearance of desire satisfied. But just as desire must be overridden by the anorectic in order for her to assuage her profound neediness, so the large compulsive eater in overriding her appetite in the opposite manner also denies her need for the other or others. Fat (like emaciation) provides, in fantasy, a symbolic bulwark against desire and against the dangers of sexuality (Orbach, 1978). Both extreme body distortions provide evidence that object relations has a physical component as significant as the psychical component.

The false body

I shall now turn to the second proposition, that the woman with a distorted body image has a 'false body' experience. During the last several years working with or supervising the work of psychotherapists treating anorectics, bulimics and compulsive eaters, as well as women who are not symptomatic in this way but express great distress about their inability to 'live in their bodies', I have found myself thinking about Winnicott's (1965) explication of the 'true self' and the 'false self'. I have been thinking about the protective defensive functions of the latter, the notion of compliance and its implications for ego organisation, and I wish to extend his ideas about the false self to the body proper. As Winnicott expressed his ideas, they are almost palpable and have a physical feel to them. It is this aspect of his work – the resonance of his words with my experience of the anorectic within the therapy relationship – that has led me to see whether his concepts can be usefully extended to a discussion of the difficulties that anorectics have in attaining a corporeal sense of self.

I situate Winnicott's notion of the false self within the developmental model that informs the thinking of writers on whose work I have drawn. Broadly, they would all argue that the psychological development of the infant is dependent upon the relationship between it and its mother.

Psychological growth proceeds on the basis of the 'good-enough' mother or mother substitute responding to the baby's initiations, providing a containing experience in which the undifferentiated neonate develops out of absolute dependence into subjectivity. In so far as the mother is emotionally unavailable, thwarts the baby's initiatives or disregards its dependency needs, the developing psyche will incorporate a range of defense structures. The potential self develops a split, with good experiences forming the basis of satisfactory ego development while bad experiences become elaborated into highly complex internal good and bad object-relations representations (Fairbairn, 1952).

What is interesting to think about in the context of the bodily difficulties that anorectics express is just how much – as far as we can surmise – of the baby's earliest experiences are primarily those of sensation. In these first few months, the physical exchanges that occur between caregiver and baby dominate the relationship. The baby is caressed, fed, hugged, changed, wiped, dressed, undressed, bathed, dried, rocked, winded and carried. These activities may well be accompanied by cooing, singing, talking or melodious soothing of one kind or another. Physical relating is a primary mode of contact and infancy is characterised by sensual exchange between mother and child. The emotional ambience that the baby takes up is dependent on the conscious and unconscious actions and feelings of the baby's caretaker; so too the physical sensations which the baby experiences are interpreted for it by those who care for it. Depending upon how accurately its caregivers are able to perceive the baby's physical needs, the baby will come to have more or less confidence that what emanates from it will be responded to.

Several writers have considered the processes of the somatisation of mental distress (for example, Pines, 1980; McDougall, 1989) or the way in which the physical contains the mental distress (Bick, 1968). Here, I want to emphasise the physical basis of early human experience as opposed to considering the physical as a mental container for unprocessable feelings.

> The False Self defends the True Self; the True Self is, however, acknowledged as a potential and is allowed a secret life. . . . The False Self has as its main concern a search for conditions which will make it possible for the True Self to come into its own. . . . The False Self is built on identifications . . .   (Winnicott, 1965, p. 143)

Thus Winnicott (1965) lists some of the critically important defensive functions of the false self. The aetiology of the false self is the failures in good-enough mothering:

> The mother who is not good enough is not able to implement the infant's omnipotence, and so she repeatedly fails to meet the infant gesture; instead she substitutes her own gesture which is to be given sense by the compliance of the infant. This compliance on the part of the infant is the earliest stages of the False Self, and belongs to the mother's inability to sense her infant's needs.   (p. 143)

If we extend the notion of the false and true self to include the body we have a handle with which to understand important phenomena in women with severe body-image distortions. Winnicott's concept of compliance helps us make sense of the woman's capacity to change her body, her weight, her size or shape to comply with what she imagines is acceptable.

A woman may come to feel that her body is not really for her or of her; rather it is a malleable vehicle for survival through attempted compliance. Like the unintended development of a false self to shield an embryonic true self, the woman with a distorted body-image finds herself with a body that feels wrong. It doesn't seem to be her.

If the false body can be understood as having similar defensive functions to the Winnicottian false self, we can then see statements she makes about her hating her body as authentic statements which relate to what she feels lurks behind the false body, i.e. an embryonic-hated-body. Just as the true self fears that it will be found to be unattractive and that disclosure will bring rejection, and just as the true self has little facility for being, so the true body is an unknown entity. The true body does not exist within her imaginative possibilities except as a ghastly expression of unmet need. The creation of a false body is developed to comply with the felt demands of an inner object.

She does not know her true body: it has never been welcomed into a relationship and been authenticated. Just as the true self needs to be received within the therapy relationship in order that truncated development processes can be put in train again, so the true body – with all the attending hesitation that accompanies revealing it – needs to enter into the therapeutic dialogue in order for it to come to life.

Of all the body-image distortions, the anorectic's distorted sense of her body is most palpable. She powerfully feels that her body is not right. Let us see here if we can understand what occurs in the mother–daughter relationship that leads to a mother's misinterpretation of a daughter's cues, the substitution of mother's gestures and, ultimately, the creation of a false body sense in an anorectic.

The gender prescriptions that have such a profound effect on all aspects of mothering (Eichenbaum and Orbach, 1982; Orbach, 1986) are no less important in the development of a girl's corporeal sense of self. In trying to separate out the various influences that come to be expressed in the relationship to the body, four areas need to be considered.

First we need to consider the fact that in raising a daughter a mother will be inclined to shape her physical development in line with accepted social practices. While girls of today's generation may well not experience a message of physical restraint and caution, girls growing up 10, 20, 30 and 40 years ago were certainly the recipients of a pattern in which they were counselled to show restraint in physical and sexual matters. From the playground to the dating arrangements of teenage years, girls' and boys' behaviour continues to be rigidly divided along sex lines. Beginning with the daily life of an infant and toddler, this division involves more than the obvious observable differences such as encouraging a boy to climb a ladder while sending warnings of caution to a girl attempting the same task. The need to teach a girl to be physically a little girl involves three processes: one of negation, one of omission (teaching a 20-month-old girl to kick or throw a football is not common practice) and one of positive encouragement.

Girls learn from an early age to take an interest in particular aspects of their physicality. Little girls hear so frequently about their prettiness that they take in the idea that being pretty and having pretty clothes are crucial and important attributes. Looking attractive is essential to their well-being, to attracting a partner and so on. As they get older they learn the physical gestures that ensure that they are feminine. They learn how to hold a cup gracefully, to wipe their noses daintily, to run and walk in a 'ladylike manner'. As a result girls walk around with a sense of being watchful about their bodies. They know not to sit with their legs apart, they become fearful of vaginal odours, they know to harness their breasts in bras, they know to be careful lest they show evidence of an unexpected or particularly heavy menstrual flow and so on.

In contrast with girls, boys grow up learning that their bodies are powerful for *them*. They learn to push their bodies and to take pride in stretching their physical capabilities. It is as though we are looking at a mirror image: girls learn to restrain or contort or give up a potential, boys to extend a potential.

The same teaching extends to sexual matters. Girls are still learning that they shouldn't be giving their bodies away too hastily. This sentiment exposes the idea that a girl's body is essentially for another, her enjoyment of her sexuality will come through entrusting her body to another. In contrast a boy learns that his sexual appetites are legitimate and for him, something he is entitled to act upon. Ideas about gender and sexuality are not simply acquired in adolescence; they are part and parcel of what is conveyed to little girls and little boys in the process of growing up. Girls learn that a kind of physical demureness is appropriate and that a sexual relationship is part of the obligation of being a wife and mother rather than a proper female desire in itself.

Second, in the last 20–30 years, this injunction of physical and sexual restraint has also extended to girls' management of their appetites. Current child-rearing concerns express fears that children and especially daughters will grow up fat or with food problems. Much of a mother's concern for her family and an approved aspect of her social role is shown through food and so she is invested in her children enjoying it. She may, however, give confusing messages about food, especially to a daughter to whom she imparts the crucial lesson of being watchful of her desires in that area lest she be seen to be greedy and unattractive.

On the one hand she wishes her daughter to show pleasure and enjoyment in the food that she has prepared for her while on the other hand she directs her to be heedful of the food needs of others. There are significant differences in how girls and boys are breast-fed related to time and amount and even weaning practices. In cultures which value breast-feeding boys tend to get more of it for longer and are weaned more gradually (Belotti, 1975). As children develop, the message of restraint is one a girl hears frequently. She sees and hears about other females being involved in food in a particularly intense way. She learns about good foods and bad foods, foods that make you fat and foods that make you thin. She learns there is something naughty about bad foods and they become particularly attractive to her. Food and eating takes on all manner of symbolic meanings so that it frequently loses its fundamental relationship to appetite (Orbach, 1978, 1982, 1986).

Mediating the learning process by which a girl acquires her sense of physical restraint is the dynamics of the mother–daughter relationship. Mothers may well wish to give their daughters a far less conflicted notion of sexuality. They may well wish their daughters to be free of the food and weight problems that they may have experienced in their adult lives. And they may be able to convey to their daughters that their bodily desires and appetites are wonderful and wholesome. But such a message is unlikely to be unambivalent, for each woman internalises the dictates of the culture in which she lives and her personal desires interact with wider cultural practices. More importantly, and this is the third point I wish to raise, most mothers themselves experience a measure of discomfort with their bodies. The same practices they are passing on to their daughters are practices that they themselves have learned and internalised. This means that it is unlikely that mothers themselves will be relaxed in their physicality. The mother's body is more likely to be the site of a kind of discomfort itself, to express the injunctions that have been absorbed in relation to sexual and physical appetites of all kinds.

Thus many a daughter has heard her mother sigh about the shortcomings of her body, many a daughter has witnessed a mother dieting and sneaking food, many a daughter has watched a mother put on her 'face' – the mask of make-up that women learn to don in order to feel alright in themselves. This physical ingestion into the heart of the corporeal sense of self means that a girl will introject her mother's feelings about her body. If mother experiences the discomfort so endemic in Western female experience of the body, then a version of this will be introjected by the daughter. If the mother feels confident and at ease with her physicality, this will likewise be imbibed by the daughter. Hence, the daughter's corporeality embodies the mother's feelings about her body, her experiences of the physical interactions between them, as well as the instructions and modelling about appropriate physical femininity.

Fourth, beyond instruction, beyond the observances of the mother's physicality, the daughter also has another even more direct experience of mother's body which plays a significant role in the daughter's perception of self. The process of psychological development discussed before involves the 'taking in' of the mother's emotional presence in the formation of the girl's identity. The essence of emotional growth depends upon the relating that occurs between mother and child. Part of what the baby is taking in in the forming of its own personality is the *physical* sense of mother's body. It is actually mother's body that seems to provide or withold succour; she gives the breast as it is wanted or she seems to press it on the baby or withold it without the baby being able to comprehend or control its actions. The baby is scooped up and held in mother's arms in a comforting manner, but again not at its whim, at mother's. The physical presence of mother is potentially containing but also potentially disappointing. In crude terms, the mother's body is loved for meeting the baby's needs appropriately and hated for mismatching.

Just as the baby introjects mother's personality so, too, the baby takes into itself the physical presence and ambience of mother and develops its own physical sense of self with this physical imago of mother.

All these experiences are folded into the complex of interactions that occur between mothers and daughters in relation to the critical areas of body/physical awareness. The misdirecting of internal physical cues, the introjection of the mother's body, the experience of the maternal body and the gender-specific focus on a girl's body undermines the possibility that the daughter will develop a secure body image. A daughter's initiations are not authenticated, her gestures misconstrued and her mother's gestures offered in place of her own. This mismatching provides the preconditions for symptomatology which includes body-image distortions.

Some clinical implications

A common occurrence during therapy with an anorectic is that a woman may at first say her body is alright, that there is nothing wrong with it and she doesn't know what all the fuss and focus is about. She may shun discussion of her body size, she may hide herself in oversized clothing; if pressed she will most frequently utter the sentence 'it's too fat, it's horrible'. During the course of therapy she is able to acknowledge that there is something wrong and that she does hate her body. Without wishing to press my idea into Winnicott it does seem to me that when this happens in therapy the potential true body has come to treatment. I recognise this point as having a parallel with Winnicott's observation that before the true self has come to treatment, the therapist can only talk with the false self about the true self. In other words, until the hatred and fear and the shakiness of the body are experienced and acknowledged, one has to respect the protective functions the false body embodies.

Perhaps a way to look at this is by seeing that the anorectic despises her body and that hatred of her body is a reflection of a more general kind of self hate, despair and hopelessness not able to be experienced directly. The hatred then is an authentic experience which has arisen out of failures in the early environment. It is a parallel development to feelings of self loathing or hate commonly seen in women which, when reached in therapy, are often a sign that potent defences have been lowered – thereby opening up the possibility of direct engagement with the embryonic self. Such ideas are often expressed in a different form in the anorectic. With her they make their appearance firstly and most forcibly around how she feels about her body.

What this means clinically is that it is fruitless to dissuade the anorectic – except in the reality aspect of the therapeutic relationship – that her body is hateful. It denies her getting to a true experience. That hate needs to be acknowledged and received within the therapy relationship. And the hate that she carries needs to be expressed not just once but many times. When it is felt to have been heard, the way is open for the feelings projected onto the body to be integrated into the psychosomatic gestalt of the person. A productive way to discuss it might be as follows:

Patient: I really hate it. It is so fat and ugly.

Therapist: I think we have come to understand that despite the fact that your body is not in any objective sense hateful, you experience it as hateful and the horrible part of you.

Patient: I wish I could just do away with it, I hate it so much. Every hour of every day I am accosted with horrible feelings about my body.

Therapist: These powerful feelings of hate and horror for your body are feelings we need to face and understand together. . . .

At another time one might have taken up the meaning that the hated 'fat' body is invested with, but in this instance I wish to point out the importance of the therapist's *accepting* the feelings of hatred, not by accepting the patient's definition of the body, but by receiving the patient's *experience* of it. In doing this one is interposing a bridge against the division between a felt 'OK self' and a hated 'body'. The anorectic has designated her body as the source of her problems and the changing of her body as the solution to her problems. While the therapist needs to generalise the distress, he or she cannot do this by disregarding the actual phenomenon of body hatred that the anorexia expresses. And just as the patient comes to use the constancy and rightness of the therapist's interventions in the building of an authentic self, so the patient will come to use the body and the physical presence of the therapist in the making of an integrated psyche–somatic sense of self.

Pamela

P. sought treatment for her eating problems in her late thirties. She presented as a large compulsive eater and during the course of twice-weekly psychoanalytic psychotherapy lasting six years she had two brief periods of anorectic symptomatology. P. is a professional woman in a stable marriage. She has three children. When she originally came to therapy she presented as an enthusiastic earth mother who took care of everyone, her children, husband and relatives. Her work in medicine mitigates a self experience of being unworthy.

In the beginning phase of therapy she described herself as a compulsive carer. She needed to do this in order to feel of some value. She identified with the recipients of her own care and experienced short-term (narcissistic) gratification that her needs were being attended to in the process.

Alongside a need to administer to others was the world's experience of her as capable and competent. This was confirmed by her professional status and people's regard for her. However, her interior experience was one of fraudulence. She was unable to hold together a sense of her accomplishments as being other than tricks she could pull off or 'naturally endowed skills' which she could claim no credit for. Her considerable abilities were disavowed or rather hung outside of her finding no internal reflection and thus could only be used in the service of survival rather than as nourishment.

This was mirrored in relation to her body, which she felt was counterfeit and towards which she felt only critical. Here, where she felt she did have some responsibility and expert knowledge, she experienced herself as refusing it. Often it felt to her as though her body 'was in control' not her – she could exercise no authority over it. She described it as a self-willed child. Her body was a lump she was forced to accommodate to but one she refused to inhabit.

Her physical shape when she entered therapy resembled her paternal grandmother's body. Grandmother had been a figure of warmth and steadiness. Grandmother had lived in the family home when P. was a child and P. experienced some tension between mother and grandmother over how much P. should be 'spoiled and fussed over'. Grandmother's body was not experienced consciously in any negative way. Rather P. took comfort on grandmother's lap as a child and in grandmother's physicalness around the house.

P.'s mother's body was sturdy and trim but quite unwelcoming. P. remembers running to hug her mother after an absence of several weeks when she was 15 and mother *physically* recoiling. P. was of 'normal' size at the time but this experience translated inside of herself into the notion that there was something physically repulsive about her; that in her very being, in her spontaneous physical gesture, she was unacceptable and too much.

P. went on a diet, became briefly anorectic (for about six months), then bulimic (for a period of 18 months). For the last 20 years she had been a compulsive eater – sometimes briefly within normal range, more frequently 20 kg larger than she wished.

During therapy, P.'s experience of mother's recoil was repeated at both the physical and emotional level several times. P. found these experiences deeply shocking for in part of her unconscious she had split off the rejecting aspects of mother from that of the good aspects of mother who could be embracing. Up to that point she was only aware of the physically welcoming mother. The pain of her actual physical encounters with her mother were too distressing to bear and she had recreated mother as a physically alive and engaged person inside of herself. P. responded to the shock by eating more to obliterate and cushion the pain, but as the therapy progressed she dared to encounter the feelings more directly and to absorb and express the pain these encounters held for her. During this process her awareness of my lack of recoil, my physical and emotional acceptance of her assured her that she was not only capable of evoking rejection.

P. realised that she had two distinct experiences of her own body: one which identified with that of her paternal grandmother which was warm, fleshy and abundant, and another which was 'absent in its presence' – that is to say, not stable, not knowable, unreliable.

It was this unreliable experience of her body, an elusive body that matched her early and continuing experience of mother, and it was this aspect of her own corporeality, the unstable, almost non-material aspect of her body, that provoked her to try to transform that body – to make it comply with what was wanted. She experienced her mother's recoil as a recoil of her physical and mental existence. But at the same time, she had physically internalised her mother's 'absent presence'.

Her physical sense of herself contained both an absent body (the maternal introject) and a present more welcoming body. This split experience, entwined as it was with her early development, meant that she had alternating views and experiences of her body. Her grandmother's physical and emotional presence probably protected her from more extreme symptomatology as it offered her some form of identification with a reasonable physical and emotional subject. However, the mother's disdain for grandmother and the conflicts between them meant that she could not unambiguously identify with her, for this would have represented abandoning her internal relationship with mother.

Her body instability was linked with mother and this instability strove to find some security and recognition through the remaking of itself when she became anorectic. But the anorexia, while bringing her close to her internal world of denial, failed to offer her the imagined acceptance and recognition she would receive when she allied herself with the still-much-needed but rejecting object. Her continuing need for the rejecting object provoked her into a Winnicottian 'compliance'. She created the imagined 'false' body.

Her alliance with the grandmother's body was also a 'false body' experience. Through identification she attempted to have a body like the body of her grandmother, but this was no more authentically her own body. Often the most accurate reflection of her corporeality was paradoxical. She either experienced her body in bits held together by a broad piece of elastic or as its opposite: an undifferentiated lump that could absorb anything, mould itself to anything, become almost inanimate one moment and highly adaptable the next.

In the therapy, my body came to represent both mother's body, grandmother's body and an ideal body. It so happened that during the course of her therapy, I became pregnant. This event interposed my body into the therapy in an extremely vivid way and became the basis for much discussion, a certain amount of projection and a perhaps unique opportunity to work on her difficulties with having a body that was hers.

My body was experienced in a range of different ways from embracing, to withholding, to contained. I explored P.'s perceptions of my body as one might any other aspect of the transference and to the best of my ability I endeavoured to sort through the projections while allowing for identification and disidentification with my body. The pregnancy with its dramatic physical changes highlighted the impossibility of her having a stable sense of her body. At times she felt herself to be very fragile and frail. She was fat but this fatness covered up a physical delicateness. She had in fact been a rather sickly baby (or so she was told) and this sense of physical fragility alarmed her. It seemed at odds with her physical presence and yet there was something authentic about it. She imagined that I felt similarly delicate during my pregnancy (although she had remembered feeling robust during all her pregnancies except for the latter part of her third). It was as though she needed acknowledgement of delicateness; she needed recognition and legitimacy of it and when she could see me as delicate she could begin to allow her body to develop and strengthen from its weak roots rather than through 'over feeding'.

As the therapy proceeded we worked on the dilemma of her having a body that was neither grandmother's, nor mine nor her mother's, but hers. In time, her body changed and became similar to mother's physical shape although the ambience that infused her body was far from one of an 'absent presence'. P. felt at this time a certain fear that she would become her mother and that her attributes would be inverted and she would discover herself to be a cold, uncaring, physically distancing person. The therapeutic dialogue was able to hear and work through her fears of her own psychic and physical coldness. My physical and emotional engagement acted as a counterpoint. She could risk restructuring her internal world in the presence of someone whose physical–psychic engagement she could begin to trust.

In working with P., as is the case in work with other women with distorted body image, the therapist's body can become a prominent feature of the therapeutic milieu. It will at times be experienced in dramatically different ways, receiving the projections of the patient, being felt at one moment to be comforting and embracing, at another to be large, invasive and too present. These feelings on the part of the patient will be an important thread running through the therapeutic dialogue. The patient has only a crisis relationship to her body and cannot imagine that in any sense the body in which she lives will be a source of strength for her. By using the body of the therapist to work through her feelings about her own body and her mother's body she begins to introject a different physical presence and different physical possibilities for herself. As Winnicott has written in relation to the false self:

> Survival is sought in the management of crises. In other words the person has no real sense of continuity, of being an ongoing proposition themselves. They provide this continuity for themselves through the creation, management and survival of crises ... in extreme cases the infant exists only on the basis of a continuity of reactions to impingement and of recoveries from such reactions.
>
> (Winnicott, 1965)

This statement so expresses the anorectic's relationship to her body, a relationship in which almost every half an hour a ritualistic practice of some kind is undertaken so that a continuity of experience is kept up with the false body by its being remade again and again.

For the compulsive eater, a parallel process is in play. The act of eating without regard to hunger means that physiological processes that could provide for a sense of continuity are continually disrupted. There is an internal drama played out around hunger and satisfaction. Whether in dieting behaviour or in bingeing, the compulsive eater lunges from one crisis to another which she survives. The diet is the task she sets herself up to conquer, she manages and then fails, thus creating a series of exigencies that must always be overcome.

Conclusion

I have suggested in this chapter, then, several things. I have proposed that we need to take account of the process of corporealisation and to see how it is linked in with psychological development in general. We can see how problems in corporealisation express difficulties in object-relations and how the body comes to take on aspects of those object-relations. In the clinical situation I am suggesting that we need to look more closely at the actual particulars of the relationship a woman with a distorted body-image has to her physicality in order to understand the developmental problems that have occurred and in order to help her restart developmental processes around the true body: processes that I suggest are akin to the Winnicottian notion of the growth of the true self. And I have been proposing that to look at body-image distortions in this way can be seen as the physical expression of the developmental level of object-relations.

References

BELOTTI, E. (1975). *Little Girls*. London: Writer's & Readers' Publishing Cooperative.

BICK, E. (1968). The experience of the skin in early object relations. *International Journal of Psycho-Analysis* **49**, 484–486.

EICHENBAUM, L. and ORBACH, S. (1982). *Outside In Inside Out: Women's Psychology: A Feminist Psychoanalytic Approach*. London: Penguin. (Revised 1983 and published as *Understanding Women*. London: Penguin.)

EICHENBAUM, L. and ORBACH, S. (1983). *What Do Women Want? Exploding the Myth of Dependency*. New York: Coward McCann.

FAIRBAIRN, W. (1952). *An Object Relations View of Personality*. New York: Basic Books.

MAHLER, M., PINES, F. and BERGMAN, A. (1975). *The Psychological Birth of the Human Infant*. New York: Basic Books.

McDOUGALL, J. (1989). *Theatres of the Body*, London: Free Association Books.

ORBACH, S. (1978). *Fat is a Feminist Issue*. London: Paddington Press.

ORBACH, S. (1982). *Fat is a Feminist Issue II*. London: Paddington Press.

ORBACH, S. (1986). *Hunger Strike: The Anorectic's Struggle as a Metaphor for Our Age*. London: Faber.

PALAZZOLI, M. (1974). *Self-Starvation: Femine Intrapsychic to the Transpersonal Approach in Anorexia Nervosa*. London: Chaucer Publishing.

PINES, D. (1980). Skin communication: early skin disorders and their effect on transference and countertransference. *International Journal of Psycho-Analysis* **61**, 315–323.

RYCROFT, C. (1985). *Psychoanalysis and Beyond*. London: Chatto & Windus.

SPITZ, R. (1965). *The First Year of Life: Psychoanalytic Study of Normal and Deviant Development of Object Relations*. New York: International Universities Press.

WINNICOTT, D.W. (1965). *The Maturational Processes and the Facilitating Environment*. London: Hogarth Press and the Institute of Psycho-Analysis.

Chapter 8
The value of emotional awareness in general practice

Sotiris Zalidis

Introduction

For the past five years I have been a general practitioner working in a busy, training, inner city group practice of six general practitioners, one professor of general practice, two trainees and three practice nurses. We are responsible for the primary health care of a multi-ethnic population of 10 000 people, many of whom come from a deprived background. We know from NHS data (Fry, 1985) that when people have symptoms, only one in five will visit their general practitioner. At least one-third of the practice population do not consult their doctor in the course of the year. An increasing number of patients, however, need to consult us; in the East End of London, where our surgery is situated, we have to meet considerable social need and pressure. As general practitioners we also face pressure from the Health Service with its managerial, target-oriented climate, which tends to foster quick interventions based on the medical model. Unfortunately, a conventional medical approach can all too often lead to a therapeutic impasse because it ignores the needs of the individual.

For me, one of the most exciting aspects of working in general practice is the opportunity to know my patients as people and to understand the intrapsychic, familial and social contexts in which they fall ill. Psychodynamic theory provides me with the scientific basis for exploring my patients' life problems and in this chapter my focus will be on an individual psychotherapeutic approach, rather than on those familial interventions which can also be helpful.

When a patient feels unwell he or she may present to the general practitioner with symptoms which can be the physical accompaniments of anxiety, or with anxiety that is precipitated by physical symptoms, or a combination of these. Both the symptoms and the anxiety have to be attended to before it is legitimate for the general practitioner to attend to any underlying life problems about which the patient often does not complain. The patient may or may not be aware that there is a connection between his symptoms and his life problem. A great deal of trust is needed for the patient to confide his intimate worries and fears. Where there may still be genuine uncertainty about a diagnosis, there is a very real need for careful, physical examination and physical investigation. A physician who pretends that he does not need to do these things fools himself and the patient and runs the risk of missing serious physical illness. In this way the patient feels that his physical problems are being taken seriously and it becomes possible to build a sense of trust. It is only if the patient can trust the doctor with his body that he can venture further and trust him with his soul.

'Whole person' model

It would be relatively simple if we could separate the physical symptoms from the emotional complaints so that doctors could deal with either according to their preference and skill. There is, however, a vast literature on psychosomatic* medicine (Taylor, 1987; Cheren, 1989; Paulley and Pelser, 1989; Wilson and Mintz, 1989) documenting clearly the interaction between physical complaints and emotional states of mind. Very often the physical problems will not resolve until the emotional blocks to recovery have been dealt with. Attention to both 'psyche' and 'soma' is needed, in varying proportions, according to the patient's need. In this endeavour, the psychodynamic approach complements the conventional medical model.

One of the greatest influences on my practice has been the pioneering work of Michael and Enid Balint who were the first to apply a psychodynamic approach to primary care. Michael Balint asserted that the field of 'whole person' medicine was the particular province of the general practitioner. His own holistic approach was based on the notion of the 'basic fault' (Balint, 1968). He believed that the early months of a child's life brought about an inevitable mismatch between individual needs and environmental care. This resulted in a constitutional vulnerability or 'basic fault' in the psyche–soma of the individual: the depth of that fault depended on the content of the mismatch and on individual temperament. The 'basic fault' predisposed the individual to problems which could be psychological and/or somatic and which tended to appear at times of stress.

Michael Balint (and later Enid Balint) began to lead training groups with general practitioners in the 1950s. This work resulted in his book *The Doctor, his Patient and the Illness* (1957). Gradually, over the years, his ideas evolved and research groups under the guidance of Enid Balint developed the 'Balint approach' (Balint and Norell, 1973; Elder and Samuel,

---

* Within a biopsychosocial model, all health and illness can be said to be psychosomatic. However, I use that term to denote cases where psychological factors are particularly salient.

1987). This was a move away from elaborate assessment and analytic interviews to the study of the here-and-now relationship with the doctor. The doctor's increased understanding of the relationship with his patient enables him to become more tolerant and more receptive to what his patients are telling him, without necessarily attempting to challenge their defences or make interpretations. The resulting improved relationship with the doctor can lead to a therapeutic change in the patient.

A second important influence has been the work of Donald Winnicott (1972) who studied the interaction between mother and baby, and wrote in detail about what the ordinary devoted mother does naturally in order to prevent the mismatch between the needs of her baby and the caretaking environment. He believed that the psyche and the body do not start off as a unit. They form a unit if all goes well in the development of that individual. This depends on the capacity of the good-enough mother to identify with her baby and adapt to his dependency needs, thereby making a satisfactory relationship both to the body and the person. Of all the functions of the 'good-enough' mother which Winnicott described, the concept of 'holding' and of a facilitating environment are of particular relevance to the work of general practitioners. When an ill patient consults a doctor, the doctor ideally responds to need with adaptation, concern and reliability. This professional attitude of holding which meets the dependency of ill patients and facilitates growth and healing should also help the patient to find a personal solution to the complex problems of his emotional life and of interpersonal relationships. Winnicott's approach to psychotherapeutic consultations with children (1971) has encouraged me to take a more active exploratory role in consultations.

This work is based on the belief that, in the professional relationship, a patient who is given the opportunity will bring, and may display, his current emotional conflicts. By providing a freely moving human relationship within that setting, the doctor or therapist makes it safe for the patient to explore ideas or feelings that have not previously been integrated into the personality. Such ideas or feelings may have been experienced in a crude form as somatic symptoms and considered by the patient not to be part of himself. This attitude may be responsible for the common presenting complaint of certain patients that they have 'not been themselves lately'.

A third influence has been the increasing emphasis on affect development and affect regulation within a psychodynamic framework (Krystal, 1988). Krystal postulates that the neonate has internal tensions which are perceived not as a mental experience but as diffuse tensions on an undifferentiated sensorimotor level. Within a short time, this general excitement becomes differentiated into two general types of emotion: distress and delight. Out of the state of distress evolve all the affects we experience as distressing, and out of the state of well-being evolve all the emotions we experience as pleasurable. There are two developmental lines of affect:

affect differentiation and affect verbalisation with concomitant desomatis-ation. Because there is a reciprocal relationship between verbalisation and desomatisation of affects, psychosomatic diseases may be viewed as regressions of affect to a total somatic expression. Just having an emotion does not prove that the subject is aware of having it and is able to name it or use it as a signal or as information to himself.

In a seminal paper, Lane and Schwartz (1987) propose that emotional awareness is the consequence of cognitive processing of emotional arousal, and that the cognitive process itself undergoes a sequence of structural transformations during development which, in turn, determines the structure of subsequent emotional experience. They described five levels of emotional awareness:

1. Awareness of bodily sensations only. At this level the awareness of the separate existence of the other is minimal or non-existent.
2. Awareness of bodily sensations and action tendencies.
3. Awareness of individual feelings.
4. Awareness of blends of feelings.
5. Awareness of blends of blends of feelings.

At this level the major advance is the development of empathy. The person can appreciate the experience of others in the context of an ongoing differentiated awareness of his own emotional experience. These affective developments take place in the context of the infant's experience with what Winnicott called the good-enough mother.

As verbal skills develop, the precision and effectiveness of words demonstrate language to be the preferred way of handling affects. Using language and fantasy, the individual gradually develops new ways of representing experiences that are more flexible and can capture more of the information contained in the emotional arousal. Slowly the capacity to contain more of the arousal increases and the individual becomes more capable of regulating his own emotional state without needing to rely so much on outside caretakers. Encouraging the patient to experience, identify and name his emotions increases his emotional awareness by raising his emotions from a primitive sensorimotor level of experience to a mature representational level where they are experienced mentally as feelings. This psycho-therapeutic approach can help diminish prolonged states of emotional arousal which may be conducive to disease.

In my own work I am very selective in applying a psychotherapeutic approach. When such an approach is needed for the management of a patient with persistent physical symptoms or a somatic illness, I start by taking an exhaustive history of the physical complaint.

Usually, during the consultation, a lot of emotionally charged information about the patient's life emerges spontaneously. I assess the patient's defences and when it is possible I encourage him to identify and talk about his feelings and explore the life situation. We have to bear in mind, however, Winnicott's (1989) warning that the real illness in psychosomatic disorder is not so much the clinical state expressed in terms of somatic pathology, but the persistence of a split in the patient's personality organisation. The forces maintaining the dissociation serve an important defensive function and vary in intensity from patient to patient. This dissociation can lead patients to divide their care among many practitioners, to avoid recognition of their emotions and to avoid making the connections between their emotions and the somatic accompaniments of these emotions.

These defences must be respected. Michael Balint (1957) has pointed out that, in general practice, time is on our side. We need not be in a hurry. If the patient's resistances are too great, there is no need to take on the battle with these resistances there and then. If the psychotherapeutic approach is blocked then the doctor can continue by prescribing some sensible medicine such as a vitamin, a cough mixture, something against headaches or something to regulate the bowels. If this fails we can send the patient for some sensible investigation such as a full blood count, X-rays or an electrocardiogram. The patient will come back in a couple of days, weeks or months, and the psychotherapeutic work can be picked up where it stopped. In other words the general practitioner has a long-standing relationship with the patient and this provides a sense of holding (Zalidis, 1992).

All this can put a great strain on the doctor. He has to be aware of his emotional responses to his patient's personality and behaviour and be able to discriminate between his own contribution to the emotional atmosphere of the consultation and that of the patient. He needs to tolerate his feelings instead of acting them out. Both through his demeanour, and through appropriate words, he has to convey new ideas about emotions to the patient. Gradually the patient needs to learn that emotions are not discrete entities to be suppressed or discharged through immediate action but, rather, valued aspects of experience that signal important information to himself. When reflected upon, such information can help him respond more effectively to stressful events and to the vicissitudes of his interpersonal relationships (Greenberg and Safran, 1987). For all these reasons, I think that the doctor is in a much better position to offer a psychotherapeutic approach to his patients if he has dealt with his own blind spots in a satisfactory way through personal analysis, psychotherapy or regular case discussions with colleagues.

In general practice we see a great variety of problems. Some patients can be helped in two or three sessions and some may take years, depending on their defences. In the following two cases I would like to illustrate how I apply my psychotherapeutic approach to complex clinical problems in the general practice setting.

Two case histories

David

David, one of my patients, developed herpes zoster. Herpes zoster or shingles is a manifestation of recurrent infection with varicella virus which also causes chickenpox (Zuckermann, Banatrala and Pattinson, 1990). Chickenpox has now been found to be the primary varicella infection and zoster the manifestation of reactivated varicella virus which follows a period of latency, usually lasting several decades. Recovery from the primary infection results in life-long immunity to exogenous infection. However, following the primary infection, the virus remains latent in groups of nerve cells in the brain or the spinal cord. When the host's immune defences fail to contain the virus, it reactivates in the group of nerve cells and progresses peripherally down the sensory nerve to produce the typical blistery rash which is restricted to the area of the skin supplied by the nerve.

Although rarely a life-threatening disease, herpes zoster is of concern because of the painfulness of the acute lesion and of the post-herpetic neuralgia that may follow the acute lesion. The failure of the host defence mechanisms to contain the virus in the group of nerve cells after such prolonged periods of time is not understood. Inadequacy of cell-mediated immunity is likely to be of critical importance. Recent advances in psychoneuroimmunology (Ader, 1991) suggest that there may be a connection between depressed cell-mediated immunity and an unsuccessful mourning process (Pollock, 1989).

In the series of 20 patients that I have studied in the last five years, it is my experience that shingles is preceded by a period of emotional distress of which the patient may be unaware. The distress is usually intensified through reactivation of unresolved mourning from the past. I have found that those patients who are unable to make any connection between the eruption of shingles and their emotional distress or to express any feelings are more prone to develop post-herpetic neuralgia, and may need treatment with tricylic antidepressants as the only means of obtaining pain relief.

In May 1992 David, a 54-year-old teacher, was the last patient on my morning surgery list. David is a tall man with gentle features and a soft voice. He told me that he was still concerned about a painful sensation on the left side of his chest that felt as if somebody had punched him. The doctor he saw the week before had reassured him that the pain was not cardiac. It had not gone away. He felt occasional sharp jabs below the left breast and sometimes the pain radiated to his head and made him feel light-headed. The previous day he could not concentrate at work and felt drained of energy.

When I examined him I noticed a small cluster of blisters below the left nipple and another one in his left armpit. I told him that he was developing shingles. As he was getting up from the examination couch I asked him whether he had been feeling run-down lately. He denied this, and dismissed any worries about friends or relatives. I asked him whether he had had any shocks lately, or any life or work changes, but he said not. He had started a new post a year previously which was less stressful than the one before and he was very pleased with it.

I then asked him about his family. He was single and lived on his own. His mother had died of a brain tumour 25 years before and his father had died six years before in his mid-seventies, from the side effects of the drugs he was taking for rheumatoid arthritis. He was the second of five children, all of them healthy. His younger brother, Peter had come back from America two months previously and had gone to stay with his sister Anne in Cornwall.

He started telling me that Peter and Anne had helped to look after his father when he was dying . . . but he stopped in mid-sentence. His lower lip began to quiver and he was overcome with sadness. He started weeping faintly. He said that he was a little different from everybody else in his family because his own interests were artistic, but overall they were a fairly close family. His father died before they could get to know each other. He was a baker and worked very hard. As a boy, David used to spend time with him at the shop in Cornwall, but his father was always working, so there was no time to talk.

During his father's last illness in the hospital, David had had to leave for a few days. His father died before he returned. He was sobbing by now. He added that he was not aware he was thinking about all this.

'Has anything happened to bring these memories back?' he asked.

'Perhaps your brother's arrival from America has something to do with it,' I suggested.

He planned to go and visit his brother soon, but he could not imagine what might have brought these thoughts on. I handed him a tissue and told him that these very painful feelings at the back of his mind could lower his immunity so that the chickenpox virus, which until then was in check, could become reactivated. If he had a chance to experience these feelings it was possible that the pain could be milder and last a shorter time.

He looked at me in surprise. I gave him topical antiviral treatment and invited him to come again the following week with a double appointment.

A week later the cluster of blisters had coalesced and formed a band along the left side of the chest. His pain was mild, but he complained of a mild headache which had woken him up the night before and stayed with him the whole day. He asked me whether the headache was part of the shingles. I told him it was probably not directly related to the shingles and I reminded him of the very painful memories of his father that had emerged in the last session.

He said again that he was not at all aware that he had all these thoughts. The eruption caught him unaware. He talked again about never having had a personal talk with his father. Their interaction always consisted of questions and answers, and they were never able to relax into a personal conversation. His father was not open with his feelings, nor was his brother Peter. When as a child he helped his father at the bakery, it was always work, work, work. Even though he was only two years younger than David, Peter did not have to help his father at the bakery. During the summer Peter used to go with his eldest sister to his aunt's house in Cornwall.

David regretted that there were so many things that he had not learned from his father. For instance, he did not know how his parents met. He saw his nieces and nephews knowing so much about their parents' lives whilst he knew so little. 'Perhaps the generation difference explains it,' he mused.

When David came to London to become a teacher, Peter stayed in Cornwall and lived with his father. Very often David was told by his relatives that they did not ring him in London because he was so busy and they did not want to disturb him. He wondered whether inadvertently he had given the message that he did not want to be disturbed.

David then talked about visiting his father in hospital. His arthritis had worn him out and he had become very weak. David wished he had been at his bedside when he died. But he had not wanted his father to see him crying. He had to cry away from his father. He said that when he gets together with his brothers and sisters now they remember the past and he realises that they had some very good times together, but at the time when it was all happening he did not appreciate it.

I told him that the headache probably had something to do with these sad memories and invited him to come again in a week's time.

He never came.

This case illustrates how my psychological management was associated with a marked reduction of pain. It may well have brought about a shift of symptoms from pain at the site of the rash to a mild headache. I understood this to represent a lessening of the dissociation because headache can be accepted as associated with feelings of sadness and mental pain in general.

I saw David a year later. He was worried about an ache behind his right ear. He had always been anxious about sensations around his right ear because this is the only normal ear; he is congenitally deaf in the left. On examination his right ear was found to be blocked with wax. I asked our practice nurse to syringe it and his symptoms disappeared. There was no need for a psychotherapeutic intervention on this occasion.

Laura

Laura was 47 years old when she first came to see me in February 1988. She is a short, plump Spanish woman who speaks fluent English with an attractive Spanish accent.

Since she registered in our practice in 1980 she has suffered from a variety of psychosomatic symptoms such as allergic swelling of the face and hives, hayfever, severe headaches, bouts of abdominal pains, recurrent attacks of diarrhoea and vomiting, dyspepsia, breathing difficulties and generalised aches and pains. Lately she had started having occasional falls and developed a fear of going out of her flat.

At the start of our relationship she used to present her symptoms with an anguished expression and dramatise her suffering by wincing at every twinge of pain and rubbing the part of her body that hurt her at the time. She would complain with exaggerated intensity, often beginning the consultation by saying that she was not better and the pains were killing her.

I remember being filled with dismay at the beginning of every consultation when I realised that none of my conventional remedies worked. As investigations and treatment of her physical complaints had given no result, I decided that I had to adopt a different approach. I asked her to make a double appointment – that is, 20 minutes – every time she came to see me so that we had time to talk. My aim was to give her the opportunity to explore her feelings and ideas and talk about them so that the physical symptoms would lose their intensity and would stop being the main form of communication between us.

Gradually I learned that Laura was the second youngest of 16 children, and lived alone with Sally, her 17-year-old daughter, since her divorce two years after Sally's birth.

She described her husband as a 'Jekyll and Hyde' character. One day he told her a terrible secret and after that she did not let him touch her again. She felt that if she could share this secret with somebody she would not get any more headaches, but just the thought of it choked her and she did not want to talk about it.

She was almost crippled by her intolerance of anything smelly or dirty. What stopped her from going out of the flat was her repugnance of dirty, scruffy people who spit in the street. She was disgusted with sexual fluids and had had to have a shower as soon as she and her husband had made love. Later, when her daughter was born, she was so disgusted with the dirty nappies that she started potty training her from the age of two months.

She had always lived with her daughter in a close, mutually dependent relationship, but recently seemed to feel increasingly threatened by Sally's developing independence and budding sexuality. She said that she could not keep up with her brilliant daughter and preferred the relationship she had with her up to the age of 15. She would get furious with Sally for smoking or coming home tipsy after a few drinks with friends. After a row with her, she would develop a number of frightening physical symptoms which would intimidate Sally into submission. Sometimes she would have a fall after such a row. The clamour of her rage and the accompanying physical symptoms would protect her from experiencing any anxiety about the changing relationship to Sally, or from thinking about it in order to adapt to her new circumstances.

From the day of her first appointment with me in February 1988 until her most recent in February 1992, I counted that I saw her one hundred times.

I would like to present a few sessions from the beginning, the middle and the current point of our relationship in order to demonstrate her progress.

Laura developed severe back pain a few weeks after we first met and she stayed in bed for about a month. I treated her at home with analgesia and domiciliary physiotherapy. Sally had to do everything for her during this illness: bath her, cook for her and when she became constipated she even gave her enemas. When she recovered she started coming to see me regularly.

One day she came to the surgery complaining of severe headaches. In our discussion it emerged that her downstairs neighbour made a lot of noise and, when Laura complained, the neighbour swore at her. Laura became very annoyed and when she was annoyed she worried and got a migraine. I asked her what the worry was about? She said that she worried that she might crack up in the same way that she had done at the Council several years ago before she moved to her present address. She had gone to the Council to complain about her neighbours, whom she described as 'blacks, Irish, madmen' who made a lot of noise, and with one of whom she had had a fight. She 'went mad' in the housing officer's office, screaming and shouting, overwhelmed with rage. I said that it seemed as though she lost her head then, and that now the headaches seem to be an attempt to keep her head.

Laura's symptoms deteriorated. She missed the following appointment because she was too ill to get out of bed and came to see me a week later in an agitated state of mind. She complained of a multitude of physical symptoms. She had a chill from the top of her head to her toes as if somebody was 'walking on her grave', constant headaches, a tickling cough, a pain in her throat and breathlessness. She was breathless all the time, but she would also wake up in the middle of the night gasping for air. She said that 'it' woke her up at three o'clock in the morning and she could not breathe. The air would not come out because there was a knot in her throat as if somebody was strangling her. Sometimes she developed a heaviness on her chest and then she could not take a breath. It felt to her as if her chest had sunk into her tummy. Not surprisingly she wanted me to examine her.

I was so overwhelmed by her anxiety about the frightening and bizarre symptoms, that I did not think of the hyperventilation syndrome at the time (Lum, 1976; Magarian, 1982). I examined her and all I could find were some tender spots on her ribs. I told her that her symptoms were probably related to muscle tension due to her anxiety and listened to her anger about her neighbour who was annoying her so much recently. Laura found it easier to talk of her rage with her neighbour than with her daughter, and considered the neighbour responsible for her state of mind. When Laura said that 'it' woke her up at three o'clock in the morning she was also expressing her belief that she had no responsibility for her symptoms. She was the passive victim of something alien out there which attacked her in the middle of the night.

Krystal (1988) has pointed out that in the permanent blocking of affectivity by long-lasting defences, the emotions are experienced as 'attacks'. During such attacks the affects may not be consciously recognised as such, as in the case of hyperventilation. This subjective experience is the cause of the tendency found in both patients and doctors to experience their emotions as if they were part of a physical illness. My aim in treating Laura was to help her recognise her emotions as her own and her symptoms as the somatic accompaniments of these emotions. Thinking about and expressing these emotions in words could modify their intensity and make them a source of information about herself and her relationship to others. This was not an easy task with Laura. Apart from her fear that she might become overwhelmed by the intensity of her emotions and go mad, there was also a fear that her magical powers would make the wish contained in the emotion come true. One day she told me that she was trying hard not to have bad thoughts. She had the impression that she was psychic, that if she thought of something it would happen. 'Nothing good ever happened to me,' she used to say. When her brother-in-law developed leukaemia she felt responsible and guilty. She remembered an argument they had in Spain long ago, when she lost his dog and he told her off angrily. She was annoyed with him and she thought 'Why don't you get lost like your dog'. Now she considered herself to be the cause of her brother-in-law's illness.

About a year and a half after I first met Laura, Sally found a well-paid executive job in an advertising company and to celebrate her success she went for a trip to Spain to visit her maternal grandmother. Laura developed severe back pain about a week before Sally left and colicky abdominal pains, diarrhoea and vomiting during Sally's absence for which she made several requests for home visits.

I felt dismayed that in spite of spending so much time with her the previous year I had made so little impact on her neediness. Her symptoms did not improve after Sally's return. She complained of severe abdominal pains for which no drug was effective. Sally made an appointment to come and see me and find out what was wrong with her mother. Laura had become afraid that she was suffering from a peptic ulcer and had asked me to refer her for a barium meal. Even though I knew intuitively that her symptoms were related to her feelings about being abandoned by Sally during her trip to Spain, at some level I experienced her request for physical investigations as a vote of no confidence. I felt that my authority was challenged, that it was my job to decide when physical investigations are needed. Her request implied that I was neglectful and this annoyed me.

I was able to hold my anger and modulate it by reflecting on it with the help of my previous experience with psychosomatic patients (Zalidis, 1991). This experience has confirmed Winnicott's view that their tendency to consult many therapists is a symptom of the split in their personality organisation. There is little to be gained by forbidding this tendency. The patient will consult other therapists without the doctor's knowledge if he thinks that his doctor disapproves or expresses his anger. Much more can be gained if the doctor tolerates his own anger, stays in the background and maintains a unified view of the patient's progress. In relation to Laura, I could have either refused her request, on the grounds that a similar test several years before was normal, or given in to it and done exactly what she asked by giving her a request form for a barium meal. Both options would have been dismissive, giving vent to my annoyance.

After reflection I thought that the most helpful course of action would be to refer her to a consultant gastroenterologist for a specialist evaluation of her symptoms. Apart from reassuring her, the referral would free me from the pressure to do something about her physical symptoms in order to concentrate on the psychotherapeutic management. Besides, as her symptoms were not improving, I was also beginning to consider a possible organic lesion. I wrote to the consultant explaining to her the background of Laura's symptoms and personality and asking her to rule out organic pathology. Fortunately all the investigations were normal except for a raised eosinophil (a particular type of white blood cell) count which necessitated examination of her stool for ova and parasites. I remember, with a certain vengeful glee, the combination of amusement and horror on her face when she told me of the ordeal of having to put her stool in a pot and take it to hospital for examination.

Very little had changed in her behaviour or her complaints since I first met her. The main gain was that by now she considered me to be her doctor and she always came to see me with a double appointment, something that was beginning to contain her distress within the practice.

I would listen to her symptoms and then guide her to talk about whatever upset her most. Sometimes she was angry with her neighbour but more often she talked about Sally. She would become furious if Sally came home drunk, jealous if she talked of her boyfriend, promotion and payrise at work, tearful when she discussed her plans of going to work abroad, annoyed because she spent all her money too easily without saving for the future. Very often she commented that their roles were reversed and Sally behaved towards her with the authority of a mother. One night she dreamt she was a cripple and was driving around in an electric wheelchair. In November 1990 she developed sudden crippling back pain. The duty doctor had to visit her at home twice in order to assess her condition and treat her. She arranged for domiciliary physiotherapy and I visited her three days later.

Laura was in bed with a lot of pain and she greeted me with a barrage of complaints. 'The stupid tablets made me dopey . . . the physiotherapist was no good . . . her treatment was too short and ineffective.'

I asked her whether she felt Sally was caring enough and Laura wondered whether the pain had anything to do with her daughter.

I asked how the pain started.

The day before the onset Sally came home tipsy, giggling. Laura was furious. They had a violent row which lasted for three hours. At the height of the argument Laura slapped Sally and Sally slapped her back, breaking Laura's glasses. After this Sally stormed out of the flat and Laura spent all night sobbing on the floor. The following morning she went out into the garden to cut some flowers to decorate her father's photograph. As she stretched her arms to cut the flowers she heard three cracks in her back and felt excruciating pain. She said that it was all Sally's fault and she wanted to scare her into not drinking. Seeing her drunk reminded her of her husband. It was not ladylike. She behaved like a tart and Laura was afraid that any man could take advantage of her in that state. I commented that it would be an awful shame if she tried to control Sally with her back pain, but she took no notice.

Laura said that there must be something wrong with her back and perhaps she needed an operation to put it right. I was worried about this trend towards invalidism in her. Becoming a back cripple in a wheelchair, totally dependent on Sally, was a possible outcome that I wanted to prevent.

I visited her again two days later. Her pain was no better and she appeared to be in agony. Every movement caused excruciating pain and made her scream. I examined her and listened to her complaints about Sally who had left her alone for the day to go to a conference. She did, however, acknowledge that Sally did everything for her. She washed her, cooked for her, and if her constipation persisted she would give her an enema.

I asked about enemas in childhood.

She remembered her mother bringing her children breakfast in bed: first a cup of capuccino and then a deep plate of boiled chestnuts to regulate their bowels. If she did not open her bowels for three days her mother would give her an enema. When Laura was about 12, she told her mother to stop because she found it humiliating.

I visited again a week later and she complained bitterly of constipation. Sally had refused to give her an enema. She had rung the duty doctor at three o'clock in the morning to complain but she did not find his advice at all helpful.

We talked again about her childhood in Spain. Her mother had to go back to work in a tomato factory after the birth of her youngest sister and one of her older sisters became the 'little mother' for her.

She became the cleanest, tidiest child under the tutelage of that sister who was more fanatically clean than her own mother. She would run her fingers on surfaces that Laura had missed dusting and she would wipe her dusty finger on Laura's mouth. Her father was very much respected. He was, according to Laura, 'a lovely man'. When the family would sit down to dinner, Laura would complain that her mother had given more food to her brothers and sisters. Father would ask her to hush and would give her a spoonful from his own plate. She missed him very much. She did not remember her mother ever kissing her, whereas her father did.

Her condition was not improving and I had to reassure her physiotherapist, who anxiously rang me, that she was doing a good job.

When I visited again three days later, Laura was in pain and full of complaints. Nobody was doing anything for her. She was angry with Sally who was not devoting herself completely to her mother's care. 'She could have given up her job for a few days,' she said. 'Is her job more important than me? She does not care for me.' She was annoyed with Sally's chatter about her excited preparations for her company's Christmas party. She experienced Sally's behaviour as a 'stab in the back'.

A week later she felt a lot better. She could limp around her bed without much pain and she was not complaining any more. My visit had a social character. During my visit Sally came home with her new dress for her company's Christmas party. She was cheerful and excited and she put it on to show us. I expressed my admiration but Laura said nothing and looked at it disapprovingly. When Sally went to the kitchen to make a cup of coffee, Laura said that she did not like the dress because it did not have any class. She went to her wardrobe and took out a black dress of her own that she had bought 15 years ago to show me how much better class it was than Sally's. She had lost all interest in dressing up 15 years ago, she said sadly.

Then came a turning point. In January 1991, six weeks after the onset of her back pain, she was able to come to the surgery again. She looked somewhat amused and told me that she had dreamt she had sex with the Pope.

I asked her for the details of the dream. She dreamt that she was in St Peter's Square. The Pope came up to her and held his hand out to her. He led her up to his chambers, sat next to her and started talking to her. He put his hand under her skirt and started fondling her. Gradually he made love to her and the whole thing was celestial, beautiful and refined. When Sally came into the room in the morning Laura felt so embarrassed. 'You will never believe what I have been dreaming,' she told her. Sally laughed and laughed when she heard. Since then she had been dreaming of the Pope every night. They did not make love anymore. He cuddled her and it felt so good. All his entourage in the dream treated her with respect as though she was a member of his family. She was worried that she was going mad. She was not even religious. She thought of writing to the Pope to ask him what he was doing in her dreams!

I told her that it was she who put him in her dreams. It was like putting a picture of the Pope in her sitting room, and writing to him to ask what he was doing in her sitting room. I reassured her that it was perfectly alright to have these dreams and asked her to come again in two weeks time to talk more about them. In retrospect it was clear that this reassurance did not address the anxiety as will be apparent from the ensuing guilt.

When she arrived she started complaining of headaches and dryness of the skin on her nose. I asked whether she was going to waste her time instead of discussing her dreams as we agreed. She looked at me craftily. 'I don't want to tell you my dreams. They're saucy.' Then she burst into laughter and said that a week previously she had dreamt of Patrick Swayze, the hunk who plays in 'Dirty Dancing'. He was teaching her to dance and she could do everything he taught her. Then she told me of another dream with a different mood which she had after the Patrick Swayze dream. She dreamt that she was a Jesuit and she was running through a forest. Hanging branches were whipping her face and she woke up with a feeling of suffocation, gasping for air. She often got this feeling of suffocation, she remarked.

I asked her what the Jesuits would think about her dreams of having sex with the Pope?

'They would whip me, they would cut my head off,' she said in alarm.

I interpreted that in that case her dream expressed her guilt about all the good times she had in her previous dreams. She asked me what her dreams about the Pope meant and I suggested that the Pope stood for her father. She wanted her father to come and rescue her. Her back pain started when she stretched her arms to cut some flowers to decorate his photograph.

She marvelled. 'What a good memory you have,' she said. She had never accepted her father's death. She had not dreamt for 10 years yet for the last two months she had been dreaming all the time.

She also remembered dreams of being invited by the Queen to the Palace for tea. She went to the Palace but was never given tea. When I told her that the Queen might stand for her mother she remembered how stingy her mother was, both with affection and money. Her father would not hesitate to spend money on her or encourage her to buy an extra pair of good shoes.

Laura's improvement was clearly signalled by the ability to remember her dreams. Although I did not make an interpretation, the Pope dreams expressed her wish for care and affection from me as well as from her father. Its sexualisation led to a sense of oedipal guilt expressed in her Jesuit dreams. This was so strong that it could not be contained by the dream but woke her up with a sense of suffocation. I wonder whether similar unconscious emotions and phantasies underlay the hyperventilation attacks that woke her up several times at night in the past.

Laura continued to come to the surgery regularly but her physical symptoms had lost some of their urgency and now she could discuss her feelings. In November 1991 her mother became terminally ill with cirrhosis of the liver and her brother-in-law's leukaemia took a turn for the worse. She had to go to Spain to be with her mother, who died at the end of November. Laura came to see me as soon as she returned. She told me how amazed she was with herself for finding the strength to overcome her disgust and nurse her mother. She had to feed her, wash and wipe her bottom. She cried a lot when she died and now she felt empty.

Two weeks after Laura's mother's death, in the middle of evening surgery, I had an urgent request from Sally to go and visit her mother who was writhing in agony with severe abdominal pain. With a sense of exasperation, I interrupted the surgery and visited her immediately. She was groaning with pain, twisting and turning in a world of her own. On examination she was tender all over. The slightest movement caused pain. I knew intuitively that her pain was related to her feelings about her mother's death, but she was beyond words. I gave her an injection of pethidine and went back to the practice to continue my surgery.

The injection did not work and at three in the morning Sally called the duty doctor who admitted her to hospital under the surgical team. In the morning Sally rang me at the practice. She was crying. Her uncle had just died of leukaemia and she was very worried about her mother. She wanted to know what was wrong with her. I explained to her that with such a degree of physical pain it was impossible to be sure that there was nothing seriously wrong going on in her mother's tummy. We would have to wait and see.

That evening I visited Laura in hospital. She was drowsy from the analgesia and had a drip up. The surgeons suspected intestinal obstruction. I sat by her bedside and we talked for half an hour. She remembered that something similar had happened to her when her brother died and she could not go to the funeral. She also remembered that her mother was complaining of abdominal pain while she was dying and Laura had to go out of the room because she could not tolerate her moans. She felt so helpless. She had heard about her brother-in-law's death. She had known he was poorly but she did not expect him to die so soon.

'You have to bear so much pain Laura,' I said. 'It is like becoming your mother and brother-in-law in one.'

She groaned with pain. 'What can I do about it?'

Because I was worried that the surgeons might operate prematurely before giving her the benefit of the doubt, I rang up the surgical registrar to inform him of Laura's personality and of her tendency to respond to death events with severe pain. He had already noticed her capacity to dramatise and he was interested in what I had to say. He was aware of an association between acute emotional crises and paralysis of the bowel.

The following day Laura's pain resolved and she was discharged. Four days later she went back to Spain for her brother-in-law's funeral. She suffered no more pain.

When she returned she came to see me. She was sad and subdued and complained of her feelings of emptiness and of shivering at night. She talked of her anger with her mother's helplessness. She was afraid that if she became paralysed Sally would have to do for her what Laura did for her mother and she did not want this to happen. Life was so cruel and she felt so angry with it. I asked her whether it was possible for her abdominal pains to be due to this anger. She looked at me in silence.

A month later she came back and complained of numbness in her hands and feet and a feeling of suffocation. She could not take a deep enough breath for the last three weeks. She was also waking up at night, gasping for air. She wondered whether all these symptoms were due to her anxiety because Sally had gone to a conference in Greece and with all the news about young girls being abducted and raped she was worried. I explained the hyperventilation syndrome to her and taught her diaphragmatic breathing (Lum, 1976). When she came back three weeks later, she told me that she found the breathing exercises very helpful but she still had a lot of headaches. We discussed her money worries and how angry she can get with Sally who spends money without a thought for the future. Then she paused and said that sometimes she thinks that she makes herself ill. I took notice of this phrase. It represented a significant change from the phrase four years earlier that 'it' woke her up at night.

Laura had begun to develop the capacity for reflective self-awareness and had stopped seeing herself as the passive victim of alien forces. She had begun to recognise that she owned her emotions and that her symptoms were the somatic accompaniments of these emotions. It was crucial to this change that she had formed a relationship with me in which her long-standing depression, rage and denied sexuality could be acknowledged and contained rather than expressed in symptoms and fights with her daughter and neighbours.

When I looked in her medical notes after this period of intensive treatment, I realised that the number of consultations had fallen from 30 a year for the years 1989, 1990, 1991 to 15 for the year 1992. However, 15 was the average number of annual consultations before I adopted a psychotherapeutic approach towards her. The dramatic change was not so much in the number of consultations but in their quality.

There is no longer a sense of insatiable neediness and agitated demandingness which made her come to the surgery as an emergency without an appointment, complaining of aches and pains and being oblivious to the disruption she caused to the doctor's work. She still attends frequently but she always makes a double appointment one or two weeks in advance and she discusses her feelings, such as her anger with her demanding invalid brother, or her apprehension about following her daughter to America where she is tempted to live and work.

She has been transformed from a patient about whose urgent, incomprehensible, agitated complaints I felt exasperated, to a person whose progress in life I follow with interest.

Summary and conclusion

In general practice we routinely see a large number of patients. In the majority of cases we only have to deal with their immediate complaints and provide symptomatic relief. A lot of the symptoms patients complain of are the bodily accompaniments of emotions of which the patients are not consciously aware. At the first contact it is often hard to recognise what may become a significant emotional theme. When the symptoms are difficult to explain in terms of physical pathology, I tend to write something like 'What is going on?' in the notes to remind myself to be on the look out for further information to make sense of the patient's complaints.

When the symptoms do not resolve spontaneously and quickly or they are recurrent, the patient may attribute them to a frightening disease, increasing his anxiety, and demand from his doctor that he makes a diagnosis which can make sense of his suffering. Alternatively, the emotional arousal which is not contained mentally by the information processing of the cognitive elements of affects can activate neuroimmune or neuroendocrine mechanisms that can lead to physical breakdown. This will need further management in its own right. When this is the case, the general practitioner can rely on the patient's trust to go beyond common-sense and explore the emotional setting in which symptoms arise.

The psychodynamic approach provides the basis for this exploration which has to include the identification and verbalisation of affects.

The two cases I have presented illustrate my way of working. I have first to earn the patients' capacity to trust me with their body by taking their physical complaints seriously. I am also active in eliciting the patient's emotional response to the symptoms and, once this emerges, I acknowledge it and allow it time to develop. At the same time I assess the patient's vulnerability and resistance and seek the right moment to link physical symptoms with emotional state. The patient is then given the opportunity to express his emotional conflict in words. If he feels that the doctor listens with interest and acceptance, he may then feel safe enough to explore the conflict further and thus go on to experience a lessening in severity of the physical symptoms. Hopefully he will feel sufficiently supported to find his own solution to his problems.

This work is delicate, demanding and has dangers. David's case shows the need for the doctor to know just how much emotional work a patient is prepared to risk at any given time and to be prepared to wait, perhaps for years, before the next moment of insight. Laura's case shows how the doctor's necessary identification with the patient has to be watched so that it does not become overidentification which might then propel the doctor into action rather than thought.

The doctor's ability to meet the demands of the work can only take place through continuous monitoring and awareness of his own feelings and the capacity to tolerate and contain them. Primarily this serves to contain anxiety which the patient finds unbearable, until in time the patient can perform this function for himself.

Bibliography

ADER, R.(1991). *Psychoneuroimmunology*. London: Academic Press.

BALINT, M. (1957). *The Doctor, his Patient and the Illness*. London: Pitman Medical.

BALINT, M. (1968). *The Basic Fault*. London: Tavistock Publications.

BALINT, E. and NORELL, J.S. (Eds) (1973). *Six Minutes for the Patient. Interactions in General Practice Consultations*. London: Tavistock Publications.

CHEREN, S. (Ed.) (1989). *Psychosomatic Medicine Theory, Physiology and Practice*. Madison, CT: International Universities Press.

ELDER, A. and SAMUEL, O. (Eds) (1987). *While I'm Here Doctor. A Study of the Doctor-Patient Relationship*. London: Tavistock Publications.

FRY, J. (1985). *Common Diseases: Their Nature, Incidence and Cause*. London: MTP Press.

GREENBERG, L.S. and SAFRAN, J.D. (1987). *Emotion in Psychotherapy*. London: The Guilford Press.

KRYSTAL, H. (1988). *Integration and Self-Healing: Affect, Trauma, Alexithymia*. Hillsdale, NJ: The Analytic Press.

LANE, R.D. and SCHWARTZ, G.E. (1987). Levels of emotional awareness. A cognitive developmental theory and its application to psychopathology. *American Journal of Psychiatry* **144**, 133-143.

LUM, L.C. (1976). The syndrome of habitual chronic hyperventilation. In: O.W. Hill (Ed.), *Modern Trends in Psychosomatic Medicine*, Vol. 3. London: Butterworth.

MAGARIAN, G. (1982). Hyperventilation syndromes: infrequently recognised common expressions of anxiety and stress. *Medicine* **61**, 219-236.

PAULLEY, J.A. and PELSER, H.E. (1989). *Psychological Managements for Psychosomatic Disorders*. Berlin: Springer-Verlag.

POLLOCK, G.H. (1989). *The Mourning Liberation Process*. Madison, CT: International Universities Press.

TAYLOR, G.J. (1987). *Psychosomatic Medicine and Contemporary Psychoanalysis*. Madison, CT: International Universities Press.

WILSON, C.P. and MINTZ, I.L. (Eds) (1989). *Psychosomatic Symptoms*. New York: Jason Aronson.

WINNICOTT, D.W. (1971). *Therapeutic Consultations in Child Psychiatry*. London: Hogarth Press.

WINNICOTT, D.W. (1972). *The Maturational Processes and the Facilitating Environment*. London: Hogarth Press.

WINNICOTT, D.W. (1989). Psychosomatic illness in its positive and negative aspects. In: C. Winnicott, R. Shepherd and M. Davis (Eds), *Psychoanalytic Explorations*. London: Karnac Books.

ZALIDIS, S. (1991). Psychosomatic encounters and the scope for interpretation in general practice. *Journal of the Balint Society* **19**, 16-22.

ZALIDIS, S. (1992). Holding in general practice. *Journal of the Balint Society* **20**, 4-7.

ZUCKERMANN, A.J., BANATRALA, J.E. and PATTINSON, J.R. (Eds) (1990). *Principles and Practice of Clinical Virology*. London: John Wiley and Sons.

Chapter 9
'The body goes mad':
hospital liaison psychiatry in sickle-cell disease

Sebastian Kraemer

Introduction

This narrative begins in a hospital where the weekly liaison meeting in a very busy inner city paediatric department is taking place. It is attended by doctors, nurses, paediatric social workers, child psychiatrists, physio-therapists, dieticians, speech therapists, liaison health visitors, hospital teachers, medical students, and sometimes others. The case being pre-sented is Michael, nearly 13, who has sickle-cell anaemia, as does his mother, Linda.

Bad blood

Together with the related disorder, thalassaemia, sickle-cell anaemia is the most common single gene disorder in humans (Weatherall, 1991). It is a nasty disease (Anon, 1989) in which the red blood cells collapse and become extraordinarily sticky when the person is stressed, such as by getting cold, ill, tired or by being emotionally upset. The result is a potentially fatal loss of oxygen supply to, and severe pain in, various parts of the body. There are about 50 000 carriers of the disease in Britain, who are themselves barely, if at all, affected. Most of them are of African descent. If two carriers have children together, one in four of them will have the full-blown disease. In both senses of the phrase, this is bad blood; 5000 people in Britain have sickle-cell anaemia, and almost half of them live in London. Over 10% of sufferers in a North American study were dead before their twentieth birthday (Leikin et al., 1989), and death is most likely in the under-fives. Besides painful crises, sufferers can get sequestration (trapping) of blood in organs, such as the spleen or liver, often leading to serious collapse; infections such as those from pneumococci which can kill small children; strokes; damage to the retina of the eye; gallstones; kidney failure; destruction of hip and shoulder joints; and much else. If it has become enlarged, it is sometimes helpful to remove the spleen. Damaged joints can be replaced by artificial ones.

Besides the physical complications of sickle-cell disease, there are also psychological effects, as shown in North American and African studies (Nevergold, 1987; Iloeje, 1991). In the latter Nigerian study, affected children showed greater evidence of emotional and behavioural disorders, measured on standardised parent and teacher questionnaires, as they grew older. This suggests that the psychological effects depend primarily upon the child's increasing awareness of having a chronic and dangerous disease, rather than any direct bodily effect of the illness itself. Nevergold's review (1987) focuses on the effects of parental guilt and the stigma of having an inherited disorder, and on the chronic stress (including financial) of having a child who needs repeated and unpredictable hospitalisations. Family routines are interrupted, and the other children are neglected. The patients themselves are fearful of independence and have low self-esteem, particularly in adolescence when their development, both emotional and physical, may be delayed. Poor school performance is common.

Brown et al. (1993) found a high incidence of depression and self-blame among adolescent patients (a finding confirmed in many other studies – reviewed by Midence, Fuggle and Davies, 1993), who were generally less popular than their peers. Many families are ignorant of the nature of the disease. Similar ignorance, to which is added prejudice, is widely prevalent among health workers, which led to the publication of a series of lectures designed to inform clinicians in the Chicago area of USA (Hurtig and Viera, 1986). The editors of this collection also note the astonishing paucity of research on the psychological and psychosocial issues of sickle-cell disease, which they see as further evidence of neglect. 'Often these patients are perceived as malingerers, drug addicts, and nuisances and, at some level, this problem may be attributable to the "hidden" nature of the disease. For example, patients complain of symptoms such as pain, which the health care practitioner cannot see or verify. At a deeper level, however, it appears that the very attitudes of health care staff toward the individuals presenting with sickle-cell disease are implicated' (p. 5). In Britain, official neglect of sickle-cell disease has been noted by Streetly, Dick and Layton (1993). Little is known of its epidemiology, and there is no national programme for dealing with it.

For reasons that are unclear some people are very ill with sickle-cell anaemia and others have hardly any symptoms. Some, like Linda, have good periods and bad ones, for no obvious reason. Patients are advised to keep well hydrated and to avoid sudden changes in temperature (Davies, 1991), but this does not always prevent crises, and many patients are plagued by the threat of an attack of horrendous pain at almost any time, without warning. A lifelong relationship with hospitals ensues (Brozović, Davies and Brownell, 1987). This chapter is primarily about the effect of sickle-cell disease on the hospital staff who have to deal with it.

Prevention of sickle-cell anaemia is possible through antenatal diagnosis in susceptible couples. Affected mothers may then have an abortion. Before second or further pregnancies, genetic counselling is available. Linda's parents were first cousins, which increases the risk considerably. Though bone marrow transplantation has been attempted in some centres (Vermylen et al., 1991; Davies, 1993), it is in practice rarely done. The transplant must come from a close relative, such as a sibling. This is risky, and highly traumatic for the family (Kodish et al., 1991; L. Zirinsky and R. Emanuel, 1994, unpublished material) particularly for the donor, whose marrow has to be 'good enough', otherwise it will be rejected. Worse still, the recipient can become very ill, or even die, from a reaction to the transplant – the 'graft-versus-host disease'. Trials are currently underway of intravenous treatment of sickle-cell anaemia and thalassaemia with arginine butyrate, which increases the proportion of fetal haemoglobin in the patient's blood (Perrine et al., 1993). Fetal haemoglobin does not sickle.

Liaison meetings over a two-year period

The rest of this chapter is written in the form of a diary that records the interactions of one family with a large number of hospital staff, and their interactions with each other. The principal characters, besides the family, are a consultant paediatrician, a consultant haematologist, two consultant child psychiatrists (one of whom is me), a junior paediatrician, a ward sister and her team of nurses, and a sickle-cell counsellor. The story of Michael and Linda is being presented.

March 1990

Michael was causing enormous anxiety and irritation in the ward. Staff thought that he pretended to be in pain, or exaggerated it. He and his mother had often been admitted to hospital at the same time, but to different wards, quite far apart. Michael would ring his mother to complain about the treatment he was receiving. Then, from her bed, Linda rang the children's ward and demanded that Michael be given more pain relief. The junior doctor responsible for Michael's day-to-day care felt that she had to give him pain relief when he asked for it, but found it hard to believe that he was really in such pain. As soon as he had had his injection he was immediately up and about in the ward, watching television. He was written up by the doctors for two-hourly doses; but about half an hour before his next dose was due he pestered for it, and when given it would ask for more.

I said to the liaison meeting that Michael was in terrible pain, and was begging for relief from it. I had briefly seen him being interviewed by a junior paediatrician in a crisis some weeks before and witnessed the impossibility of any kind of conversation with him. He was abusive and impatient. He could not say how bad the pain was, nor where it was, nor for how long he had had it. 'Just get rid of it!' was what he was effectively crying. The doctors and nurses were not able to see it from Michael's point of view, as they could not accept his cries of pain as genuine. They felt that they were being tricked by him, so that he effectively assumed control of his own treatment. By trying to point out how real his pain was, I and my psychiatric colleague seemed to be siding with the child against the staff. They felt that we just weren't seeing how manipulative Michael was – 'You can't just give in to him every time he asks for opiates!'.

The liaison psychiatrists were getting nowhere, and the atmosphere of mutual incomprehension was increasingly uncomfortable. My fellow consultant psychiatrist broke through the barrier by saying that the child was not simply in pain, he was terrified of dying too, and wanted the drug to ease the fear. He recommended that a nurse or a doctor should try to address this terror with Michael. Although this clear observation was undoubtedly correct, it was not yet possible for any of us to see the complexity of this drama. The discussion itself was tense, as if a fierce row could erupt at any moment. Whatever it was, we all knew that *something* was intolerable, and had to be got rid of.

Referral

After the meeting, Michael and his mother were referred by one of the consultant paediatricians to the child and family psychiatric service.

June 1990

Consultation with the family, including haematologist and nurse

I arranged to see Michael with his mother and her partner. The consultant haematologist and a nurse from the children's ward were also present. This began as a conventional family consultation in which I tried to link Michael's anxiety not simply with his condition, but also to an impending life event in the family, namely his mother's marriage, and the beginning of his teenage years (Kraemer, 1983).

He had not known his birth father and had, as the only child, a very special relationship with his mother. Because of this I called him the 'King', and pointed out that he would now have to accept demotion to the level of a 'Prince', since his mother was about to marry (for the first time). It was clear that his devotion to Linda was full of fear – an anxious attachment (Bowlby, 1973, 1988) – mainly because of her very serious sickle-cell crises, particularly in recent months. (The consultant haematologist admitted that she had no idea why this deterioration had taken place.) I supported Michael's devotion and anxiety, but said that this did not mean that he needed to be admitted to hospital every time his mother had a crisis. We discussed who would look after him when she was ill. His new stepfather works shifts and would probably not be able to take over. Linda's mother was the most suitable alternative. Michael could, of course, visit Linda every day when she was in hospital, something he had not been able to do when he himself had been admitted.

Michael was most anxious about his forthcoming operation, in which his spleen was to be removed. He thought that he would die during the operation, or die without his spleen. Even if he had no operation he feared that he might die during a crisis, something he had read about. An even greater fear was that his mother could die in a sickle-cell crisis. Both were impressed to be told by the consultant haematologist that this was highly unlikely, and that she has a sickle-cell patient who is 65.

Michael seemed to be interested in the discussion, but he complained that his schoolteachers did not understand his condition, so the consultant haematologist gave him a card to carry with him at school, and elsewhere, that shows he has sickle-cell disease. Both he and Linda also felt that the hospital staff are unsympathetic to their condition, and that they do not realise just how bad the pain of a crisis can be. Linda spoke of how she had enraged the paediatric nurses by telephoning the ward to complain about Michael's treatment, or the lack of it. Later, during one of his tantrums, one senior nurse had said to Michael 'You're just as bad as your mother!' and had to apologise some days afterwards.

I felt I engaged well with the boy and his mother, both of whom I admired, and thought that the haematologist and I had together been helpful. I somehow hoped that the consultation would help the ward management. It did not. Admissions continued as before.

October 1990

Consultation with the family, including haematologist and junior paediatrician

A follow-up consultation had been arranged at the end of the first one, and to this I invited the consultant haematologist again, but also the junior paediatrician most involved with Michael in the tussle over pethidine. This is a powerful painkilling drug, chemically related to morphine. Doctors invariably hesitate when prescribing what is in effect a dangerous drug.

We heard some more of this family's history. When her mother knew what was wrong with Linda, she at once decided not to keep her. She was brought up by her mother's sister, whom she assumed to be her real mother until adolescence, and whom she still refers to as 'mother'. Her father, meanwhile, had disappeared and was later killed in a car crash. Linda produced from her purse a rather crumpled black and white photograph of him and explained that neither her mother nor her aunt ('mother') would acknowledge that he was her father. We learned, too, that before Linda was born, her aunt had had a baby who died at three weeks, in a fit.

Michael's preoccupations were apparently elsewhere. Rather than follow his family history he was more intent on educating his doctor. He gave a coherent lecture to the junior paediatrician on his requirements. What he wanted was simply someone to give him painkilling treatment when he is in pain, no questions asked. He confirmed the other psychiatrist's hypothesis – that fear makes it worse – when he said that in a crisis he is already relieved when he hears the ambulance coming. The pain subsides, because he knows help is at hand. But he would not accept that anxiety could play a part in his hospital admissions. He had said he was not interested in being in hospital when he is well, and dismissed any idea of his being addicted to opiates. He is addicted to football, and his home computer.

The haematologist then explained to all of us that the pain of a sickle-cell crisis is the pain in a part of the body suddenly deprived of its blood supply, just like the heart muscle in angina, or during a heart attack. So, as I put it to Michael and his mother, a sickle-cell crisis is like a heart attack inside a bone. The difference is that the patient in sickle-cell crisis is quite well once the pain has gone. He is not ill any more, unlike the coronary patient, who wants to stay in bed even after the pain is removed.

For me this was a revelation. Up to that point I had not been able to imagine the nature of the pain itself. My medical training had simply not prepared me for it. Besides being enlightened, however, I was also relieved. Linda's tragic story was obliterated by Michael's brilliant performance as a medical adviser. Carried away by that, I was no longer required to be a psychotherapist. I could ignore the family's unbearable catalogue of loss, and dispense with the obligation to make links between past history and present anxiety. I could instead adopt Michael's simple and necessary solution and become a campaigner, together with him and Linda, for adequate pain relief. The family dynamics now became irrelevant. This background information helped me to understand some of the burden that Michael was carrying, particularly as he had himself once had a fit after a pethidine injection, but it did not sufficiently account for the difficulties he was having in the ward.

Armed with Michael's view of the matter, I swept aside any thought of his particular anxieties and concluded that the problem belonged in the hospital. All he needed, I thought, was a change of policy by the hospital, to give immediate opiate pain relief on admission.

January 1991

Meeting with Michael and his mother

Mother and Michael came for a further follow-up appointment. Michael had by now had his spleen removed and there had been no crises since then. Linda's view, like Michael's, had an impressive clarity. As she saw it, the problem was primarily one of racism. She had been admitted once, a few weeks before, during which she had had a row with the nursing staff on the ward. She walked out after being told that she was not to use the 'phone. Later she complained in writing to a hospital manager. She described her fury at the attitude of nursing staff towards both her and another young black woman with sickle-cell disease, and particularly at the official response to her written complaint. In his reply the manager wrote that there had been a cardiac arrest on the ward, which was the reason she could not use the 'phone. She did not believe this. 'I know about hospitals. I know when there has been a cardiac arrest.'

I said that I had learned a great deal about sickle-cell disease both from her and Michael, and from my haematology colleague. I suggested that instead of writing to the hospital she sought a wider audience and wrote something about her experiences for doctors and nurses to read (and I gave her, for inspiration, a copy of a published article written in a medical journal by a sickle-cell patient [Daniels, 1990]). I wanted Michael to do this too. He is a bright and articulate boy.

Both of them spoke quite impressively about their embarrassment after a crisis was over. When they are in pain and waiting to get pethidine they behave very badly. They know how rude and impatient they are, and feel that they should apologise afterwards.

January 1991

Visit from the consultant haematologist

The consultant haematologist came to see me about the hospital staff's attitude towards adult sickle-cell patients. She described the episode just reported in greater detail. The nurses, she believes, regard these patients as ambitious and non-conformist young black people who make themselves too easily at home in the ward. In fact the sickle-cell patients are admitted to a variety of wards so that there is no possibility of specialisation in the nursing care of this unusual group. As in the paediatric ward, they provoke mistrust in the staff, because they often seem to get well so quickly when effective pain relief is given. The haematologist asked me to meet with the relevant staff. I offered a time a few days hence, but it was not possible to get everyone together on that day and the meeting was postponed. In fact the requested consultation never happened, but in its place I was able to present some of this material to the hospital staff and students, including most of the people involved in the story so far. The presentation took place in April, three months later.

March 1991

Report from the paediatric ward, and from school

Michael had again been admitted to the paediatric ward in a crisis, but one which was far less severe than previously. He was still as unpopular on the ward as ever. The staff found him dishonest and malicious. I went to see him but was told he had been discharged – 'Thank goodness!'. The senior nurse who said this told me how Michael tortured another child by telling him that he was going to kill him with a knife. She said he has no friends of his own age. She thinks that he is a very disturbed and rather evil child. She repeated the statement that he cannot really need his painkillers because he is up and about within seconds of his intramuscular dose. (I suggested that he might be anticipating the pain relief he knew was on the way, which she acknowledged.)

I rang his school the following day and heard how popular he is with the other children. He is of average ability, but does rather little work. He tends to chatter a lot, and is quite a powerful personality. Sometimes he uses his illness to protect himself, saying that the other children are not allowed to hit him. Using their disease to manipulate others has been observed in 25% of a sample of North American children with sickle-cell disease (Nishiura and Whitten, 1980). (By implying that he was similar to a haemophiliac, Michael was exploiting others' ignorance of his condition, which is not difficult to do. Even doctors can be poorly trained in the management of sickle-cell disease.) Apart from that, the teacher thought that he was an ordinary naughty boy, just like her own son. His attendance had been excellent recently.

April 1991

Case presentation in the hospital

At one of the weekly 'grand rounds', in which case material from different clinical teams is presented, I told Michael and Linda's story, followed by contributions from my haematology and paediatric colleagues. The discussion which followed was illuminating.

The first point is that I was not alone in my ignorance about sickle-cell disease. This is partly due to its rarity. Most doctors or nurses do not meet sickle-cell patients unless they work in particular areas where black people live. Furthermore, standard medical textbooks (e.g. Houston, Joiner and Trounce, 1982) merely mention that pain may be a feature of the crisis. There is rarely any suggestion that it can be overwhelming. Sickle-cell anaemia would have been regarded as an exotic tropical species by previous generations of doctors. But now the population of sufferers, often called 'sicklers' by themselves and their caretakers, is increasing because medicine is able to save the lives of the younger children. In the past, many patients would have died in childhood, as they still do in less developed countries.

Some junior doctors then complained that they had not been trained to deal with crises, and that they were not given time off to attend the courses available. We went on to talk about the need for a specialist unit in the hospital, where skills could be concentrated and in-service training could be given. Commenting on this, a senior nurse, who is very experienced in work with these patients, revealed that few nurses would wish to work in such a unit, because these patients are so unpopular. 'You can't trust sicklers,' she said. From the way that she was speaking I could tell that she was not intending to make a racist statement. Even so, it sounded quite shocking. The fact is that sicklers in crisis communicate the most terrible agony, which is simply unbearable to the majority of nurses and doctors. Another senior nurse spoke powerfully of the intimate and inevitably torturous relationship that develops between them and the hospital. 'They know us,' she said. 'Fear, not pain, is the problem.'

May 1991

News from the sickle-cell counsellor

I received a phone call from the sickle-cell counsellor saying how worried she was about Michael's mother, who was in hospital again. She said that Linda was very depressed.

Liaison meeting

At the weekly liaison meeting an hour later I was surprised to see the senior nurse who had in March spoken to me in such negative terms about Michael. For many months she had not attended these meetings, so that her presence suggested she had something important to say. Michael had just left the hospital, having been readmitted, as so often in the past, a few days after his mother. We spent the whole meeting, which lasts an hour and a half, on this case alone.

The nurses repeated what had been said before, that Michael is abusive to them and to other children. He was particularly nasty to another sickle-cell patient whose mother had died of cancer two years ago. A junior doctor sensitively linked that to his concern about his own mother, but the senior sister said that he is not bothered about his mother, he just rings her up to taunt the nurses. 'He plays power games with us,' she said. He had telephoned a former partner of his mother's, who promptly came to the ward demanding that the boy be given the right dose of pethidine. 'Michael never lies,' he had said to the incredulous nurses. Sister continued, 'Michael goes over us; we're like turds on the floor . . . he needs to be in control, to have power. Pain is not the problem.' I tried to explain that his need for power stems from his lack of it, from his sense of being victim to these terrible random attacks. The fear of pain is made so much worse by its unpredictability.

The doctors had been very quiet, but it was clear that they did not feel so badly about Michael, who was always quite nice to them. After all, they have the power to prescribe. I should not have been surprised at what then occurred. The senior nurse burst into enraged tears: 'The doctors don't listen! . . . for four years they have not listened!' When he has just been admitted there is no dispute, since he is obviously in great pain. But after a day or two the problem develops. Michael summons any passing doctor and demands his pethidine. Rather than put up with his performances, tantrums and groans, the doctors give in to him. The nurses, enraged at not having been consulted, give him one-third of the dose he is written up for – 25 mg instead of 75 mg – while telling him that he is getting the full dose. He demands to see the syringe. A corrupt power game has been set up, with imperious, even hysterical, performances responded to by lies.

June 1991

Consultation with the family, including haematologist and counsellor

I met with Michael and his mother, together with the haematology consult-ant and the sickle-cell counsellor who had rung me the previous month. I asked Michael why his stepfather had not come. 'He is in the shower,' he replied. Mother was depressed, as the counsellor had warned. Although she was not at this moment in crisis, her hip was in constant pain, which she said was nearly as bad as the pain of a sickle-cell crisis. She felt, however, that she was now receiving better treatment in casualty and in the ward. Although Michael's illness had become less severe, his identification with his mother was no different. As on many previous occasions, his admission to the ward was again simultaneous with his mother's.

September 1991

At the next appointment none of the family attended. The sickle-cell counsellor and I sat and talked about them instead.

Discussions with colleagues, May–September 1991

All along it would not have been possible to think about this work without the help of other colleagues, particularly those who are not involved in the care of this family. In a discussion about the pain of sickle-cell crises, my psychiatric colleague reminded me that the experience of someone with sickle-cell disease is not so different from someone expecting to have repeated heart attacks. 'What would you do if I told you that in two hours you were going to have a heart attack?' he asked me. In my wish to support and understand these two patients I had ignored the mental methods of defence that they must employ to keep themselves sane when they are well. They simply split off the fear of pain, and of death, and thus become 'supernormal' people. This state is at once destroyed as the pain approaches, and is not easily recovered. Many colleagues from other institutions made helpful comments about this process, when I presented this story to them. I had focused on the pain, and on the disagreements that arose from trying to control it, without being fully aware that it is during the recovery phase that the most difficult management problems arise. In one of these discussions, a child psychotherapist attempted to describe what it would be like going through a crisis in such pain that you want to die. Your whole self begins to disintegrate. When the pain is reduced, it takes time to put the pieces together again. Other colleagues used phrases such as 'psychic death', and 'the body goes mad', making the point that the severity of the pain, and the fear it causes, is equivalent to a temporary breaking up of the personality, in effect a temporary psychosis. No wonder that patients like Michael demand medication in this phase, not so much for pain as for the terror.

A consultant haematologist from another hospital wrote to me: 'I have often been impressed by the haunted look in the faces of [sickle-cell] patients who I see a week after discharge – a terrible anxiety at the back of the eyes. The only other patients who I have ever seen with a similar feel about them are those who are recovering from recent open heart surgery. The mechanism is clearly the same and reflects the great struggle to make themselves whole again' (Roger Amos, 1992, personal communication).

Final diary entry, February 1992

Two meetings with Linda

Months later, I saw Linda, at her own request, at an unscheduled meeting in the ward, as she was recovering from the worst pains she had ever experienced. She was drowsy and desolate. I was sympathetic but saw no opportunity, and had too little time, to make sense of all this. Although I was in a rush, it was impossible to leave her, and I missed an important appointment. I asked the ward doctor to prescribe antidepressants, something I had never before done in the hospital. Two weeks later, in outpatients, she was in less pain, but no happier. She wanted to sleep for ever. 'What is the point of staying alive to suffer like this?' She said that Michael still dreaded her coming into hospital and dying there, yet at the same time she thought that he could look after himself without her. She did not mention her husband at all. She had in the meantime had an operation to replace the joint in one shoulder, which was damaged by sickling (as also were her hips). This took place in another hospital, where she went through many of the same indignities that had previously occurred here. She had finally rung our consultant haematologist at home to get her to order proper pain relief.

She seemed to be saying that no one cared for her anymore, and I linked this with her mother's rejection of her in infancy, as soon as she had her first pains. She was immediately roused from her gloom, and quite animately said that she had been thinking a lot about this. Her mother had just sent her a birthday card, with quite inappropriate messages on it, as if she had always cared for her. Suddenly there was hope that something could yet be achieved. By making sense of her misery, there was at least a chance that it could be managed. I felt that this was the first really psychotherapeutic moment in my contact with this family.

Discussion

Pain

The pain of a sickle-cell crisis is caused by the distorted red cells blocking the blood supply to various organs. When this occurs in bone the pain is greatest, of the same order as that of a heart attack. The treatment of both is the same – rapid and powerful pain relief. For these severe pains only opiates, of which heroin is the most potent and well known, will do.

Pain is never simply a physiological process, in which some hurt part sends messages to the brain. This linear process is always modified by psychological factors such as attention, distraction, mood, expectations and personality (Melzack, 1983). Michael reported, for example, that his pain is slightly relieved when he hears the ambulance coming. This means that the management of pain is never simply the prescribing of drugs. It must, in addition, include attention to the conditions in which help is given. Essentially, the sufferer needs to know that the pain *can* be controlled. A battle of wills between nurse and patient will not achieve that reassurance.

A patient in severe pain is in any case a problem for doctors and nurses because they have to rely entirely on the patient to define it. In most illnesses a symptom can be checked during the physical examination, or by a laboratory test. Even a heart attack can be confirmed by an electrocardiograph, but there is no corresponding test for bone pain. In the management of sickle-cell disease, without careful preparation of medical and nursing staff, the usual balance of power between patient and helper is easily disturbed. Here is an individual thrashing about, screaming abuse at the casualty staff, demanding a high dose of a dangerous and addictive drug, to be given at once. This is not what doctors and nurses have been trained for. Patients, even when they are very ill indeed, are meant to be grateful and deferential.

A primary problem is our attitude to pain relief. By making an explicit commitment to pain-free death, the hospice movement has shown just how cautious the medical and nursing professions usually are when it comes to handing out large doses of painkillers. Hospices have pioneered continuous infusions of opiates in the management of terminally ill patients, where the fear of causing addiction can be set aside. The acceptance of these humane practices in medicine is welcome, but why do they have to be confined to the care of the dying? Why are kind and sympathetic people commonly so careful with pain relief for other patients? The usual answer refers to the risk of creating addiction. This argument seems hard to refute since, indeed, most patients do not become addicts. This appears to support the prevailing cautious practice. However, even when there is no doctor to limit the dosage, addiction to narcotics is relatively unlikely. For example, only 4% of Vietnam veterans who used heroin regularly during the war continued to do so when they returned home (Robins, 1978). A recent study of adult leukaemic patients undergoing bone marrow transplants reached an interesting conclusion. Patients who administered morphine to themselves used less drug and weaned themselves off the analgesic more quickly than a control group receiving intravenous injections 'as required' (Chapman and Hill, 1989; Grundy, Howard and Evans, 1993). Thus, when the conditions for the power struggle over pain relief between the patient and helper are removed, the amount of painkiller required is actually less. The patient can be trusted to control his or her own pain relief, even with these dangerous drugs (Grundy, Howard and Evans, 1993). Not one of the 610 sickle-cell patients of a North London Haematology Department was known to be a drug addict (Brozović et al., 1986).

Opiates *are* dangerous. They can cause depression of respiration, and fits (Pryle et al., 1992), but the risks can be minimised, both with child and adult patients. Some children in pain will actually deny it if they think they are going to get an intramuscular injection (Williams, 1987). Giving the painkiller in a 'drip', i.e. in a liquid, such as saline, flowing slowly into the blood stream via a vein in the arm or leg, is preferable. Using simple graphic pain charts which the children complete, a recent trial of continuous infusion of the opiate drug papaveretum (Omnopon) for sickle-cell crises showed more effective pain relief, with fewer unwanted effects, than intramuscular doses prescribed to be given 'when required' (Sartori, Gordon and Darbyshire, 1990). Only one of the children in this series had his treatment stopped, because of drowsiness, and this occurred on a dose which he had previously exceeded.

My paediatric consultant colleague had sent me a reprint of this study. When I asked her why continuous infusions are not used in our hospital she said, 'The children don't like it – they don't get a buzz!'. In saying this she was implying that pain relief is not the only goal of medication. By using a language that belongs to the drug-abusing subculture, however, she also implied that sicklers might be similar. Patients who, otherwise well, suddenly need dangerous and usually addictive drugs to relieve pain, which only they can accurately identify, must stir up in doctors the most primitive suspicions.

The fear of creating addiction is, however, not the only source of medical caution. It is hard to understand, for example, why newborn babies undergoing major surgery are frequently deprived of effective pain relief, given the evidence that their postoperative recovery is much improved if they have it (Choonara, 1989). Professional disbelief that babies can experience pain is a powerful example of a general problem. We just cannot bear to think of it, so it is denied.

The general problem is our capacity for sympathy. It is a commonly observed irony that those who care for others often wish to make up for the caring they themselves have lacked.* This is not usually a conscious process. According to this view, we doctors and nurses are inevitably at risk of running into debt with our generosity, because we can never quite remove our own depriving parent from our minds. At moments of greatest pressure, such as being confronted with a patient noisily and imperiously demanding instant relief from pain, we are most likely to become just like that impatient parent of long ago, who had little time for crying babies or whingeing children. Most of us can in any case admit to feeling extremely irritated with certain sorts of patient, particularly the ones who seem ungrateful, demanding and unconvincing. A familiar example of this is the hysteric, who seems to exaggerate everything out of all proportion, and who provokes such thoughts in the doctor or nurse as 'if you go on making such a fuss, you will just have to wait. I refuse to be controlled by this sort of behaviour!'. This is a very primitive state of mind, rarely conscious except for a sense of mounting annoyance, and one in which it is quite easy to be cruel. At times like this we fear most of all being taken in, and thus humiliated, by a trickster who is just pretending to be in pain. We are tempted to think: 'No one could have pain *that* bad!' This extreme picture is not usually so explicit, but any patient whose pain cannot wait is in danger of provoking such a reaction. Whether there is 'real' pain or not, we do not like to be caught out by performances. The fact is, as Freud and many before him observed, people in severe pain become totally selfish – 'so long as he suffers, he ceases to love' (1914) – and test to the limits the patience of their caretakers.

Michael exceeded this limit on many occasions. When he was admitted simultaneously with Linda, the staff just could not believe he was in a crisis. His anxious attachment to his mother was acted out in a dramatic and unconvincing way. Instead of worrying about her, he simply imitated her. This process, which can be called hysterical, is not deliberate or conscious, and rarely achieves any of the goals the patient wishes. In this sense Michael is not a 'good patient'. He has got the worst out of his caretakers. They are not always so provoked, even by other patients with unbearable pain, yet a third of sickle-cell patients studied by Murray and May (1988) experienced long delays in treatment and inadequate pain relief. Michael's contribution to this breakdown of trust is his conviction that help will not be available,

---

* The notion of the 'wounded healer' is not, however, a cynical one. From the beginning of history, and probably before that, healers (shamans) have been gifted individuals who have suffered serious crises at crucial points in their lives (Eliade, 1964; Bennett, 1979).

however generous and frequent the dose of painkiller. I suspect that from the first day that he was diagnosed as having sickle-cell disease, his mother had to relive her own experience. Even if she did not reject Michael, she could not bear the part of him that was in pain, and rejected that.*

Because she could not contain and think about Michael's experience, he had no way of learning how to do so himself. Because he cannot think about his pain, he cannot listen to helpful interventions. All the frailties of the helping system are amplified in this kind of case. By the time the pain is at its height, the patient cannot be reassured about anything, and becomes almost impossible to manage, like a screaming baby.

Racism

A further problem in the management of sickle-cell anaemia in this country is the fact that almost all sufferers are black. Even giving the patients a haemoglobinopathy card has been experienced by some as discriminatory. Specially trained sickle-cell counsellors play an important part in the community care of these patients but are less involved in their hospital care.

One common prejudice against black people is the supposition they are more likely than white people to be drug addicts. This is probably due to the more widespread use of cannabis among young black people, at least in previous decades (Weiner, 1970). Addiction to narcotics among black people, however, is no greater than in any other group (O'Donnell et al., 1976). The usual difficulty that doctors and nurses have in giving addictive painkillers may be amplified when the patient is black. As sicklers often appear to recover very rapidly from severe pain if given a big enough dose of opiate, it is not difficult to suppose that they are malingering. Armed with this unconscious prejudice, the doctors and nurses can then contain their own reactions to the unbearable state of the patient in a crisis. After all, it is not possible to imagine such pain, which is so bad that it makes the sufferers wish they were dead. Instead of being overwhelmed by empathy, the hospital staff are easily tempted to see the demanding and the screaming only as a performance. Most people in the health professions would deny that they were prejudiced but, like it or not, we are all capable of such fantasies at any time.

In the inner city boroughs of London, and no doubt in other major cities of Britain and Europe, there is an increasing consciousness of the corrosive effects of racism. Although there is legislation in force to ensure equal opportunity, regardless of race or creed, the fact remains that being black is

---

* It is quite common for parents to be quite unable to tolerate the child's pain, and to leave them when in a crisis. Sicklers as young as the age of eight may have to arrange their own emergency care, for example, and are expected to call the ambulance themselves (M. Meleagrou, personal communication).

a disadvantage. Some local authorities have therefore taken up the cause with enormous vigour, to the point that anti-racism has become virtually their primary moral position. Because there is such clear racial injustice at almost every level of society, it is right to make a priority of removing it. The danger of this policy is that any other kind of explanation for the difficulties of individual black people is pushed very far to one side, even to the point of invisibility.*

If sickle-cell anaemia were inherited only by white Anglo-Saxons, there is no doubt that it would have a far higher profile in the public imagination. Famous people who suffered from it would be asked to support charities and we would all know how much it hurts to have a crisis (Cox, 1991). There are signs of increasing awareness, however. Questions have been asked in parliament about the management of crises, suggesting that this is no ordinary pain (Hansard, 1991, 1992).

The splitting process

While it is necessary to deal with institutionalised racism in the management of sickle-cell disease, this could never be sufficient on its own. These patients are suffering from an illness that is inherited. This has nothing to do with social attitudes. They just happen to be black people, who have been betrayed by fate.†

Regardless of their personal history, then, those with an inherited disorder that visits them out of the blue with terrible attacks of pain are going to feel like victims. This is only compounded by other conditions that also foster a sense of helplessness, such as being black, and being rejected. The particular shame and helplessness in the parents (of carrying genes that cause lifelong damage) must also have a powerful effect on the child they produce. It is hard for such people to feel that they have any responsibility at all for managing themselves as patients. Instead it is split off and handed over entirely to doctors and nurses. My clinical attitude to this family was clearly organised by such a process. The most famous split in the popular mind is between a kindly doctor and his night-time monstrous opposite. In this story the split originates in the patients instead. Both Linda and Michael are pleasant and thoughtful people when well, but become impossible

---

* A similar process takes place in the management of the child victims of sexual abuse. Almost any symptom can follow from the trauma and betrayal of sexual assault by a trusted person, but it then becomes enormously difficult to consider any *other* reasons for the child's distress. Abuse of children and of black people both stir up overwhelming storms in our minds, and professionals can easily lose their heads trying to keep a sense of proportion (Kraemer, 1988). After all, the proportions themselves are decided by the prejudices of racism and patriarchy.

† One irony of this fate is that carriers of the sickle-cell gene, that is those with the trait but not the full blown disease, have also inherited some protection from malaria. This accounts for the prevalence of sickle-cell disease in the people of tropical Africa.

patients when in pain. Most medical and nursing staff who meet them become familiar with only one of these facets, rarely the whole. The outpatient helpers – consultant haematologist, sickle-cell counsellor and myself, for example – do not usually have any direct contact with these terrible scenes. On the other hand, the inpatient staff, ward doctors and nurses rarely see anything else. Of course by the time of discharge, Michael and Linda have recovered some of their poise, but, significantly, not all of it. On more than one occasion, Michael took his own discharge from the ward, against medical advice, suggesting that he was not leaving in a comfortable state of mind. In the recovery phase it is clear that these sufferers may be free of pain, but they are not yet back to their 'supernormal' state.

With much help from colleagues in the child and family psychiatric team (a group of social workers, psychiatrists and a child psychotherapist that meets weekly before the paediatric liaison meeting), I came to see how much I idealised the 'good' outpatients. After my first meeting with them, I had abandoned most of my usual therapeutic attitudes, and had instead become an advocate, in the hospital and beyond, for these misunderstood people. While there is no doubt that they needed this, they were at the same time deprived of any help in understanding their own experiences.

I do not entirely regret this. Although not planned, the consequence was an opening up of a much-needed discussion in the hospital about the management of sickle-cell crises. Had I successfully engaged primarily in therapeutic work with the family, this might not have happened. In retrospect there did not seem to be much choice. The pull to idealise and to identify only with the patient's point of view was impressively strong.

This is evidence of the protective mental mechanism of these patients, which splits their experience into two unconnected parts. Between attacks the good part can tell a story of the terrible pain, almost as if it belonged to someone else. The bad part is the one that suffers. This process is, of course, not unique to sickle-cell patients. It is typical of those who have suffered in unbearable ways, for example, children who have been abused by trusted adults.

Michael's behaviour (and the reactions of his carers) is reminiscent of encounters with abused children – that is, children who have suffered experiences that are too awful to think about. These cause psychic wounds that Kinston (Kinston and Cohen, 1986) has referred to as 'holes in the mind'. Sickle-cell disease certainly provides very painful experiences for the child, but then so do many other serious childhood illnesses that do not seem to elicit such difficult behaviour. Could this be because parental support is sometimes diminished in sickle-cell disease? The illness is often seen as a family curse, associated with great shame, and may simply not be talked about. In these circumstances the child is left alone to manage the unmanageable, and is thus abused, even though no abuse is intended. His terror and rage are split off and remain unavailable to thought. This accommodation preserves good functioning when all is well ('supernormality'), but leave the child helpless and terrified whenever another episode of sickling occurs.

Lacking any model of somebody who will help him manage his experience, he ruthlessly seeks *not to feel it* which may well be best achieved by being in an opiate haze. As he has been abused, so he now abuses the would-be helpers, and also his fellow sufferers. When the episode is over, the terrified helpless self is once again split off from conscious awareness, leaving what seems like a different child (Peter Loader, personal communication).

Therapeutic considerations

The therapeutic task, when it is finally under way, will be to put together the fragments of personality that have been shattered by pain, by fate and by rejection. It will be necessary to distinguish between different kinds of pain. For those who have experienced crisis pain from early childhood onwards there is a sense of being attacked from somewhere inside themselves, and a corresponding wish to get rid of that source. This produces a ruthless split between pain and no-pain, one that does not distinguish mental from physical pain. Psychotherapists believe that mental pain can be faced, and that this can be a healing process. For the sickle-cell patient this is meaningless. All pain is bad (M. Meleagrou, personal communication).

From the beginning it was obvious that Michael was intensely identified with his mother ('I have always thought of them as one person', said the consultant paediatrician), and that he and she would find it hard to let a man get between them. I only met the new husband once, and later had the impression that he was totally overwhelmed by the illness in the family. My initial hypothesis about Michael was that he did not want to give up being the 'King'. I never got very far with it in work with the family, but the dynamics of parents divided by a child reappeared with great force in the professional network, when the doctors and nurses were in such conflict. This remarkable process, in which intense family dynamics are replicated in professional systems, has been described often (Mattinson, 1975; Reder and Kraemer, 1980; Britton, 1981). Staff groups and case conferences, for example, can be quite taken up with the drama of the family they are discussing, as if they have all been given parts to play. It is helpful to be aware of this possibility in any gathering, especially when the story involves some kind of abuse. Partitions of opinion, held with quite primitive ferocity, can of course spread more widely onto a national level, as happened in Britain after the sexual abuse revelations in Cleveland (Kraemer, 1988).

Discussions of outcome

If the only primary task of liaison psychiatry were to aid the patients one is asked to see, then this case would be a failure. Michael's modest improvement was largely due to his having had his spleen removed. His mother has got worse. But there are other tasks to accomplish. Liaison is also an intervention in an institution and some promising changes have taken place there, although it is not possible to identify precisely how. For example, Michael's mother says she has experienced better care in casualty. Where I know I have been helpful is in providing her with the opportunity to speak (and to write) about her experiences in the hospital, even if it has not altered the physical progress of her disease. There has also been a change in me. I have begun to understand the complex relationship between black people who have inherited a painful disorder, and the hospital upon which they have to depend.

Some of the changes that Michael and his mother asked for are beginning to occur. Although there has for some years been a written policy of generous and instant pain relief for sickle-cell patients, it has needed open, and often heated, discussion to allow its implementation. To achieve this it is necessary to have informal meetings where free expression of opinion is encouraged. A central part of the liaison task is to facilitate this culture, which in my experience takes many years to happen.

Other changes, such as a small ward dedicated to these patients, would need more money. Even then, it would only be provided when there is consciousness in the health authority of the issues I have discussed; otherwise, few would be willing to see why this was a special case.

Finally there is one inexpensive initiative that could undermine the split between the 'good' outside and 'bad' inside patients. If paediatricians were to ensure that the ward staff got to know the sicklers when they are quite well, it would be much easier to manage them when they are ill. This suggestion was made by the consultant paediatrician, but has not yet been put into practice. It would entail inviting the patients on to the ward, perhaps to talk to staff about their experiences, as Michael had done in one of the early sessions with me. Linda has always been willing to talk to professional audiences.

When her mother knew what was wrong with Linda, she at once gave her away. This is a rejection which is brought about not by race, but by shame. As soon as they had the diagnosis, both parents must have known that their union had caused Linda's illness. Although they were themselves quite well, they now felt contaminated by an invisible stain, that no one should know about. Linda in her turn carries the stigma of an inherited disorder, that she has already passed on to her child. The experience of betrayal is therefore multiple. Ostracism for being black is just the surface problem. Underneath is the further insult of knowing that the parents' intercourse, instead of producing the perfect baby we all desire, was somehow tainted.

The story of Linda helps us to understand the abuse that she experienced in the hospital on so many occasions. Because she has come to depend on the hospital like a parent she would, without thinking about it, expect some of the same treatment. She was betrayed by her parents, and the experience of such abuse is rekindled when she is most in need of being looked after. This is during and after a crisis, when she is as vulnerable as a baby who feels she is falling apart. The only way a baby can manage intolerable feelings is to get rid of them, and put them instead into someone else close by. To some extent this powerful and primitive process takes place every time a patient in severe pain is admitted to a hospital. Medical environments, particularly accident and emergency departments, need to be able to tolerate and contain such distress. In the case of sickle-cell disease – particularly in countries like Britain, where it is rarely seen – it is only after considerable pressure (Sickle Cell Society, 1992) that such environments are beginning to be created. Ignorance and misunderstanding constantly threaten these patients, who may also have the added burdens of parental guilt and rejection.

Acknowledgements

Thanks to 'Michael' and 'Linda', Dele Akinlade, Roger Amos, Carol Edwards, Peter Loader, Heather MacKinnon, Mando Meleagrou, Liz Pillay, Beatrice Wonke, the Editors and many colleagues at the Tavistock Clinic.

References

ANON (1989). Sickle cell disease and the non-specialist. *Drug and Therapeutics Bulletin* **27** (3), 9-12.

BENNETT, G. (1979). *Patients and their Doctors: The Journey through Medical Care*. London: Ballière Tindall.

BOWLBY, J. (1973). *Attachment and Loss*, Vol. II, *Separation, Anxiety and Anger*, Chap. 15. London: The Hogarth Press.

BOWLBY, J. (1988). *A Secure Base: Clinical Applications of Attachment Theory*. London: Routledge.

BRITTON, R. (1981). Re-enactment as an unwitting professional response to family dynamics. In: S. Box, B. Copley, J. Magagna and E. Moustakim (Eds), *Psychotherapy with Families*. London: Routledge and Kegan Paul.

BROWN, R.T., KASLOW, N.J., DOEPKE, K., BUCHANAN, I., ECKMAN, J., BALDWIN, K. and GOONAN, B. (1993). Psychosocial and family functioning in children with sickle cell syndrome and their mothers. *Journal of the American Academy of Child and Adolescent Psychiatry* **32** (3), 545-553.

BROZOVIĆ, M., DAVIES, S. and BROWNELL, A. (1987). Acute admissions of patients with sickle cell disease who live in Britain. *British Medical Journal* **294**, 1206-1208.

BROZOVIĆ, M., DAVIES, S., YARDUMIAN, A., BELLINGHAM, A., MARSH, G. and STEPHENS, A. (1986). Pain relief in sickle cell crises. *The Lancet* **ii**, 624-625.

CHAPMAN, C.R. and HILL, H.F. (1989). Prolonged morphine self-administration and addiction liability. *Cancer* **63**, 1636-1644.

CHOONARA, I.A. (1989). Pain relief. *Archives of Disease in Childhood* **64**, 1101-1102.

COX, I. (1991). 'Rap epitaph': Medicine and the media. *British Medical Journal* **302**, 1613-1614.

DANIELS, D. (1990). Sickle cell anaemia: a patient's tale. *British Medical Journal* **301**, 673.

DAVIES, S.C. (1991). The vaso-occlusive crisis of sickle cell disease. *British Medical Journal* **302**, 1551-1552.

DAVIES, S.C. (1993). Bone marrow transplantation for sickle cell disease. *Archives of Disease in Childhood* **69**, 176-177.

ELIADE, M. (1964/1989). *Shamanism: Archaic Techniques of Ecstasy*. London: Arkana.

EVANS, J.P.M. (1989). Practical management of sickle cell disease. *Archives of Disease in Childhood* **64**, 1784-1751.

FREUD, S. (1914). *The Standard Edition of the Complete Psychological Works of Sigmund Freud*, Vol. XIV, p. 82. London: The Hogarth Press.

GRUNDY, R., HOWARD, R. and EVANS, J. (1993). Practical management of pain in sickling disorders. *Archives of Disease in Childhood* **69**, 256-259.

HANSARD (1991). Sickle Cell Disorders. **233**, 18.4.91, London: HMSO.

HANSARD (1992). Sickle Cell Disease. **529**, 13.1.92, London: HMSO.

HOUSTON, J.C., JOINER, C.L. and TROUNCE, J.R. (1982). *A Short Textbook of Medicine*. London: Hodder & Stoughton.

HURTIG, A.L. and VIERA, C.T. (Eds) (1986). *Sickle Cell Disease: Psychological and Psychosocial Issues*. Chicago: University of Illinois Press.

ILOEJE, S.O. (1991). Psychiatric morbidity among children with sickle-cell disease. *Developmental Medicine and Child Neurology* **33**, 1087-1094.

KINSTON, W. and COHEN, J. (1986). Primal repression: clinical and theoretical aspects. *International Journal of Psycho-Analysis* **67**, 337-355.

KODISH, E., LANTOS, J., STOCKING, C., SINGER, P.A., SIEGLER, M. and JOHNSON, E.L. (1991). Bone marrow transplantation for sickle cell disease. *New England Journal of Medicine* **325**, 1349-1353.

KRAEMER, S. (1983). Who will have my tummy ache if I give it up? *Family Systems Medicine* **1** (4), 51-59.

KRAEMER, S. (1988). Splitting and stupidity in child sexual abuse. *Psychoanalytic Psychotherapy* **3** (3), 247-257.

LEIKIN, S.L., GALLAGHER, D., KINNEY, T.R., SLOANE, D., KLUG, P. and RIDA, W. (1989). Mortality in children and adolescents with sickle cell disease. *Pediatrics* **84**, 500-508.

MATTINSON, J. (1975). *The Reflection Process in Casework Supervision*. London: Institute of Marital Studies.

MELZACK, R. (1983). *The Challenge of Pain*. Harmondsworth: Penguin.

MIDENCE, N., FUGGLE, P. and DAVIES, S.C. (1993). Psychosocial aspects of sickle cell disease (SCD) in childhood and adolescence: A review. *British Journal of Clinical Psychology* **32**, 271-280.

MURRAY, N. and MAY, A. (1988). Painful crises in sickle cell disease - patients' perspectives. *British Medical Journal* **297**, 452-454.

NEVERGOLD, B.S. (1987). Therapy with families of children with sickle cell disease. In: D. Rosenthal (Ed.), *Family Stress*. Rockville, MD: Aspen Publishers.

NISHIURA, E. and WHITTEN, C. (1980). Psychosocial problems in families of children with sickle cell anemia. *Urban Health*, 32-35.

O'DONNELL, J.A., VOSS, H.L., CLAYTON, R.R., SLATIN, G.T. and ROOM, R.G.W. (1976). *Young Men and Drugs: A Nationwide Study*. Research Monograph Series, Vol. 5. Rockville, MD: National Institute on Drug Abuse.

PERRINE, S., GINDER, G., FALLER, D., DOVER, G., IKUTA, T., WITKOWSKA, E., GAI, S., VICHINSKY, E. and OLIVIERI, N. (1993). A short-term trial of butyrate to stimulate fetal-globin-gene expression in the beta-globin disorders. *New England Journal of Medicine* **328** (2), 91–86.

PRYLE, B.J., GRECH, H., STODDART, P.A., CARSON, R., O'MAHONEY, T. and REYNOLDS, F. (1992). Toxicity of norpethidine in sickle cell crisis. *British Medical Journal* **304**, 1478–1479.

REDER, P. and KRAEMER, S. (1980). Dynamic aspects of professional collaboration in child guidance referral. *Journal of Adolescence* **3**, 165–173.

ROBINS, L.N. (1978). The interaction of setting and predisposition in explaining novel behaviour. Drug initiation before, in and after Vietnam. In: D.B. Kandel (Ed.), *Longitudinal Research on Drug Use. Empirical Findings and Methodological Issues.* Washington DC: Hemisphere.

SARTORI, P.C.E., GORDON, G.J. and DARBYSHIRE, P.J. (1990). Continuous papaveretum infusion for the control of pain in painful sickling crisis. *Archives of Disease in Childhood* **65**, 1151–1153.

SICKLE CELL SOCIETY (1992). *Sickle Cell Disease: The Need for Improved Services*, 3rd edn. London: Sickle Cell Society.

STREETLY, A., DICK, M. and LAYTON, M. (1993). Sickle cell disease: the case for coordinated information. *British Medical Journal* **306**, 1491–1492.

VERMYLEN, CH., CORNU, G., PHILIPPE, M., NINANE, J., BORJA, A., LATINNE, D., FERRANT, A., MICHAUX, J.L. and SOKAL, G. (1991). Bone marrow transplantation in sickle cell anaemia. *Archives of Disease in Childhood* **66**, 1195–1198.

WEATHERALL, D.J. (1991). *The New Genetics and Clinical Practice*, Vol. 3. Oxford: Oxford University Press.

WEINER, R.S.P. (1970). *Drugs and School Children*. London: Longmans.

WILLIAMS, J. (1987). Managing paediatric pain. *Nursing Times* **83** (36), 36–39.

Chapter 10
Pain tolerable and intolerable:
consultations to two staff groups who work in the face of potentially fatal illness

Deirdre Moylan and Jon Jureidini

Introduction

A 17-year-old boy has been readmitted to hospital. The bone marrow transplant that followed eight months of intensive treatment has failed. When first told, the boy says that he wants to die, but over the next few days he seems to change his mind. A week later he is deteriorating rapidly, and one of the staff speaks to him and asks if he feels like fighting or has he had enough? The boy replies that today he feels like fighting, but admits that yesterday he wanted to give up. The doctors meet with his parents to discuss his treatment and tell them that their son is likely to die. The only chance of survival would be further intensive chemotherapy over the next year, followed by a second bone marrow transplant. The new treatment would cause great discomfort and distress to their son, and the chances of his surviving are one in a thousand. They may wish therefore not to renew treatment so that his remaining time is more comfortable or, on the other hand, they may want to know they have done everything possible to help him to live. The parents are asked to make a decision.

As the above vignette illustrates, on a ward providing bone marrow transplantation, uncertainty about death remains until the last moment, and hope can be a persecutor. Bone marrow transplantation can be taken as a paradigm of risky, life-threatening medical intervention for otherwise fatal disease. Much literature on consultation to bone marrow transplantation units (e.g. Rappaport, 1988) interprets the psychological consultant's role as being to provide psychological and/or psychiatric services to patients and advice and education to staff, but there is an increasing recognition of the importance of understanding the functioning of the staff group (Patenaude,

1990; Stuber and Reed, 1991). Our focus will be the psychological impact on staff groups of undertaking such work and we will demonstrate why the work group set up to carry out such treatment is fragile and vulnerable.

The authors worked separately with staff groups in units providing bone marrow transplantation. One group, in England, consisted mainly of nurses, while the other, in Australia, was multidisciplinary. The similarity of our experiences with these different units led us to wonder what themes might be specific to work in the face of potentially fatal illness. Although we have different professional backgrounds – psychology and psychiatry respectively – we came to this work from a similar mixture of interests: the application of psychoanalytic ideas outside the context of individual psychotherapy, the psychological impact of severe physical illness on the individual and the family, and the functioning of groups and organisations.

Previous consultation work in hospitals has provided compelling evidence of the value of bringing together these interests, e.g. the work of Dartington, Henry and Menzies-Lyth (1976) in children's orthopaedic wards was built on the work of James Robertson (e.g. 1958) and led to further understanding of the crucial importance of the presence of the mother or caretaker in hospital, both to the success of the physical treatment and the future psychological well-being of the child. Menzies-Lyth's (1960) understanding of the group defences against the anxieties inherent in the work of a ward led to changes in the training of nurses and in the organisation and structure of the nursing environment.

Menzies-Lyth had been invited in as a consultant to help the understanding of a particular problem in planning the training of nurses. By observing the nurses at work, she was able to formulate from a psychoanalytic perspective the social systems that had unconsciously evolved to protect individual nurses from anxiety. These included rigid routines that led to nurses waking sleeping patients in order to give them sleeping pills, or the way student nurses were moved about so frequently to avoid their becoming 'over-involved' with their patients. She was able to show how those defences were failing, and how the system was at the point of breakdown (for example, when junior nurses were treated as irresponsible and incapable of undirected actions, patient care suffered and job satisfaction was minimal), and was able to work together with the organisation to find creative solutions.

These examples of consultation work in hospitals form part of a growing body of literature on psychoanalytic conceptions of organisational behaviour (e.g. Bion, 1959; Kernberg, 1984; Hirschhorn, 1988; Menzies-Lyth, 1988, 1989; Trist and Murray, 1990; Gould, 1991; Kets de Vries, 1991). Our work was informed by this tradition.

We embarked on our work with a less specific contract than did Menzies-Lyth. In both bone marrow transplantation units, at the preliminary meeting between the consultant and the potential group, it was agreed that the focus of the group would be the work on the ward. We made it clear that we saw their work as highly distressing and both units responded that they would be grateful for whatever we could provide. Each of us then provided consultation from a psychoanalytic perspective, which in practice was not so gratefully received. Perhaps this mirrors the situation of parents seeking help for a child with a lethal illness. They may similarly request 'anything that will help', but in practice, their gratitude for what is offered may be complicated by other reactions, especially when the results are not what everyone hoped for.

We asked our groups to bring to the sessions whatever material seemed most appropriate to them. Our function would be to help them to think about this material. As consultants we did not seek to organise the content of the individual sessions, but to engage actively with whatever was brought to our attention – not only what was being said, but also what was *not* being said, and what was being communicated non-verbally. We believed that if the material about the ward, and the staff's reaction to it, was allowed to emerge in its own way, we would be less likely to contaminate the consultation with our own expectations or assumptions. It is the staff of the wards, not the consultants, who have the expertise in their work. Our hope was that together with the group we would come to a greater understanding of what it was like to work on a bone marrow transplantation unit, an understanding that would inform their future work and might lead to suggestions for organisational change.

Bone marrow transplantation: an outline of the procedures involved

Bone marrow produces red blood cells which carry oxygen, platelets which are important in controlling bleeding, and white blood cells which are part of the immune system and help to fight infection and to reject foreign protein. Bone marrow transplantation is usually a treatment for cancer, most often leukaemia. It is a potentially lethal procedure and is only used when other treatments are inappropriate or have very little chance of being curative. Less malignant types of leukaemia are treated with drugs alone.

Bone marrow transplantation increases the chance of survival, but also carries the risk of shortening life. It is a matter of balancing the odds. A patient faced with a 15% chance of being alive in five years without bone marrow transplantation may be offered a 50% chance with the transplantation but must also take into account the fact that the procedure itself may kill him or her.

Bone marrow for transplantation can come from a donor, preferably an immune-matched sibling or, in certain circumstances, the patient's own bone marrow can be removed, treated and reinfused after the patient has been subjected to other treatments. In the latter case the immune reactions between the marrow and the recipient will not occur.

Bone marrow transplantation is still in some ways an experimental procedure. Although survival rates are around 50% the outlook for any individual case might be much better or much worse than that. Overall survival rates do not seem to have improved over the last 10 years, although the outcome is better for people with certain specific diagnoses, and new drugs have speeded up engraftment, reducing the risk of infection.

The physical procedure of bone marrow transplantation is quite minor for the recipient, comparable to a blood transfusion. But the transplantation must be preceded by a preparation called 'conditioning' or 'build-up' which is psychologically and physically most demanding. In order to avoid the host immune system rejecting the new bone marrow as foreign and causing the transplant to fail, the patient's own bone marrow and immune system must, as far as possible, be destroyed. Before the transplantation the patient is subjected to procedures that would in the ordinary course of events be lethal, and he is then rescued from almost inevitable death via the transplantation of marrow. (This is similar to what happens in cardiac transplantation, but different from renal transplantation, where failure means return to dialysis rather than death.)

Bone marrow transplantation is such a difficult procedure psychologically (Gardiner, August and Githens, 1982; Futterman and Wellisch, 1990) not only because of the awfulness and devastation of what the patient, family and staff must go through, but also because this devastation is juxtaposed against great hope. This is grief without moratorium – there is no time or space to process what is being experienced. Instead there are constantly new tramas to face:

1. Conditioning involves the administration of otherwise lethal doses of chemotherapy, and sometimes total body irradiation. The latter involves spending up to an hour alone inside a frightening machine. This can result in sterilisation in 50–60% of patients.
2. Because the bone marrow and immune system have been destroyed, and there is a delay before the donor immune system becomes effective, there is a great risk of infection. In most units, patients are isolated in a single room for anything from 3 to 10 weeks (Lesko, Kern and Hawkins, 1984). The patient may not leave his usually very small room. Visiting is often restricted, and visitors may be required to wear gowns, masks and gloves. Physical contact may be limited.
3. As it is immune tissue that is being transplanted, the donor's bone marrow carries the capacity to reject the host. In essence this means that the patient is attacked by the transplant causing anything from skin rashes and abdominal pain to death.
4. The patient is living under the threat of death (Patenaude and Rapper-

port, 1982) and other patients with similar conditions may be dying in the same ward. The setting is one where the staff may interpret death as failure (Marsden, 1988).

5. Meanwhile debilitating nausea, pain, fever and other unpleasant symptoms are common.

Thus there is massive and repeated physical and psychic trauma. In addition, throughout the procedure and the time that follows, cure remains a tantalising and perhaps even persecuting hope – persecuting because if the procedure is successful, peak relapse is still a year or so away. Staff report that patients sometimes seem to welcome relapses as an end to doubt. Furthermore, in leukaemia, unlike solid tumours, there is no clear point at which the patient is totally beyond hope, and thus more and more aggressive and experimental therapies can be justified. The relentlessness of this led us, when we first entered the wards, to make comparisons to concentration camps, as we wondered how anyone could survive. Clearly this represents a moment of despair in us in response to just what is involved in the work. But can patients and staff afford to realise how awful it is?

In 1960 Menzies-Lyth wrote of the task facing nurses:

'Their work involves carrying out tasks which, by ordinary standards are distasteful, disgusting and frightening ... The work arouses strong and conflicting feelings: pity, compassion and love; guilt and anxiety; hatred and resentment of the patients who arouse these feelings; envy of the care they receive.'

The major advances in medical science in the past three decades add a further dimension. The highly technical work of the staff on a modern bone marrow transplant unit involves carrying out some tasks which, by ordinary standards, are horrific. The anxieties that are thereby aroused are more primitive and have the quality of psychosis. Anxiety of this kind may be well-nigh intolerable, resulting in a rigidity of defence mechanisms which allows the work to proceed, but only at a high cost to individuals and to the group.

Two consultations to bone marrow units

During the consultation experiences, both authors felt something of the awfulness that is being encountered daily on these wards. Human beings communicate on many different levels. In what Klein (1946) has called 'projective identification', the individual unconsciously transmits his experience to another, who then finds himself having to cope with these feelings and emotions, as it were, on behalf of the first individual. We see the clearest examples of this when a baby is crying, and the mother 'knows' that her baby is hungry or thirsty, in pain, bored or frightened, and deals with it accordingly. To a stranger the cries sound the same, and he is impressed by what he calls 'mother's intuition'. But it is the baby's ability to communicate so clearly that is impressive, though of course a sensitive receptive mother (or other carer) is essential to the process.

This early communication method is used much more often than we are aware. It can of course be used defensively when we 'get rid of' our worrying and troublesome emotions by evoking these emotions in others while losing contact with them in ourselves. It is as if we still expected that a mother would process our feelings and deal with them as she once did when she provided a drink for her thirsty baby or changed the nappy of her sore and uncomfortable child or held and comforted the frightened one. The patient, facing the terrors of death, seeks desperately to rid himself of his feelings into a mother who will know exactly what to do to take the fears away and make the world 'right' again. The staff on the wards are frequently on the receiving end of these powerful unconscious projections from their patients. Given the highly stressful environment, they are often unable to process these projections.

When a psychotherapist arrives, offering consultation to the staff about their work, he or she in turn may feel bombarded with primitive emotions which must be processed in order to understand fully the experiences of this particular group of people, both staff and patients.

One of the strongest feelings around is the desire for that all-powerful mother of childhood who *could* make the world right again for her baby. We think that this feeling was behind the initial welcome to us on the wards, the sense that anything we could provide would be gratefully received. What we were offering – psychotherapeutic understanding – might be for a ward the equivalent to maternal understanding for a baby. Psychoanalytic theory also teaches us that the baby's perception of an all-powerful mother can be negative as well as positive: the all-powerful evil one who brings disturbance and terror is well depicted in children's fairy tales as the wicked stepmother.

Very quickly, in the consultations in both units, we were seen as making things worse, not better. The consultation time was not welcomed but avoided, the consultants seen as unhelpful, disagreeable and threatening. This pattern applied to both consultations, despite being conducted thousands of miles apart, with no prior knowledge of what was happening in the other consultation (as they were more or less contemporaneous) and with the consultants having different personal styles. We believe that what emerged may give valid insights into the problems of staff working on a bone marrow transplant unit and into the difficulties of consultation to medical units of this kind.

Unit A
Unit A was a large, well-funded research-based unit in England which did a bone marrow transplantation every week, mainly on

adults. The request for consultation emerged while J.J. was acting as a more conventional liaison psychiatrist to the unit. Gradually more and more revelations were made to him about how distressing the work was, culminating in a request for a group of nurses to have some allocated space to talk and think about their work. As J.J. was returning to Australia, the group consultation was conducted by D.M. We recognised that the loss of the consultant whom they had begun to trust a little with their confidences would have some effect on the subsequently formed group. Ideally J.J. would have conducted it. But we believe, with hindsight, that the results would have been similar.

As it was, D.M. began the consultation work bearing in mind J.J.'s absence. After conversations with some senior nurses, and a meeting with a large group of the ward's nurses, it was agreed to meet weekly for an hour, with nurses being asked to bring whatever issues on the ward were of most importance to them at that time in relation to their work with the patients. Although the material brought was frequently very painful and complicated, what was most striking about the sessions was the atmosphere that surrounded them. The pattern was quickly set of assembling only after the consultant had been seen on the ward. There would then follow a flurry of activity, until a group of 'conscripts' would eventually turn up. The sense was of a punishment squad or of having been assigned the most difficult of duties. The following week those who had attended would claim, 'But I did it last week'. It was clear that they felt they had come together for the benefit of the consultant, and they resented any implication of need in themselves.

Within the sessions, a pattern was discernible too. Initially the resentment about being there was found to predominate, with complaints about the consultant: how deliberately unhelpful and disagreeable she was. After considerable effort on the consultant's part, the nurses would begin to talk about their work, and the material brought was often very moving. Care and concern about the patients were obvious. The staff were able for brief periods to talk about the difficulties of working on a ward where such raw and primitive emotions had to be experienced. At such times it seemed there was some relief that these painful issues could be brought into the open and talked about. But once they were said, the meeting had to be avoided for weeks thereafter, with the consultant treated as if she were a noxious substance. The complaints from the new 'conscripts' for the following week became more virulent.

It seemed it was too dangerous to recognise how painful and difficult the work was. The sense was conveyed that to notice rather than to minimise or ignore the difficulties was a betrayal, and the consultant was made to feel she was forcing something on the staff. The painfulness of the meetings was not seen as reflecting anything about the work, but as a response to the consultant's behaviour, lack of initiative or prompting, and her disagreeable manner. The relentlessness of this eventually became unbearable for the consultant, who felt she had 'had enough' and decided to 'let the patient die'. At the pre-planned review of the meetings after the consultation had been running for three months, the consultant informed the nurses that she had decided to stop, having taken seriously their feelings about the difficulty of the meetings. They were shocked and disappointed, and proceeded to have a discusison of their problems on the ward which they felt was the most fruitful and helpful of the entire consultation. Thereafter they tried to persuade the consultant to continue.

It was as if the ward was reluctant to lose the person in whom all their complaints had been safely located over the past few months. The consultant was then faced with a dilemma; given the previous history of the group, the chances were probably a thousand to one that this 'remission' would last. Knowing that further intervention of this sort would continue to cause discomfort and distress to the group and it was likely not to survive, was it worth attempting a 'further course of treatment' which might merely prolong the agony rather than achieve the aim of furthering understanding? Was the slim chance of success at this point worth the risk of lengthening something which seemed so painful? This dilemma will be all too familiar to those involved in experimental medical work. In this instance, the consultant decided to terminate the consultation. It had not achieved what was wanted, and needed to be rethought.

Unit B

Unit B was a haematology/oncology unit that performed bone marrow transplantations in a large teaching hospital in Australia. The consultation began when J.J. was invited to speak to the unit about his previous experiences with bone marrow transplantation in Unit A. Because J.J. was unavailable to offer direct psychiatric services to the patients, the Director of Unit B requested that he run a staff group. Although this option was regarded as second best by the unit, nevertheless there was general support for the group and interest in, for example, the concept of nurses carrying uncomfortable feelings for the group as a whole.

Half an hour a week was set aside for the groups. What could be done in this amount of time was limited, but the consultant felt that it would be counterproductive to push for more time for a way of working that was new and strange for the staff involved. The groups were initially well attended by physicians, residents and nurses. Without any discussion about how the time should be used, the group would select topics, seemingly by silent consensus. The first sessions were encouraging, and the group seemed receptive to the consultant's interventions. For example, when the staff were discussing disagreements between the parents of a patient who had recently died following a bone marrow transplantation they were able to build on an interpretation by the consultant to discuss disagreement between doctors and nurses about active treatment versus nature taking its course. In the second month, they were able, over a number of sessions, to discuss what they saw as the dismissive treatment of their patients by the Intensive Care Unit, who regarded oncology patients as hopeless. Arising out of this discussion, meetings were held with intensive care staff resulting in improved relationships between the units.

But coincident with the decreased animosity towards the external 'bad guy', animosity within the team seemed to increase, together with disparagement of the consultant. Medical staff made their dissatisfaction with the staff group known to another psychiatrist within the hospital, but it was not expressed directly in the group. Instead, the consultant was informed that the hospital palliative care specialist had been invited to the next staff group to give teaching input, thus effectively cancelling the consultation session that day, and a suggestion was made that perhaps educational films might be shown at subsequent sessions. The group disagreed with the consultant's opinion that this was an attack on the consultation.

In the third and fourth months the numbers of staff, especially nurses, attending sessions began to drop. The sessions were still focused on important issues, such as how to allocate diminishing resources, the distress at having to choose which patients to say 'no' to, and resultant hostility towards health authorities. But, increasingly, the consultant felt that he was disappointing the staff group through not being 'part of the team', not working directly with patients, not having enough that was useful to say to the staff groups, and, when he did speak, being an obtuse psychiatrist.

By the sixth month there was more open animosity expressed towards the consultant, who was thought to see hostility between staff where it did not exist, and to lack commitment to the Unit. Having openly expressed such animosity, however, the team became anxious that they may have hurt the consultant. The Director of the Unit rang the consultant later in the week and told him that the staff had stayed discussing the group for an hour after it had finished. He suggested that the consultant might like to take a break from the next session. The consultant instead negotiated with the Director to come to the next session to discuss his continued involvement with the group as a whole. The group ultimately decided that they wished to continue meetings without the consultant.

Discussion

It is painful to reflect that the groups to which we consulted did not benefit as much as we would have wanted from our intervention. Nevertheless we learned a great deal from our work. We recognise that there are ways in which the intervention could have been made 'easier'. There were strong pressures on us to do it in a different way, e.g. to provide teaching input about psychological illness, to supervise counselling of difficult patients, or negotiate with management about problems and structures on the wards, all of which would have been welcomed, and might have been helpful. But to do these things would have prevented us from doing what we had hoped to do: to try, together with the staff, to understand in-depth the experience of working on a ward providing dramatic medical intervention for otherwise fatal disease.

To continue in the way that we did required much soul-searching along the way: were we really being inept, unpleasant and cruel as we were being told so consistently? Was our manner of conducting ourselves causing unnecessary discomfort and pain? Should we give up on our attempt to understand and, instead, merely provide a service which focused on what was already known? Support and supervision from colleagues were invaluable at this time.

Our understanding is that the pain of the consultations was an *unconscious* way of letting us know about the painful process of the work, and our soul-searching mirrors the soul-searching undertaken by all the staff on medical wards attempting new techniques where the results are uncertain.

Palliative care or aggressive treatment?

The question was often raised, 'Is it more cruel to carry on, or to stop treatment and let this patient die?'. Think of the dilemma for the parents of the boy described in the opening paragraph of this chapter (a dilemma mirrored in the consultation described on pp. 227–229). Should they choose the treatment that might give their son a chance to live, but which would be painful and debilitating? Would it prolong his life, or merely prolong his suffering? Or should they tell the doctors to stop treatment, watch their son die and spend the rest of their lives guiltily wondering if they had refused his one chance of survival? It is a cruel choice to make, and it seemed unfair to offer it to the parents given that whatever they choose they would feel guilty. But if the parents (or the patients) do not choose then the doctors and staff of the ward have to. To the relief of the consultants the boy died before his parents had to go through the pain of making a decision. But witnessing the family's open grief at the loss of their son was virtually unbearable for many of the staff on the ward, and everybody concerned was caught up in the sense of failure.

The choice between palliative or aggressive treatment, and the issue of experimentation, were mirrored in the consultations themselves. The staff felt that we were experimenting on them. They seemed to be confused by our openness about what we did not know and our expressed wish to learn together and they seemed fearful of our therapeutic skills. They found themselves talking more freely about their emotions than they had been prepared to initially, and felt manipulated. Sadly, in neither unit did staff and consultant feel that they were experimenting or exploring together in trying to understand the difficulties of the work. It was not possible to get beyond the point, familiar in psychoanalytic therapy, where incomplete under-standing felt more persecutory than helpful. A patient who longs for certainty might also feel persecuted by her doctors' incomplete knowledge and their need to experiment with different treatments to further that knowledge. It is hard for a patient who is distressed and in pain to hold onto an idea of an eventual good outcome which might only benefit others after his or her own death. A sense of cruel persecution can easily break through and a patient may convey images of, for example, the perverse sadistic experiments of the Nazi concentration camps.

Working in the face of potentially fatal illness, one has to choose between letting the patient die or offering aggressive invasive treatment. What happens inside you when you watch a patient who is clearly suffering as a direct result of the treatments you have given him? The unconscious feelings that have to be dealt with are very frightening as anxieties about 'playing God', the battle between Good and Evil, and issues about sadism, power and control are stirred up. Staff may experience frightening feelings of omnipotence like the young infant who feels that everything is his responsibility/fault. As with the infant, defences of denial, splitting and projection may become essential to hold back intolerable anxiety. But if you stay with the work, you still have to choose. Do you offer the patient palliative or aggressive treatment?

In the consultations we were under pressure to provide a palliative service, to take away the pain and provide comfort. However, we took the more 'aggressive' approach of trying to widen understanding. The members of our groups seemed to hope that understanding could be achieved without pain or distress. But when it caused pain, our work was perceived as an aggressive assault. Instead of the hoped-for fairy godmother who magically makes things better, our attention to the pain made us each seem like the wicked witch.

In Unit B the consultant attempted to link the staff's experience of the sessions with the experience of their patients facing treatment. Like the patients, they had to ask themselves whether it would be preferable for the consultation to have an 'aggressive' rather than palliative approach which made them feel worse now but, in the long term, would lead to real improvement. Although the discussion enabled the doctors and nurses to know each other and to appreciate the concerns of the other, the insight did not extend to the consultation. There was little understanding that the consultant might be attempting to hold in mind a possible good outcome for this 'aggressive' approach.

We recognise that it is difficult to maintain confidence that work of this type might lead to real improvement when the worker's internal experience of the moment is of being attacked or treated badly; similarly, patients' internal experience of feeling under attack may be so acute that they too experience their doctors' interventions as merely making things worse. Having this discussion in the consultation enabled the senior doctors to talk about times of their own despair when *any* intervention seems to make things worse, and how difficult it is at that time to keep in mind the possibility of a good outcome. However, as we know, on the wards there are many examples of a good outcome following aggressive treatment to balance the 'cruel failures' when treatment prolonged suffering without preventing death.

In the units doctors are often seen as the perpetrators of aggressive treatment, whereas the nurses argue for time for palliative care (Marsden, 1988; Futterman and Wellisch, 1990). In Unit A the nurses complained frequently that the doctors 'refused to let the patients die'. Experiments with new treatment regimes were initiated, invasive treatments were continued when it seemed obvious to the nurses that the patient was beyond hope. These patients were not then given the space, clear from the hope that treatment offered, to prepare for the death that 'everyone knew' was inevitable in the near future. The practice of offering invasive treatment right up to the time the patient was dying meant that the nurses had little time to do what they felt more expert in, i.e. helping the patients to die with dignity and peace.

Thus it can be seen that in practice the dilemma of palliative versus aggressive treatment is often split in the team, with some members arguing for each side. In this way the team protects the individuals from having to hold both sides in mind simultaneously, an emotional position which makes decision-making very painful indeed. This splitting could be seen in many different contexts, not least in the perennial inter-disciplinary rivalries. Sadly, parents and families also often found it too difficult to help each other to tolerate the complicated emotions, becoming rigidly split into factions and then literally splitting apart. On one occasion when the sister of a young man was told of his death, her response was, 'Oh good, now at least we won't have to put up with his awful wife any more'. Staff reported that divorces are not uncommon among the parents of children in treatment.

According to psychoanalytic thinking, splitting is a defence mechanism used when anxiety becomes intolerable. The young child makes sense of his confusion about his world by splitting the complicated creature who looks after him into a good mother (fairy godmother) who loves him and seems to be present when he is, for example, having a good feed, and a bad mother (wicked stepmother, witch) who hates him and seems to be present when he is frightened or in pain. To realise that both are the same person requires emotional maturation. Prior to that, strenuous efforts are made to get rid of the bad mother, and we saw this happening (successfully!) in both consultations. However, concern about the split-off good mother was also present, as demonstrated in the last sessions of both consultations. In Unit A there was a determined attempt to keep the consultant whose helpfulness could suddenly be seen; in Unit B there was concern about the health of the consultant, a wish to ensure he would survive their dismissal of him. As consultants we are able to think about what has happened and why, and try to reflect this back to the units. The results of the splitting are more tragic when a parent becomes the 'bad witch' and is alienated, or a member of staff is scapegoated and driven from the speciality or even from the profession. Staff turnover is very high in this area of work.

Alien intrusion

What the staff wished to drive away was not, we believe, the actual consultants D.M. and J.J. but something more primitive, dangerous and bad, something that we can only express as a feeling that the consultants were 'not one of us'. We were both acutely aware of this feeling throughout the consultations proper, although in the more informal contact prior to setting up the consultation itself, J.J. was accepted on the ward because he was a doctor with medical knowledge who talked to staff in their language. By being 'one of them' it seemed that he got beyond their defences and opened a path to communication (Patenaude and Rapperport, 1984). When D.M. took up the work the atmosphere suggested that the staff felt invaded by someone who seemed like an alien presence, a psychologist who was definitely not 'one of them'. Similarly, in Unit B in the time during which the consultation was being negotiated, there was welcome for Dr J.J. However, when he too used his consultation skills he quickly became an alien presence also, no longer a medical colleague, but someone 'other', a psychiatrist (an 'alienist' in former language). For both of us, then, it was the actual difference that we represented that was so threatening, with a fear that we would somehow overcome or dominate their competence with our own.

The fear of domination by an alien presence is a major aspect of the work of the ward. That we were made so aware of it in the emotional atmosphere of the consultations was in part a representation of its importance for the patients and for the treatment offered in bone marrow transplantation, which is both psychologically and physically alien and poisonous. You will remember that bone marrow is part of the immune system, whose job it is, in simplistic terms, to distinguish what is foreign or alien, to fight and reject it. In the early days, organ transplantation failed because the host rejected the graft as alien. To counteract this, the immune system must be suppressed before the transplantation is carried out. But in bone marrow transplantations, it is immune tissue that is transplanted, so that the new marrow can attack the recipient; thus the donated bone marrow necessary for long-term survival may kill the patient.

In psychological terms, this raises very confusing issues for the patient about his identity, his sense of self. What is 'me' and what is 'not me' when you have cancer? Coping with a transplant, the body has to distinguish what is benign and what malign, what should be accepted because it will support life and what rejected as dangerous. It is a matter of life and death. When it is a donor's bone marrow that is grafted rather than the patient's own treated marrow regrafted, then the patient has to come to terms with accepting inside himself a part of another person, without which he could not live. If he accepts another's 'life force', then who is he? David Rosenfeld (1992) describes how such issues can lead to psychotic anxieties, precipitating an actual psychotic breakdown in one man who was given a heart from a younger man. The patient believed for a time that he had now become his own son (who had been previously killed in an accident).

We believe that the problem of rejection is an issue for the individual as a whole, and not just his body. Modern medicine can now prepare the body by irradiation so that it is more receptive to the donated organ or bone marrow. But what is the best preparation for the mind, for the thinking, feeling individual who has to accept that he has just been given a potentially lethal dose of radiation or drugs, after which, to survive, he must accept into his body and assimilate as his own a part of another's body? In heart transplantations, there is the complication that the other is now dead. In bone marrow transplantation the other is usually a relative, separating from whom may already be complicated. Furthermore, the donor relative must also live with the success or failure of his bone marrow in his sibling or child (Patenaude, 1990). For the patient, the task of establishing and maintaining a sense of one's own identity may become impossible when psychotic anxieties about identity are evoked in this way. The treatments themselves are like the psychotic fantasies come to life, where the patient passively receives lethal rays, is 'invaded by' and 'taken over' by another, and where the tiniest bug can be life threatening. Some parallel to these fantasies may be found in our sense of being 'not one of them' in the consultations, and the staffs' fear that we might destroy their competence, replacing it with our own dangerous version of competence. No 'irradiation' was applied to the wards to prepare them for the consultation, so our rejection was perhaps inevitable at this early stage of our knowledge. More care in preparation of the ward for consultation may be essential to avoid rejection. For professions to work together to a common cause clearly requires more than good will. Understanding something of what is unconsciously evoked by coming together may facilitate multi-disciplinary work.

Doctors and nurses

When the staff group unconsciously uses splitting as a way of dealing with unbearable anxiety, what happens to communication on the wards? Predictably, difficulties abound (Hirschhorn, 1988). In both consultations there were many complaints about the difficulties experienced between doctors and nurses. At times, the presence of the consultant served to unite both professions temporarily against 'a common enemy', as the professions do unite against the common enemies of disease and premature death. In our experience, doctors and nurses within such a unit behaved as if other professional groups did not exist, the dyadic relationship thus excluding any other perspectives. It seemed that maternal and paternal functions were split, the former largely being carried by the nurses and the latter by the doctors (largely independent of the gender of the staff).

In the process of splitting, attributes become more or less stereotyped. The father/doctor is strong, authoritative, courageous and dominant; he is thoughtful and has available the defences of intellectualisation. Through research he can think about the patient of the future, even when his current patients are suffering. But he carries the burden of an overwhelming sense of responsibility. The mother/nurse is emotional, bosomy and generous. Unreplenished by contact with the father, she must give until depleted and then perhaps depart. She talks of professionalism but it lacks conviction and she hides in the toilets to cry when a patient dies.

Sometimes the father/doctor supports the mother/nurse in holding the child/patient as we see in a healthy family. However, just as often, the nurse/mother protests at what the father is doing to the child, yet reluctantly administers the perhaps beneficial, but perhaps sadistic, treatment the doctor/father prescribes. In our experience, mother and father rarely come together in this setting as a creative couple. Instead, on occasion, they engage in a somewhat perverse and essentially sterile sexual banter. For example, on Unit A, a doctor suggested that an attractive and vivacious nurse should pose topless next to a patient whose grossly swollen and deformed tongue was to be photographed. The consultant knew that this banter would not be acted out, yet it was painful to listen to. It seemed a vivid portrayal of the need to perceive only fragments of the other person, split off from the rest: the deformed tongue apart from the suffering human being whose tongue it is; the large breasts apart from the young woman who has to feed and care for her patients but who has needs and cares of her own. Sometimes it is more tolerable to interact with a 'fragment' (what Melanie Klein, 1946, called 'part-objects') such as a breast or a tongue, because to see the whole person feels too confusing.

Perhaps the frequent inability of doctors and nurses to work together as 'whole objects' expressed the need to avoid the pain that love would bring in this setting. Instead of communicating as a professional 'couple', the staff find themselves acting out these stereotypical roles with the resultant rigidity causing them discomfort and hampering their creativity. The male/female split is facilitated by the patients who tend to see doctors and nurses in stereotyped ways and develop paternal transferences to doctors and maternal transferences to nurses. It is further facilitated by the very real differentials in power, status and financial reward between the two professions. As individuals, they did respect and admire the skills of other individuals, but as groups of professionals, they would deny the contributions of the other profession, while complaining bitterly and demanding a contribution! Somehow the blamed profession colluded, feeling both guilty and misunderstood.

As an example of this, in Unit A, a junior doctor was invited by a nurse to attend the consultation set up for the nurses. In the three meetings he attended, he arrived ten minutes before the end of the meeting and, having been told they were discussing difficulties of communication, proceeded to talk, solo, for the rest of the meeting, repeating all they had already told the consultant about difficulties with the patients. It was as if the nurses did not exist. The consultant's attempts to interrupt his flow, interpret it, or to encourage any understanding of why the doctor was allowed to silence the nurses was met with hostility on the part of the nurses and with puzzlement by the doctor. Similarly, in Unit B, when the consultant attempted to address the hostility being expressed by the nurses to the doctors, it met with denial, and the consultant was attacked: 'You don't understand us here'; even though the doctor involved on this occasion stated clearly that he experienced the nurses' remarks as hostile, this could not be heard, but was treated by all (including him) as a joke.

It seemed to us that there was a sense of hopelessness about effective communication, with professional groups often believing that they carried such different aspects of the work that it was not possible to talk together in the same language. Moreover, everyone operated as if it was necessary to have these difficulties. They were 'more invested in the struggle than in its outcome' (Hirschhorn, 1988 p. 90). Any attempts to change them, to enable more effective communication, were resisted with great strength. It seemed that this 'war' between staff groups was a necessary location for hostilities, without which the anxiety, fear, hopelessness and terror of the work on the ward would become undeniable. In Unit B, when the physicians were talking about how exhausted they felt in the last month of their three-month stints of running the ward, it was pointed out that the nurses were there all the time. A doctor responded, 'But they can blame us'. A nurse replied, 'But so can the doctors blame the nurses'. The group was thus able to recognise, briefly, the hostility that communication difficulties had obscured, and the necessity to have a 'bad object' into whom all the difficulties of the ward could be projected.

Talking to patients

The difficulties in communicating with patients seemed one of the major sources of stress on those wards. In fact, it seemed to us that the set-piece battles between staff defended the organisation against the pain of communicating with the patients. Real communication seemed to be both feared and longed for (Maguire, 1985). This ambivalence led to a range of coping strategies including, at times, the doubling of the number of staff present at any interview with patients, and the proliferation of the reports and repetition of information. It seemed to resemble the image of a cancerous growth, ever increasing, rather than anything that would facilitate the flow of information or human communication. Menzies-Lyth (1960) noted that one of the ways the social system defended itself from what was unbearable was by instituting repetitive tasks, such as counting the laundry. When anxiety increased beyond what was tolerable, so the number of repetitious tasks increased.

The pain caused by difficulty in communication was graphically illustrated in Unit A which regularly admitted patients who did not speak English. The language barrier frightened the patients and left nurses feeling that they could not do their work competently, which caused them guilt. Interpreters were not always available, and 'anyway they "interpret" what is said, instead of translating it exactly'. Neither patient nor staff gets to hear the actual words of the other and much confusion can arise because of the interpreter's attempts to soften the words by not being specific. A nurse described how guilty she felt when administering treatment regimes without being able to explain what she was doing and why. She said, 'I do my work as quickly as possible and leave, and avoid going into his room if I can', because seeing the fear in the patient's face, without being able to talk to him about it, had become intolerable for her. Nurses conveyed a sense of betraying their profession, their training and the patients, by not being able to work in the way they thought best, and felt very bitter about it (see Marsden, 1988, on care-giver fidelity).

In a research-based unit, the language problem will not be uncommon. However, the problem of communication seemed not to be restricted to these foreign patients, but was conveyed in various stories told to us about the work. How do you speak of death when the patient wants to live? How do you speak to relatives and tell them to move their dead father's belongings from the room he occupied for months, only an hour after their father has died, because the bed is needed for another? How do you talk to a 22-year-old woman, pregnant for the first time, who needs immediate treatment which will kill her child and leave her sterile, but without which she will die?

The words, in any language, sometimes seem impossible. Once again, one is left with a sense of something inexpressibly cruel. One young nurse, following a discussion of the grief of parents whose only son had just died, and how helpless the staff had felt in the face of their inconsolable pain, cried out, 'The things that go on on this ward are terrible. I'm too young to have seen all this'.

The atmosphere evoked is of something horrific. Yet this work is undertaken and carried out, often with great courage and compassion, because someone, somewhere in the team is able to hold on to the hope of an eventual good outcome: hope that the word 'cure' could one day replace 'remission', and meanwhile that the good outcome of death with peace and dignity can be accomplished. As consultants we too try to hold in mind an eventual good outcome for this work while acknowledging the limitations of the two interventions described. We were able to see some changes in the organisations, for example, the improved relationship Unit B was able to achieve with other linked units such as Intensive Care, as a direct result of our work. There was, however, too much pain around for the staff to acknowledge our positive contributions. As consultants, we offer hope of change, but, mirroring bone marrow transplantation, we offer it at great risk. Change will always feel likely to plunge the staff into a frightening world, where a repository for all the bad feelings is needed. The 'wicked witch' becomes such a repository. While caught up with strong negative emotions, it is impossible to acknowledge the important developmental role that the witch plays in the fairy story. Without her 'interference', would Snow White or Beauty ever have left their fathers, braving the world of dwarves and beasts, eventually to find their princes? We hope that the learning we have arrived at from our work in these units is a step in the direction of development.

The understanding of the impact of life-threatening illnesses, and the medical and technological innovations designed to combat them, on the staff and on the patients themselves, is still at an early stage. Our hope is that it will develop further, so that an awareness of psychological and social processes, conscious and unconscious, in individuals, groups and organisations, can contribute to the growing medical and technical knowledge that is doing so much to combat such disease. This biopsychosocial understanding must extend to the work group who, as we have shown, are very vulnerable in the storm of psychotic forces unleashed by work in the face of potentially fatal illness.

References

BION, W.R. (1959). *Experiences in Groups and Other Papers*. London: Tavistock.

DARTINGTON, T., HENRY, G. and MENZIES-LYTH, I. (1976). *The Psychological Welfare of Young Children making Long Stays in Hospital*, Tavistock Institute of Human Relations Doc. No. CASR 1200.

FUTTERMAN, A.D. and WELLISCH, D.K. (1990). Psychodynamic theories of bone marrow transplantation: when I becomes Thou. *Haematology/Oncology Clinics of North America* 4, 699–709.

GARDINER, G.G., AUGUST, C.S. and GITHENS, J. (1982). Psychological issues in bone marrow transplantation. *Paediatrics* 60 (4), 625–631.

GOULD, L.J. (1991). Using psychoanalytic frameworks for organisational analysis. In: Kets de Vries, M. et al. (Eds), *Organisations on the Couch*. San Francisco, CA: Jossey-Bass.

HIRSCHHORN, L. (1988). *The Workplace Within: Psychodynamics of Organisational Life*. Cambridge, MA: MIT Press.

KERNBERG, O. (1984). The couch at sea: the psychoanalysis of organisations. *International Journal of Group Psychotherapy* 34 (1), 5–23.

KETS DE VRIES, M. et al. (Eds) (1991). *Organisations on the Couch*. San Francisco, CA: Jossey-Bass.

KLEIN, M. (1946). Notes on some schizoid mechanisms. In: M. Klein (1980) *Envy and Gratitude and Other Works*. London: Hogarth Press.

LESKO, L.M., KERN, J. and HAWKINS, D.R. (1984). Psychological aspects of patients in germ-free isolation: a review of child, adult, and patients management literature. *Medical and Paediatric Oncology* 12, 43–49.

MAGUIRE, P. (1985). Barriers to psychological care of the dying. *British Medical Journal* 291, 1711–1713.

MARSDEN, C. (1988). Care giver fidelity in a paediatric bone marrow transplant team. *Heart and Lung* 17, 617–625.

MENZIES-LYTH, I. (1960). A case study in the functioning of social systems as a defense against anxiety: a report on a study of the nursing service of a general hospital. *Human Relations* 13, 95–121.

MENZIES-LYTH, I. (1988). *Containing Anxiety in Institutions: Selected Essays*. Vol. 1. London: Free Association Books.

MENZIES-LYTH, I. (1989). *The Dynamics of the Social: Selected Essays*. Vol. 2. London: Free Association Books.

PATENAUDE, A.F. (1990). Psychological impact of bone marrow transplantation: current perspectives. *Yale Journal of Biology and Medicine* 63, 515–519.

PATENAUDE, A.F. and RAPPERPORT, M.D. (1982). Surviving bone marrow transplantation: the patient in the other bed. *Annals of Internal Medicine* 97, 915–918.

PATENAUDE, A.F. and RAPPERPORT, M.D. (1984). Collaborations between haematologists and mental health professionals on a bone marrow transplant team. *Journal of Psychological Oncology* 2 (3/4), 81–102.

RAPPAPORT, B.S. (1988). Evolution of consultations – liaison services in bone marrow transplantation. *General Hospital Psychiatry* 10, 346–351.

ROBERTSON, J. (1958). *Young Children in Hospital*. London: Tavistock Publications.

ROSENFELD, D. (1992). *The Psychotic: Aspects of the Personality*. London: Karnac Books.

STUBER, M.L. and REED, G.M. (1991). Never been done before – consultative issues in innovative therapies. *General Hospital Psychiatry* 13, 337–343.

TRIST, E.L. and MURRAY, H. (1990). *The Social Engagement of Social Science*, Vol. 1, *The Socio-Psychological Perspective*. Philadelphia: University of Pennsylvania Press.

Index

241